AFRO-CHRISTIANITY
AT THE GRASSROOTS

STUDIES OF RELIGION IN AFRICA

SUPPLEMENTS TO THE JOURNAL OF RELIGION IN AFRICA

EDITED BY

ADRIAN HASTINGS (University of Leeds)
MARC R. SPINDLER (University of Leiden)

IX

AFRO-CHRISTIANITY AT THE GRASSROOTS

Its Dynamics and Strategies

EDITED BY

G.C. OOSTHUIZEN, M.C. KITSHOFF
AND S.W.D. DUBE

FOREWORD BY

ARCHBISHOP DESMOND TUTU

E.J. BRILL
LEIDEN · NEW YORK · KÖLN
1994

The paper in this book meets the guidelines for permanence and durability of the Committee on Production Guidelines for Book Longevity of the Council on Library Resources.

Library of Congress Cataloging-in-Publication Data

Afro-Christianity at the grassroots : its dynamics and strategies /
edited by G.C. Oosthuizen, M.C. Kitshoff, and S.W.D. Dube ; foreword
by Desmond Tutu.
    p. cm. — (Studies of religion in Africa, ISSN 0169–9814 ; 9)
    Includes bibliographical references.
    ISBN 9004100350 (alk. paper)
    1. Independent churches—Africa, Sub-Saharan. 2. Christian sects-
-Africa, Sub-Saharan. 3. Africa, Sub-Saharan—Church history.
I. Oosthuizen, G. C. (Gerhardus Cornelis) II. Kitshoff, M. C.
(Michiel Casparus) III. Dube, S. W. D. IV. Series: Studies on
religion in Africa ; 9.
BR1430.A36   1994
289.9—dc20
                                   94-26023
                                     CIP

Die Deutsche Bibliothek - CIP-Einheitsaufnahme

Studies of religion in Africa : supplements to the Journal of
religion in Africa. - Leiden ; New York ; Köln : Brill.
    Früher Schriftenreihe
    Früher u.d.T.: Studies on religion in Africa
    NE: Journal of religion in Africa / Supplements
9. Afro-christianity at the Grassroots. - 1994

Afro-christianity at the Grassroots : its dynamics and strategies
/ ed. by G. C. Oosthuizen ... - Leiden ; New York ;
Köln : Brill, 1994
    (Studies of religion in Africa ; 9)
    ISBN 90-04-10035-0
NE: Oosthuizen, Gerhardus C. [Hrsg.]

ISSN 0169-9814
ISBN 90 04 10035 0

CONTENTS

FOREWORD

I remember so very well how we in the so-called "mainline" churches looked down disdainfully at the odd phenomenon called independent or indigenous churches. After all were their ministers not nearly all of them illiterate persons heading up churches (often no more than fragmentary minute congregations) with usually rather preposterous names and what was this odd mix of clearly pagan beliefs and practices which so obviously condemned them all as syncretistic—the ultimate heresy we had been led to believe? And they were not even churches, but mere sects at best with hardly any decent theology between them all.

We tended to pour scorn on these churches though now and again we had an awkward feeling engendered by the fact that there was no doubt that these strange "aberrations" seemed to be proliferating at a remarkable rate. In the process they were seemingly growing faster than our staid more western type of churches. Reluctantly, if privately, we had to admit that it appeared there was a need that these churches were meeting which our own churches with their more cerebral theologies and dignified liturgies were certainly failing to do. For instance the newcomer into the urban conurbations of our townships bewildered and lost, needing a warm welcoming environment and reassurance in a hostile setting, was more likely to gravitate to these new creations than join our huge and often unwelcoming congregations with their daunting anonymity. The independent churches provided them with the reassurance of healing when the urban setting was threatening personal disintegration and their way of doing things provided a bridge between what they came from, the familiar, and what they were experiencing in this great unknown. Our churches had tended to scorn the healing ministry, as it turned out very much to our cost.

But even more profoundly, most African members of the mainline churches discovered that they were all suffering from a strange schizophrenia. They were expected to be "circumcised" into occidental persons in the manner of their worship, their beliefs, their theology before they could be integrated into their church community. They had to deny their African-ness to become genuine Christians. Their African *Weltanschauung* was denigrated and virtually all things African were condemned as pagan and to be destroyed root and branch. They even had to adopt so-called Christian names at baptism because their beautiful African names (such as Thamsanga = blessing; Mpho = gift; Thandeka = lovable; Palesa = flower) were considered heathen. Most of us accepted this cerebrally but our psyches were being damaged with African Christians finding they were shuttling back and forth between two worlds; during the day being respectable western-type Christians and at night consulting traditional doctors and slaughtering to the ancestors under the euphemisms of a "party".

We were shaken and perhaps liberated by the publication of Bishop Bengt Sundkler's seminal *Bantu Prophets in South Africa*. Since then we have become less and less arrogant and supercilious. We have had to acknowledge the fact that the greatest growth has happened amongst the independent churches—that probably the largest church in South Africa is the Zion Christian Church (ZCC) of Bishop Lekganyane. We are acknowledging that there is a very great deal that we can learn from the independent churches. They have been a wonderful goad to our acknowledging that while the Gospel comes in judgement of much in our African ways, it also comes to fulfil what is good, that we are loved and redeemed by God not under pseudonyms but as who we authentically are—Africans with our peculiar gifts and weaknesses. And we are challenged to help root the Gospel in Africa, contextualising and indigenising it properly. We most not be uncritical in our attitudes to the indigenous churches because we are romanticising them. We must take the Incarnation seriously if we are not to become of only Antiquarian interest.

This book comes at an important time in South Africa's history, for we want to be authentically African and we must know what resources are available to us in our quest for that contextual authenticity. We must welcome every effort to inform us of our ecclesiastical, social and cultural landscape. It will be good and salutary for us in the mainline churches to be brought down a peg or two. It will be good for our souls.

The Most Reverend Desmond M. Tutu
Archbishop of Cape Town

INTRODUCTION

The African Independent/Indigenous Churches (AICs) as such need no introduction. They are not only for more than a century part of the Southern African socio-religious pattern, but they have asserted themselves as both a popular and a powerful movement.

The popularity can perhaps be ascribed to a contextualized and holistic ministry which probes effectively into the existing realities of the members and the newcomers to these churches. This ministry moves in harmony with the cosmology, values and ethos of the society and community it serves, it take seriously the physical, material, social and religious needs of the constituents. The popularity of these churches can often be related to the brief testimony, "I found healing there": meaning in life was found there, and vital relationships were experienced as being restored. Here, healing is understood in a genuinely holistic sense. The impact of these churches is connected with grassroots experiences and relationships. The emphasis in their expression of Christianity is not merely on worship but on relationships. In 1950 the 'mainline' churches had 75% to 80% of all African Christians in South Africa under their wings and the AICs only 12% to 14%; in 1980 the relevant figure for the 'mainline' churches was 52% and for the AICs 27%; in 1991 the relevant figure for the 'mainline' churches was 41% and for the AICs ±36%. During the first decade of the next century the AICs will be the predominant church movement among Africans in South Africa. There is in fact a dynamic growth of the AIC movement in Southern Africa, indeed in the whole of Africa. And yet most of the attention from the West is on the rapidly declining so called mainline churches.

The power of the AICs is not only vested in the large numbers as such, but in their relevance to the situations and needs of the day, and in the practical benefits which they provide. They generally strive to become self-sufficient, but at the same time they render collective support, making them a caring, sharing and healing movement based on African traditional spirituality in which a deep concern for one's fellow human beings finds expression and which is not disturbed by western orientated individualism as is evident in many churches.

Generally speaking, the AICs are disciplined and can be seen as oases of order amid instability and unrest. With their self-help and mutual aid schemes they assist people in transcending their economic plight.

People have become conscious of the power of this dynamic and mighty movement. Financial institutions are interested in the vast sums which are involved in the mutual aid schemes, development agencies are taking cognizance of the work done and of the potential to be exploited, medical and health care authorities are keen in using avenues opened up by the AICs and politicians, realizing the power and importance of the AICs, are sure to woo them before an election.

To understand the AICs it is necessary to consider the various causes and pattern of events which prompted the formation of independent churches. Both negative and positive factors will be found, both centrifugal and centripetal forces will be traced. Very often misunderstanding, withholding, negation and rejection in the mission churches context will be discovered as negative factors and centrifugal forces in the AICs causing members to leave the fold. Some of these are the recognition of identity, a desire to run their own affairs, a common worldview and lifestyle, traditional wisdom, the latter also seen in the context of healing and socialization.

In the first section of this volume the attention is focused on the historical aspects of a number of independent churches in Southern Africa: South Africa, Swaziland, Botswana and Malawi. An article in this section dwells on the comparison between the Black churches in South Africa and those in the USA.

Apart from the specific positive and negative factors which are highlighted in these essays, there are also more general time-related and society-related forces which played a role and which were difficult to resist because they breathed the spirit of that specific time and that specific society. These are also brought into focus.

The AICs which emerged and flourished, found themselves more often than not in the midst of two worlds: the modern Western world and the world of African tradition. When thought-patterns and lifestyles of these two worlds meet they can clash, or can result in absorption, adjustment, compromise or blend. To understand such reaction, the impelling forces must be grasped. In Section B, on values and ethos, light is thrown on some aspects of the African traditional patterns and their understanding.

Section C in this volume uses virtually the same basic material, the interaction between the different thought- and life-patterns of

African and European character, but here the emphasis is on the resultant change effected by the encounter of different worldviews and patterns of thinking. The last article in this section explores the possibility of devising a holistic approach in which Western science and Christian theology join hands with African traditionalism.

From the earliest time women have been active in the church, in a serving as well as in a leading capacity. Paul in Romans 16:6 and 12 mentioned with affection and appreciation four women who delightedly served the Lord of the church. Describing their role Paul used the verb *kopiaō* meaning "to toil to the point of exhaustion." Such respected and hardworking women are found in every church. Also in the AICs they are conspicuously active. Section D contains two papers highlighting aspects of the ministry of women in the AICs.

The final contribution to this volume is of a different character. Here the emphasis is not so much on verified research but on testimonies, on oral histories regarding the influence and fruit of the gospel of Christ in the lives of members of the AICs. These "stories of faith" are part and parcel of the life story of the AICs, a fragment of which has been described in this volume.

The contributors to this volume are:

Dr Lydia August, Christinah Nku Theological Training Centre, Johannesburg, South Africa.

Dr D. Balia, Department of Missiology and Church History, University of Durban-Westville, South Africa.

Professor R.J. Cazziol, Dean, Faculty of Education, University of Swaziland, Kwaluseni, Swaziland.

Mr Jacques de Wet, Post-graduate student, Department of Religious Studies, University of Cape Town, Cape Town, South Africa.

Mr S.W. Dumisani Dube, Director of the Institute for Education and Human Development, University of Zululand, Zululand.

Ms Rachel H. Friesen, Mennonite Mission, Gaborone, Botswana.

Rev. Darrel M. Hostetter, Mennonite Mission, Mbabane, Swaziland.

Dr Margaret P. Johnson, Clinical Psychologist, Ventura, USA.

Prof. M.C. Kitshoff, Dean, Faculty of Theology, University of Zululand, Zululand.

Prof. Julian E. Kunnie, Theological Faculty, University of Valparaiso, Valparaiso, USA.

Rev. S.I. Maboea, Transvaal Bible Society Offices, Kempton Park, South Africa.

Ms J.A. Millard, Department of Church History, University of South Africa.

Ms Hlengiwe Mkhize, School of Psychology, University of Witwatersrand, Witwatersrand, South Africa.

Dr Joshua B. Mzizi, University of Swaziland, Kwaluseni, Swaziland.

Prof. G.C. Oosthuizen, Director of the Research Unit for New Religious Movements and Independent/Indigenous Churches (NERMIC), Westville, South Africa.

Prof. C.M. Pauw, Department of Missiology, Faculty of Theology, University of Stellenbosch, Stellenbosch, South Africa.

Rev. B. Rantsudu, Church leader and researcher on Independent/Indigenous Churches in Botswana

Prof. A.S. van Niekerk, Faculty of Theology, University of the North, South Africa.

Mr Musa Xulu, Music Department, University of Durban-Westville, Durban, South Africa.

S.W.D. DUBE
M.C. KITSHOFF
G.C. OOSTHUIZEN

SECTION A
HISTORICAL ASPECTS

BETWEEN MAINLINISM AND INDEPENDENTISM:
A CASE STUDY OF AN EARLY SECESSION

M.C. KITSHOFF

Abstract

The secession of Nehemiah Tile from the Methodist Church in 1882 has invariably been considered as the beginning of the Independent Church movement in South Africa. Not much attention has been given to what may be called precursors of the African Independent Churches. This paper dwells on an earlier secession, in 1862, by black church members under a white missionary. Apart from the discussion of local and personal factors which contributed to the secession, the separation is set in the wider context of the nineteenth century with its evangelical revivals, missionary movements and liberal spirit. All these assisted in forming causal factors which prompted a church group to secede from the Dutch Reformed Church and to become, at least, a link in the chain between mainlinism and independentism.

The Independent Churches which emerged during the nineteenth century cannot be viewed or understood outside the ideological and spiritual context of their emergence, a context peculiar to the nineteenth century.

The nineteenth century has been labelled "eene eeuw van worsteling" (a century of struggling) (Van Veen, 1904 : 3). Although every century and, for that matter, every day, has its own struggles, one is certainly justified in asserting that the nineteenth century was one of diverse and far-reaching activities and turmoils. Ecclesiastically viewed, two important movements, sometimes opposing one another, at other times joining forces, surfaced with such dynamism that they profoundly influenced, if not modified, church and society. These two incisive movements were the evangelical awakening and liberalism.

The spiritual awakening was not only manifested in evangelical revival meetings, but also reflected in a missionary surge of nineteenth-century Protestantism. The rapid expansion of foreign missions brought Protestantism and its emphasis on the individual's right and duty to decide for him/herself, especially as far as religion is concerned, to almost every corner of the world. South Africa was no exception, and Natal and Zululand, in particular, were parts of the globe which were generously supplied with missionaries of diverse origin and persuasion (cf. Etherington 1978).

Although the evangelical revival and missionary endeavours were
concerned with one kingdom, the kingdom of God, revival and mission
were also dividing factors. The evangelical revival led to much separation from the establishment, and the mission churches reflected
a segmentation which not only virtually repudiated the concept of
the unity of the church, but also created the notion that segmentation
and fragmentation were acceptable, if not natural, in the church.

The other force which contributed to making the nineteenth century
an era of change and turmoil was the liberal movement, which often
linked up with eighteenth-century rationalism. Liberalism, which
considered itself the champion of the individual, of freedom, relativism,
tolerance and openness to change, left a marked influence on eccle-
siastical-religious views and practices. It revealed itself, among others,
in a resistance against authority, organised Christianity and confessional
unity. A fluid and diluted ecclesiology, or even a lack of Biblical
ecclesiology, was one of the results of theological liberalism. Often
the church and its congregations were considered as no more than
religious clubs or societies, where the individual played a leading role
(cf. Hanekom 1951 : 156–190).

Revivalism and liberalism together unwittingly promoted schisms
in the church. In many countries a tension between liberalism and
evangelical revivalism was experienced. This tension in various cases
led to church schisms. In the Netherlands, Switzerland, France,
Germany, Scotland and America, free evangelical churches were
formed. Apart from these separations, a large number of non-conformist
churches and religious bodies came into being, sometimes prompted
or influenced by nineteenth-century liberalism. Among these were the
Plymouth Brethren (1830), Catholic Apostolic Church (1835), Adventists
(1845), Jehovah's Witnesses (1870), the Church of Christ, also called
Christian Science (1875) and the Salvation Army (1878) (Walker 1985 :
644–646, 650, 663–665).

The spirit of revival and mission, but also the spirit of liberalism
and non-conformism found their way to nineteenth-century South
Africa. The church expanded but also experienced the onslaught of
division and separation. The Dutch Reformed Church, the oldest
church in South Africa, was no exception. A separation from the DRC
in Tulbagh, in 1843, to form an independent DRC congregation,
was promoted amongst other factors, by the quest for ecclesiastical
freedom and the desire of the members to run their own affairs

(Moorrees 1937 : 688). The establishment of the Hervormde Kerk ten years later, and the secession of the Gereformeerde Kerk in 1859, also breathed the spirit of ecclesiastical and political independence.

The middle of the nineteenth century witnessed the introduction of secessions with a racial element. In 1842, Rev. G.W. Stegmann and a number of Cape Coloureds separated themselves from the Scottish Presbyterian Church in Cape Town, to form an independent church. Fifteen years later, Swellendam in the Cape Province saw the rise of another independent congregation under the following circumstances: L. Witsteijn, a converted Jew from Holland, was removed from his post as reader (voorlezer) in the DRC in Swellendam, on charge of negligence. He started ministering to the Coloured section of the Dutch Reformed Church and in 1857 an independent congregation of Coloured people was established, with Witsteijn as parish minister (Claasen 1990 : 256–258).

Into the atmosphere of this dual expression of Christianity, namely missionary zeal and ecclesiastical fissure, came Wilhelm Illing, of the Berlin Missionary Society who arrived in South Africa in 1857.

Zealous as he was for his missionary task of leading people to salvation, he was also instrumental in what was evidently the first secession in South Africa involving African converts.

Having arrived in South Africa, Wilhelm Illing started his ministry on the missionary station Marthinsthal in the Transkei, where he displayed his individuality by dwelling in a hut and calling the people to his meetings by means of the sound of his trumpet. It seems as if he was following a somewhat comprehensive, if not holistic, approach by offering his charges together with the gospel, also meat, tobacco and other good things. Having been transferred to Natal, owing to disagreement and conflict with fellow-missionaries, he left the Berlin Missionary Society to work for a while under the supervision of Bishop Colenso of the Anglican Church. In November 1861, Illing met Rev. Frans Lion Cachet, minister of the DRC in Ladysmith. As Cachet was deeply conscious of the need for well-organised missionary work in Ladysmith, his encounter with Illing seemed to him to be an answer to prayer. Before the end of 1861, Illing commenced working as a missionary of the DRC in Ladysmith.

Wilhelm Illing was a dedicated and untiring worker. He preached and taught in the township called Barkerville, organised a school, visited those who were in prison, and brought the gospel to the people in the rural areas. It seemed as if the work was progressing as new members were added to the church, and the numbers of those attending his school were increasing. But Illing's connection with the DRC was not of long duration. On 6 January 1865, about three years after his appointment as missionary for the DRC in Ladysmith, Illing resigned. In a letter to the commission under whose supervision he worked, he stated that at the request of the people he served, he had decided to stay with them as a completely independent missionary (*geheel onafhanklijke Zendeling*). A letter from the congregation, dated 11 March 1865, and signed by 62 persons, endorsed Illing's statement. The letter stated that the congregation had separated itself from the DRC and had appointed Illing as minister (Hofmeyr 1973 : 216–219, Zollner & Heese 1984 : 169), Etherington 1978 : 107).

Here we have a group of blacks who, in 1865, under the leadership of a white missionary, severed ties with a mainline church and considered themselves a separated and independent church. Does this not mean that here we have, in all probability, a secession which resulted in the first independent black church in South Africa?

A consideration of a number of factors which probably played a role in the secession might help to furnish an answer to this question.

In 1897, that is thirty-two years after the secession, Rev. H.F. Schoon, who knew the history of the church in Natal, stated that the causes of the secession were unknown. This incorrect statement illustrates that the event, which had taken place three decades earlier, was still considered a sensitive issue.

Despite Schoon's view, various factors which contributed to or triggered the secession can be indicated. They are as follows:

1. *The mission factor*

Often the emergence of independent churches is seen as related to the shortcomings and failures of the churches within which these movements arose. Although the secession led by Illing cannot properly be called a wilful reaction against the DRC or its mission activities, the secession did take place in a mission context. If we remind ourselves that Barret saw the main cause of Independency as "a failure in sensitivity, the failure of missions at one small point to demonstrate consistently the fullness of the biblical concept of love as sensitive understanding towards others as equals" (1968 : 156), a possible reason for secession presents itself.

The failure in "sensitive understanding" was certainly experienced by both Illing and his congregation. Illing himself mentioned as the main reason for leaving the DRC the low status which he as missionary enjoyed. People of the community—probably he meant the Dutch-speaking whites—looked down with contempt on the "messenger of peace", as he styled himself. In stark contrast to the ministers of the church, who were called "Domini", the missionaries were considered to be people with donkey heads (*menschen met ezelskoppen*). It was also an unbearable burden that he as missionary in the DRC was not allowed to preach or to administer the sacraments in the established church.

Illing's low status as missionary, the corresponding limitations imposed on him as regards preaching and administering the sacraments, as well as the insensitive attitudes and views expressed by members of the established church, could certainly have given rise to negative sentiments towards the DRC. These matters, however, continued to be sensitive issues and continued to create resentment until the middle of the twentieth century. Although many later missionaries probably felt the same as Illing, they did not generally see their lower status as a reason for separation.

Other matters which revealed the superior attitude of the Dutch-speaking whites, as well as their insensitivity, were connected with Illing's school activities. He felt unhappy about the following:

* The Rev. Cachet and the Rev. McCarter, members of the Mission Committee, appointed themselves as examiners of Illing's school without having consulted him.
* The said two gentlemen also once remarked that his school was "miserable".
* Some people considered it ridiculous that pupils at his school should be educated in more than the three R's. This attitude reflected not only insensitivity towards Illing's community service, but at the same time insulted the people served. Illing himself believed that the black pupil was able to compete with the white pupil, and that the blacks needed as good an education as the whites. One of his pupils was even taught the French language. These views and activities of Illing were certainly not approved by all, and could have caused resentment on the part of Illing which, in turn, could have contributed to his decision to quit the DRC (Hofmeyr 1973 : 230).

The third area of possible conflict which could have generated a negative feeling towards the DRC, concerned land for a new mission station. Up to that time Illing had been using a building erected by Rev. George Barker, the first Anglican missionary in Ladysmith. The building stood on private land and, when the rent was raised to an unacceptable level, the Mission Commission of the DRC of Ladysmith decided to move the mission station to Tamboekiesfontein in the district of Newcastle.

Illing pointed out that the people under his care would in all probability not move because they would not return to an agricultural way of living. He also mentioned that in case of resettlement he would lose his flourishing school. He did, however, see merit in the idea of moving to Tamboekiesfontein because there he would be able to work more specifically among the unchristianised Zulu-speaking people (Hofmeyr 1973 : 234–235).

The fact that Illing tendered his resignation, and his congregation declared itself independent shortly after the resettlement plans were announced raises the question whether the land issue could not have been a factor in the secession event. In all probability Illing's initial reservations about resettling the mission station grew into resistance, which could only be neutralised by leaving the established church. If the Mission Commission was determined to execute the plans for the envisaged resettlement in the face of objections, a failure in sensitivity again manifested itself.

If the historical flow of events took place as reconstructed above, the mission factor contributed a fair share of the fuel which kindled the fires of dissent, resentment and finally, secession.

2. The personal factor

Before he arrived in Ladysmith, Wilhelm Illing was described as "a queer independent fellow who flitted from society to society" (Etherington 1978 : 107). The reason for this particular mobility should be sought in his personality. According to Richter, who wrote a history of the Berlin Missionary Society, Illing showed himself to be an obstinate person, inclined to extreme positions. This attitude caused conflict between Illing an other missionaries prior to his arrival in Ladysmith.

There is no clear evidence that Illing acted in an inflexible and self-willed manner at Ladysmith before the secession. However, in his letter of resignation he did reveal that there was a difference of opinion between him and Cachet regarding the function of the sacraments and the understanding of divine providence. Furthermore, Illing doubted the orthodoxy of Cachet. Nevertheless, it is clear that Illing's separation from the DRC had no connection with the teaching of the church or its ministers. He asserted that he remained faithful to the teachings since they were based on the Word of God. There is also no evidence that his differences with the ministers were expressed on a personal level with such conviction and/or emotion that it caused him to resign.

Considering that human hubris plays a disruptive and separating role in the church and that it is "one of the most potent sources of fission in the Independent Churches" (Daneel 1988 : 167), it could be worthwhile searching Illing's track record for such an all-too-prevalent human disposition. The fact that he bewailed his low status as missionary might, on the one hand, point in that direction, but then, on the other hand, he was willing to live in the township among his charges, and he fully identified himself with the people he ministered to. This fact rather points to a disposition of humility.

Conscious of the fact that hubris is harboured in every human heart, and Illing's heart was certainly no exception, there is nevertheless no evidence that Illing's obstinacy or eccentricity revealed itself in a desire for prestige and recognition, to such an extent that it became the sole or main cause of secession.

3. *The racial factor*

If it is true, as Stephen Neill says, that at the heart of the Independent Movement "directly or indirectly, will be found the sin of the white man against the black" (1964 : 164), it could be worthwhile considering this statement in the light of the separation of Illing and his congregation.

It has already been mentioned above that some prejudice and resentment existed against Illing's educational endeavours and views in favour of the black child. Whether these negative sentiments of the white members of the DRC, sentiments undoubtedly known to Illing and his group, were a contributing factor in the secession is difficult to ascertain. We have also intimated that Illing did not live among the whites but occupied a small house in the township, which was nothing but a black ghetto where poverty and crime abounded. Again, we have no evidence that this action of Illing offended the white DRC members. On the contrary, Cachet himself called this action of Illing one of no mean self-denial.

On a congregational level, the racial factor manifested itself in separate church services for white and black, in separate buildings. But this kind of separation was already prevailing when Illing arrived at Ladysmith, for George Baker, the Anglican missionary, and his flock were using a small building in the black township. When Baker left, Illing and his charges, comprising a number of Baker's converts, took over the church building (Hofmeyr 1973 : 227). But, as early as 1850, ecclesiastical separation was practised by most churches or missionary societies operating in Natal/Zululand.

In the DRC at that time a threefold arrangement was in operation:

* white and black were members of the same congregation and worshipped together;
* white and black were members of the same congregation (church) but worshipped separately;
* white and black belonged to separate congregations.

It seems as if the last-mentioned arrangement was adopted in the DRC of Ladysmith. Despite the fact that such a practice was justified on language and cultural considerations, it cannot be denied that "a failure in sensitivity", in particular a lack of "sensitive understanding towards others as equals" manifested itself in the mission situation. Just as Illing felt that he was a missionary of low status, so his congregation must have felt that they were Christians of low status. There is, however, no direct evidence that such a feeling of inferiority, or even rejection, increased to the extent that it resulted in secession. On the other hand, there is no reason to doubt that such a feeling of displeasure could have been a contributory factor in the process of separation.

4. *The ecclesiology factor*

According to Daneel, a poor ecclesiology is to be found "at the very core of Independentism" (1988 : 154). The question is whether this factor also played a significant role in the secession of Wilhelm Illing and his group.

Illing obviously suffered from a poor or even distorted ecclesiology, or perhaps one should call it an unbalanced ecumenical spirit. Coming from the Berlin Missionary Society, he voyaged to South Africa with a group of Hermannsburg missionaries, worked for the Berlin Missionary Society, was employed by Colenso of the Anglican Church and then became a missionary of the DRC, until the secession in

1865. He also knocked at the door of the Methodist Church, but without success. In 1869, his congregation was incorporated into the Anglican Church and, two years later, he was ordained deacon in that church. But still he could not find rest and in 1889 he severed his connection with the Anglican Church to become the Independent Protestant Congregation of St John's (Hofmeyr 1973 : 239–241, Etherington 1987 : 107).

This all indicates that Illing did not really see the church as the body of Christ, but as a society or club in which membership can be terminated when so desired.

It can, therefore, be assumed that the independent spirit of Illing, his poor ecclesiology, his dissatisfaction with his restrictive status, and his uneasiness with the views of some DRC ministers and their flocks, were contributory factors propelling Illing towards an independent congregation.

The congregation certainly did not find it difficult to follow their leader when he left the DRC. Because he made every effort to serve his congregation and the community they represented, he naturally enjoyed the respect and confidence of his charges.

That same poor ecclesiology, however, which in all probability was a factor in Illing's resignation, also exerted influence from the side of the congregation. Christianity, especially in the mission fields, was manifested in a confusing diversity of churches, missionaries and religious groupings, and the mission churches, including Illing's own congregation, had in all probability not been taught a sound ecclesiology.

Also the history of the congregation was not conducive to producing a strong ecclesiology. The mission station in Ladysmith had been started in 1856 by the Anglican Joseph Baker. When Illing came, most of the black members of the Anglican Church and others interested in Christianity wandered away to the fold of the new missionary. They apparently felt no special allegiance to the Anglican Church, nor to the DRC with which they became associated through Wilhelm Illing, and they too left later (Etherington 1978 : 107).

When certain factors arose which opened the way for separation the congregation had no theology, not to mention an ecclesiology, which could resist separation and the move to independency. It was a matter of easy come, easy go. Nonetheless, one may ask whether a sound ecclesiology is a bastion strong enough to resist other factors pressing for separation. The history of the church has not adequately proven this point. Illing's weak ecclesiology, manifested by his denominational transmigrations, could have been no more than a contributory factor in the event of secession.

5.   *The independency factor*

So far we have argued that the respected and strong leadership of Illing, together with the weak ecclesiology of the black congregation and feelings of discontent in both Illing and his congregation, supplied the materials for the tools which subsequently cut the ecclesiastical cord with the DRC.

But the hand which cut the cord was perhaps, in the final instance, not activated by a defect in the relationship between the DRC and the black congregation and its leader. The action came, rather, from something new, something I would like to call the independency factor.

The act of separation by Illing and his congregation was broadly comparable with the many secessions of the nineteenth century. It must also be seen against the background of the developing tendency in mission situations. Patterns of dependence were to be replaced by independent thinking and independent actions by African converts. This spirit of independency, which was in line with or was even inspired by nineteenth-century liberalism, started to appear in a missionary context in Natal during the second half of the nineteenth century. A few examples will suffice:

*   In 1860, black Christians of Edendale, Pietermaritzburg, successfully managed to remove the missionary James Allison on account of dishonesty in land dealings.
*   Between 1860 and 1870 some black Christians did not wait for missionaries to start schools, but opened their own self-supporting schools and hired their own teachers. Where use was made of missionary schools, black Christians often voiced their dissatisfaction regarding the standard of education. In 1867, Edendale parents demanded that an incompetent teacher be replaced by another one. Since 1860, some African Christians in Natal had been showing their dissatisfaction with missionary efforts in education by sending their children out of the Colony for secondary education.
*   Since 1857, black Christians were launching their own informal missions to the heathens around them. The Native Home Missionary Society, founded in 1860, also provided room for black religious initiatives.
*   This new spirit of independency was clearly signalled by missionary

Aldin Grout in 1869, when he wrote: "Up to the time when we opened our new Chapel I always felt that I had a hold on the people and could lead them ... They then said, 'Hereforeto we have been children and have followed our missionary, now we are men and may think and act for ourselves' (Etherington 1978 : 131–133, 142, 151).

It is not known whether such signs of coming-of-age, such expressions of independency, manifested themselves in Ladysmith before the secession. There is, however, sound evidence that the black converts in Illing's congregation were well aware of what was happening on other mission stations, especially in Edendale. In all probability they knew about the remarkable spirit of independency in Edendale, not only in getting James Allison removed, but in successfully continuing and controlling the work after the missionary's departure (Etherington 1978 : 158).

What is important here is that at the time of the secession in Ladysmith the spirit of independency, and not only in church and religious matters, was in the air. But it was more. This spirit of independency was becoming enfleshed in the lives of African converts, and was manifesting itself in the words and actions of African Christians. And it is this spirit which, I believe, inspired the black congregation to follow Illing through separation to independence. They were the first to initiate the process from mainlinism to independentism.

6. *Disputing the claim of independency*

Possible arguments for disputing this claim are the following:

– The leader was a white missionary, so the secession could not result in an *African* Independent Church.
– The break-away group was very small and did not result in a viable AIC.

In reaction to the above the following points are put forward: The race and colour of the leader carries no weight when determining the character of the seceding group. The fact is that the black members decided to divorce themselves from the DRC. Or does anyone want to argue that the black church members could not decide for themselves and were coerced into a position which they did not desire? The view that the majority of those who separated were blacks is supported by figures given by Illing in 1872. He listed the tribal origins of his station residents as 200 Nguni, 190 Sotho, 20 Griqua, 31 Khoikhoi, 10 Tswana and 7 Coloureds (Etherington 1978).

To return to the matter of the white leader of the seceding group, one can refer to Pieter le Roux who, in 1902, left the DRC with 400 black members to join the CCAC in Zion (Oosthuizen 1987 : 11–12). No one would say that those 400 black members did not really join an Independent Church because a white Christian worker acted as their leader. The same applies to Illing and his group.

Regarding the possible argument that the break-away group never really became a viable African Independent Church, the following points are relevant:

It is a fact that Illing and his independent congregation joined the Anglican Church in 1869 and thus terminated their independence. What happened after the act of secession could not, however, annul or cancel the *de facto* situation as at the time of secession. At the secession, Illing's group desired to be an independent congregation. The duration of the independent status does not determine the quality of the status.

That independence was an abiding ideal is demonstrated by the fact that in 1889 Illing and his group separated themselves from the Anglican Church to become the Independent Protestant Congregation of St John's. Two years later it was renamed the Independent Calvinistic Protestant Congregation of St John's and St Philip's. At the beginning of the 20th century, the congregation was incorporated into the United Free Church of Scotland.

7. *Summary and conclusions*

*   The phenomenon of Independent Churches cannot be understood without reference to the religious and ideological environment of the nineteenth century.
*   Two forces, religious awakening and ideological liberalism, assisted in moulding the ethos of the nineteenth century.
*   Both religion and liberalism emphasised self-responsibility and self-expression.
*   These spiritual forces found their way to the mission fields, where they assisted in uniting people but also in separating people.
*   The secession from the DRC by Illing and his group in 1865 could have had as its immediate or triggering causes Illing's personality; the displeasure of Illing and his group about attitudes, views and activities within the DRC and the mission; and the poor ecclesiology of both Illing and his group.

* Undergirding these possible causes, but also supplying the stimulus for separation and the forming of a new group were the emergence of black religious initiatives; and the transition from dependence on the mainline church to independence in thinking and acting.
* It therefore seems correct to say that here we have a very early example of a religious group that found itself in the force field of external and internal factors which caused the propulsion from mainlinism to independentism.
* If our analysis is correct, we have described here a secession that took place about twenty years earlier than that of Nehemiah Tile, which is usually considered to mark the beginning of the African Independent Church Movement in South Africa.
* Should there be serious reservations as to whether Illing's group could really be regarded as a part of the African Independent Church movement, the secessionists could at least be viewed as a religious group between mainlinism and independentism.

BIBLIOGRAPHY

Acta Nederduitse Gereformeerde Kerk (Natal, 1898).

Barrett, D.B., *Schism and Renewal in Africa* (London, 1968).

Claasen, J.W., "Die Kerklik-godsdienstige agtergrond en invloed van die eerste skotse leraars in Suid-Afrika", Unpublished Doctoral thesis, University of Pretoria, 1990.

Daneel, M.L., *Old and New in Southern Shona Independent Churches*, Vol. III, *Leadership and Fission Dynamics* (Gweru: Mambo Press, 1988).

Etherington, N., *Preachers, Peasants and Politics in Southeast Africa, 1835–1880* (London: Royal Historical Society, 1978).

Hanekom, T.H., *Die liberale rigting in Suid-Afrika* (Stellenbosch: CSV-Boekhandel, 1951).

Hofmeyr, A.M., "Die Sending van die Nederduitse-Gereformeerde Kerk onder die Zoeloes in Natal, 1839–1952", Unpublished Doctoral thesis, University of Pretoria, 1973.

Moorrees, A., *Die Nederduitse Gereformeerde Kerk in Suid-Afrika* (Kaapstad: SA Bybelvereniging, 1937).

Neill, S., *Christian Missions* (Harmondsworth: Penguin, 1964).

Oosthuizen, G.C., *The Birth of Christian Zionism in South Africa*, KwaDlangezwa, University of Zululand Publication, Series T4, 1987.

Richter, D.J., *Geschichte der Berliner Missionsgesellschaft, 1824–1924* (Gütersloh, 1922).

Spoelstra, B., *Die "Doppers" in Suid-Afrika 1760–1899* (Kaapstad: Nasionale Boekhandel, 1963).

Van Veen, S.D., *Eene eeuw van worsteling* (Groningen, 1904).

Walker, W., *A History of the Christian Church* (New York: Charles Scribner, 1985).

Zollner, L. & J.A. Heese, *Die Berlynse sendelinge in Suid-Afrika en hul nageslag* (Pretoria: RGN, 1984).

FACTORS LEADING TO THE FORMATION OF THE INDEPENDENT METHODIST CHURCH

J.A. MILLARD

Abstract

This study briefly sketches the history of the Methodist Church in Swaziland until 1903 when Joel Msimang broke away from the Wesleyan Methodist Church to form the Independent Methodist Church in 1906. To give more insight into the background of the secession, the history of the Msimang family is reflected on. It is pointed out that it was really Joel Msimang's concern for his family which caused the schism. This Ethiopian-type church is one of the largest in Swaziland today.

Introduction

To understand the history of the Independent Methodist Church it is necessary to have an understanding of the history of Swaziland and of the Methodist Church in Swaziland. Only then can the role played by the Msimang family in this saga be fully understood. That is why it is also important to go back into the history of the Msimang family and Joel in particular, to be able to understand why he was able to consider schism an option.

During this era there are many other black ministers who encountered difficulties and who had disagreements with their Synods, yet who remained within the structure of the mission church. One of these was Rev. Samuel Mathabathe of Soutpansberg. Like the Msimang brothers, he had been a student at Rev. James Allison's school at Edendale. After seven years, in 1869, he felt the call to return home to the Soutpansberg area (Minutes 1885 : 126). Here he worked for nine years, unknown, unpaid and unvisited by a white missionary. He was persecuted by the Chief and when the white missionaries came he worked under them and did not consider breaking away from the Methodist Church.

The Swazi people became a nation under Sobhuza 1 who was crowned king in 1816 (Matsebula 1988 : 7). He belonged to the Ngwane clan, part of the Nguni people. Matsebula writes that the Msimango clan lived somewhere between the Lusuftu and Lomati rivers and belonged to a group that were of Sotho (Pedi) origin.

King Sobhuza established a vast empire extending north as far as the Crocodile River and Delagoa Bay, south to the Pongola River and west to the Oliphants River. The Swazi people were overrun by Chaka but after the death of Dingane in 1840, and especially after the Zulu war of 1879, they felt safe again.

In 1838, the Chief of the Baraputsi (the Swazis) asked the Methodist Church, through Chief Sikonyela of the "Mantatees", to send a missionary to work among his people (Mears 1955 : 3). Mr James Allison, who was stationed at Mparani, had just been recognised by the Conference of the Methodist Church as an Assistant Missionary but at that stage was not senior enough to initiate work on a new mission. In 1843, after he was ordained, he started a school for teachers and the sons of chiefs (Mears 1967 : 4). He was later to start schools at Indaleni and Edendale in Natal. It was at one of these schools that Joel Msimang was educated. While he was at Mparani, Allison made himself very unpopular with the Boers by complaining about their treatment of the local people.

When Rev. William Shaw visited Allison in 1839, he heard reports of the request for a missionary from the Baraputsi in Swaziland but it was not until 1844 that Allison was sent by the Conference in Grahamstown to answer this request. Together with Rev. Giddy, Giddy's son and two evangelists, Job and Barnabas, who had been trained at Mparani, Allison visited the ruler, Mzwati II. The mission was finally established at Mahamba, in 1945. The following year Allison was forced to leave Mahamba due to an accusation of political involvement. One of the people who accompanied him to Natal was a young Swazi named Daniel Msimang (Bedell 1978 : 62).

At first, Allison settled at Indaleni, near Pietermaritzburg, but in 1865 it became clear that the place was too small to support the community. Several farms were bought and a community was established at Driefontein. Here Msimang was one of the leaders who cared for the spiritual and physical needs of the people (Bedell 1978 : 62). From Driefontein, mission work was carried out in the surrounding areas. It was from this community that Daniel Msimang, now an ordained minister, was to return to Swaziland to re-open the mission in 1881.

Allison left the Methodist Church in 1851, when the Church did not want to sponsor his land-sharing scheme on the farm Welverdiend, which became known as Edendale (Perkins 1974 : 107). In 1850, Rev. William Shaw wrote to Rev. Thomas Jenkins of Palmerton:

> Nothing has occurred that will induce me to speak otherwise than well, both of him and Mrs Allison so far as their zeal is concerned. . . . but (he) must be fully aware that a man may be a good and consistent missionary without being a good and consistent *Wesleyan missionary*. It is of no use for him to be connected with us unless he is willing to abide by our rules and usages. . . . It is not unnatural that they should do so.

These words were later to apply to Joel Msimang too.

Here we have the potential for the formation of an independent church. Most of the people at Edendale, however, remained loyal to the Methodist Church. The Nzondelelo movement was initiated by this group of people in 1875.

The Nzondelelo movement was a missionary outreach by the people of Edendale to other areas of Zululand. In 1877, Daniel Msimang explained what they were doing thus:

> In 1874 the Edendale people (including Driefontein) were moved in our hearts on account of the work of the Lord. We heard the cries of those who want to be saved. . . . In 1875 we met at Edendale. . . . From every side came testimony as to the sad state of the natives all over the land. . . . We felt we ought to send people to them. . . . The meeting raised 100 for this work (Hewson 1950 : 77).

This was a missionary effort by the people themselves. The word "Nzondelelo" means "to desire earnestly" and the success of the movement was evidence of their zeal. Among the leaders of the movement were Daniel and Ezra Msimang (Balia 1985 : 50). Here, Joel had evidence that the supervision of a white missionary was not necessary for a venture to succeed.

In 1880, Rev. John Kilner of the Wesleyan Methodist Missionary Society toured the South African mission field. On 3 May 1880, six workers in Zululand were ordained, among them Daniel Msimang. The people of Edendale gave generously, out of gratitude, for the work to recommence in Swaziland. In July 1881, Rev. Owen Watkins, the head of the Methodist Church in Natal, left Pietermaritzburg to visit Swaziland. He was joined at Ladysmith by "Daniel Msimang, native minister, and his son Obed". Near a mountain called "Mokebieskop", Daniel Msimang pointed out to Watkins the place where he was converted in 1845. "It was very touching to see how he recalled the circumstances. . . . and note his abounding gratitude to God" (Watkin's Journal—"Methodism re-enters the Transvaal", Sunday 31 July 1881). The whole Msimang family was dedicated to the work of the Methodist Church, so that Joel Msimang's move to break away could not have been an easy decision to make.

The old mission station "Mahamba", which Allison had established in 1845, had by this time been re-zoned within the Transvaal boundary and was in the possession of the Vermaak family. With the help of the British Government Agent, land for a new station was obtained within the Swaziland border not far from the old station. Rev. Daniel Msimang was the minister in charge of the new Mahamba Mission. In 1883, the Summary of the Reports at the District Meeting of the Transvaal and Swaziland District noted that "our devoted native minister Daniel Msimang has gained the confidence of all with whom he comes in contact and has gathered a congregation of over seventy persons". In 1885, Rev. Owen Watkins wrote to Rev. John Kilner from Mahamba, to say that on his visit he had found that "Daniel Msimang is a grand man. . . . and he occupies a position of great and increasing responsibility". A forty-foot (about twelve meters) chapel had just been built (letter in Archives at SOAS, London). In 1887, Msimang reported requests for preachers from five new places (letter from Rev D Msimang to Rev G Weavind, dated 25 March 1887). As the work grew, Joel Msimang answered the call to the ministry, especially to the work in Swaziland. In the Minutes of the 1888 District Meeting, Joel Msimang was listed as a candidate for the ministry and in 1889 as a preacher on trial or probation.

Early in the 1880s, Rev. Mangena Mokone spent a year at Mahamba. In 1880, Mokone was a candidate for minister at the age of about twenty-seven years. He had been a local preacher for four years, while working as a teacher (Minutes of the 1880 District Meeting). He was appointed to help Msimang but was later transferred to Pretoria. In 1892, Mokone would break away from the Methodist Church to form the Ethiopian Church. This contact, too, would have affected the young Joel Msimang, especially as Mokone exploited the difficulties that Daniel Msimang was having when he preached against cultural practices which he did not consider to be "Christian" (Bedell 1978 : 69, 70).

In 1890, Joel Msimang was sent to Emakosini to establish a new mission. The new mission station was near the hill which was the

sacred burial place of the old kings of Swaziland. Joel Msimang was
an excellent administrator and the new station flourished. His father
was getting old and the young Msimang took over all the administrative
work of the Swazi church. The Synod of 1902 was the last that father
and son attended together for Daniel died early the following year
(Perkins 1974 : 393). Joel Msimang expected to take over his father's
responsibility for the work in Swaziland as he had been acting in
that capacity for some time. However, the Methodist Synod decided
to send him to Mozambique to continue the work begun by Rev.
Robert Mashaba.

Joel Msimang was familiar with the conditions associated with the
work in Mozambique. It had been started in 1885 by a Mozambican,
Robert Mashaba, who had been converted through the witness of
Methodist friends while working in Port Elizabeth. In 1893, Rev. Daniel
Msimang and Rev. George Weavind had travelled to Mozambique
to investigate the work there, before the church at Lourenco Marques
was incorporated into the Transvaal and Swaziland District. In the
late 1890s, Robert Mashaba was unjustly accused of treason by the
Portuguese authorities and imprisoned on the Cape Verde Islands.
The Methodist authorities managed to secure his release but he was
not allowed to return to Mozambique. Someone else had to be found
to minister to the congregation in Mozambique and Joel Msimang
was the one chosen.

There were a number of reasons why Msimang did not wish to
go to Mozambique. He did not want to leave the flourishing work
in Swaziland which he had helped to develop. Furthermore, Mozambique
had a bad climate for people unused to it and Msimang feared for
his family's health. Lea (1925 : 44) states that with a large family
Msimang "did not want to live in that fever ridden country". His
son Richard was due to go to school at Taunton College in England
and this would have been complicated by the move (Balia 1990 : 2).

Unlike Mokone, Msimang did not actually wish to leave the
Methodist Church, but felt that he was left with no alternative. Lea
(1925 : 44) states that there was also a disagreement over class money
(the money paid weekly to the church). Money was cited as a
contributing cause for schism in a number of cases. James Dwane
of the Order of Ethiopia and Peter Mzimba of the Presbyterian Church
in Africa both disagreed with their church authorities over the use
of money that they had collected. The Methodist Church in Africa

left the mother church over a disagreement about an increase in class money.

Joel Msimang broke away from the Wesleyan Methodist Church in 1903 and he formed the Independent Methodist Church in 1906. Msimang did not forget the people of Mozambique. After he had started the Independent Methodist Church he was joined by Stephen Mavimbela (1860–1948), a policeman who had come to Mahamba because of a vision, in which he had heard a voice saying "go to Mahamba and there you will be told what to do". Msimang sent him to Mozambique as a preacher (Sundkler 1975 : 215). Many others flocked to join his church. Among them was a fellow Methodist minister from Queenstown, Rev. J Congwa (Lea 1925 : 44).

The secession of the Independent Methodist Church is the only "mass" secession from a mission church to have taken place in Swaziland. Nearly all the Methodist congregations in the south of the country followed Msimang (Cazziol : 46). Cazziol sees the causes of the schism as a refusal by the Methodist Church to appoint local clergy to senior positions and a refusal to compromise with Swazi customs and tradition. There have been many important Swazis who have been members of this church. Both Queen Mother Lomawa and her successor Queen Nukwase were members during the post-1920 period (Cazziol : 55).

The Independent Methodist Church is an Ethiopian-type church. On 17 March 1913, Rev. Joel Msimang convened a meeting to draw up a constitution. The meeting was held at Makwabe, near Wakkerstroom in the Transvaal. The organisation of the church is very like that of the Methodist Church, with class leaders and circuit stewards.

What of the future? In 1925, Rev. Allen Lea (1925 : 44) predicted that "it is questionable whether it (the IMC) will last after the passing of Rev. Joel Msimang". However Rev Joel Msimang died in 1935 and the Independent Methodist Church is the largest Ethiopian-type church in Swaziland today, as well as having branches in South Africa. There are moves in Swaziland to form a "national church" of all the independent groups without any losing its identity. Time will tell whether this "national church" will become a reality.

In conclusion, we have seen that while Msimang's background prepared him for independence, historical factors did not cause the schism. Nor was it caused by the spirit of Ethiopianism that swept South Africa after Nehemiah Tile left the Methodist Church to form the Tembu National Church in 1882, even allowing for Msimang's acquaintance with Mangena Mokone. Rather, it was lack of understanding on the part of the Methodist authorities over Msimang's concern for his family's welfare if they were transplanted to Mozambique. Added to this was his love for the Swazi church, which he had served for so many years and did not want to leave. His high regard for the church which did not understand his feelings is seen in the way he retained the name Methodist in the name of the new church, as well as the structures that he knew worked well.

The factors that led to the formation of the Independent Methodist Church may be seen as lack of understanding on the part of the mission church as well as Msimang's love for his family and the church that he had helped to establish.

BIBLIOGRAPHY

Balia, D., "A Study of the Factors that Influenced the Rise and Development of Ethiopianism within the Methodist Church", Unpub. MTh thesis, University of Durban-Westville, 1985.

Bedell, K.B., "Swaziland Methodists Experiment with Racial Blending", Unpub. MTh thesis, University of South Africa, 1978.

Cazziol, R.J., *The Swazi Zionists, An Indigenous Religious Movement in Southern Africa*, Social studies monograph, 7, University of Swaziland.

Hewson, L.A., *An Introduction to South African Methodists* (Cape Town: Standard Press, 1950).

Lea, A., *The Native Separatist Church Movement in South Africa* (Cape Town: Juta & Co., 1925).

Matsebula, J.S.M., *A History of Swaziland* (Cape Town: Longman Penguin, 1972).

Mears, W.J.G., *Methodism in Swaziland* (Cape Town: Methodist Missionary Department, 1955).

Mears, W.J.G., *The Rev James Allison, Missionary* (Cape Town: Mission and Extension Department of the Methodist Church, 1967).

Mears, W.J.G., *Methodism in the Transvaal* (Johannesburg: Goldfields Press, 1972).

Perkins, F.J., "A History of Christian Missions in Swaziland in 1910", Unpub. Ph.D. thesis, University of the Witwatersrand, 1974.

Sundkler, B.G.M., *Bantu Prophets in South Africa* (London: Oxford University Press, 1961).

Primary Documents

Journal of Rev. Owen Watkins, dated 31 July 1881.
Letters - from O. Watkins to J. Kilner, dated 1885.
          from D. Msimang to G. Weavind, dated 25 March 1887.
          from W. Shaw to T. Jenkins, dated 1850.
Minutes of the Transvaal and Swaziland District Meeting—1880, 1885, 1888, 1889.

NEW INDEPENDENT METHODIST MOVEMENTS IN SOUTHERN AFRICA

D. BALIA

Abstract

This study reflects on the emergence of some independent churches from within the ranks of Methodism during this century. The churches which come under discussion are the Independent Methodist Church in Swaziland, the Bantu Methodist Church on the Witwatersrand, the United Methodist Church in the Transkei, and the Black Methodist Consultation (BMC). The latter is discussed in more detail. Issues addressed are white racism in the Methodist Church, black awareness, black spirituality and the development of black leadership in the BMC which exists as an autonomous movement within the Methodist Church structure.

Introduction

The formation of the African independent church movement is generally located in the second half of the nineteenth century. Previous studies have documented the role of Methodist ministers Nehemiah Tile, Mangena Mokone, James Dwane and others in contributing to the spirit of discontent in a missionary-controlled church during that time.[1] Little attention has since been given, however, to the formation of independent churches from within the ranks of Methodism during this century. The momentum for secession did not subside, even though there was a lull in independent formation in Methodism between the 1940s and 1960s. The purpose of this paper is to reflect critically on the emergence of the Independent Methodist Church in Swaziland, the Bantu Methodist Church on the Witwatersrand, the United Methodist Church in the Transkei and, to a fuller extent, the Black Methodist Consultation, which continues to exist as an autonomous and independent movement within church structures.

---

[1] See for example my Master's Thesis, "A Study of the factors that influenced the rise and development of Ethiopianism within the Methodist Church in Southern Africa, 1874–1910." University of Durban-Westville, 1985.

The Independent Methodist Church

The founder of this church was Joel Msimang, a Methodist "native assistant missionary" who had been involved initially with Methodist missions in Natal. He had initiated a new work, about nine miles from the main Methodist mission station, at the foot of the Emakosini hill in Swaziland. This hill was the burial place of the famous Swazi kings. During his six months residence here, Msimang had built up a day school, with thirty children enrolled, and about sixty people attended his services regularly. Wesleyan missionary Owen Watkins said he regarded this particular work in Swaziland "as of the utmost importance", and that he was "confident it will be the means of bringing multitudes of heathen Swazis to the Lord Christ".[2]   When Daniel Msimang died in 1903, the leadership of Swaziland Methodism was thrust into the hands of his son, Joel. The white Methodist leadership, however, had other plans. Without due consideration to the parties involved, Robert Mashaba was sent to Mahamba to direct the Swazi mission, while Msimang was not appointed to Lourenzo Marques. For blacks accustomed to higher altitudes, Lourenzo Marques was particularly dangerous as it was fever stricken. Msimang did not think it safe to jeopardise his family's health by going to live in such a climate. He had been reared in the community at Edendale, where each had a right to free expression of opinion. Joel Msimang did not feel happy nor obliged to accept white decisions made at a distance without consultation. He also owned some fixed property, partly inherited from his father and partly his own acquisition. Moreover, it would have been quite difficult to simply hand over the leadership and trust of his people, which he had just assumed from his father. Msimang's son Richard was on his way to Taunton College in England for higher education and moving station would have upset family plans. The white leadership remained firm in its decision, so Msimang was forced to tender his resignation from the white church.[3] In 1904, he formed the Independent Methodist Church. Contrary to missionary predictions that it would not survive beyond Msimang's lifespan, this church has

---

[2] Cited in F.J. Perkins, "A History of Missions in Swaziland to 1910", PhD thesis, University of the Witwatersrand, 1975, p. 383.

[3] *Ibid.*, p. 430. It has been suggested that tension had also arisen between Joel Msimang and the white leadership concerning the disposition of "class money". See J.D. Taylor, *Christianity and the Natives of Southern Africa*, Lovedale, 1928, p. 81.

continued until the present day, with headquarters at Nayamane, near Mahamba.[4]

The Bantu Methodist Church

More spectacular was the forming of the Bantu Methodist church, on the Rand, in 1932–3. The leadership of this church had a flair for "stage management" and used a donkey as the church symbol. Membership was initially made up of those who were finding the financial policy of the Methodist Church quite exploitative. People on the Rand were generally experiencing a grave economic crisis and mass unemployment at the time. To compound matters, there was a simultaneous increase in church membership fees and this provided a stimulus to a discontented people to secede. Members organised a procession through the streets of Johannesburg to register their protest. A donkey led the procession with placards on which was written "Jesus Christ was sold for thirty pieces of silver. We are sold for thirty pence."[5] This was a direct reference to the new fee applicable to black Methodist members on the Rand.

Sundkler finds it interesting that a broad mass of urban church people played a key role in this upheaval and that there was "an unmistakable nationalist spirit which fired leaders and followers with enthusiasm for the break."[6] This growing feeling of national consciousness and revolt against the white oppressors was accompanied by the rapid and heavy industrialisation of the country. South Africa and its peoples were moving towards a capitalist economy, based on exploitation of cheap labour and racist class rule. The Witwatersrand was the key industrial centre and also that part of the country experiencing the most secessions from white churches. Living in the squalor of "native reserves", in an underworld of misery where, like dark phantoms, they were ceaselessly reminded of their "sub-humanity", it was not unnatural for black labourers to experience the extinction of their character and culture. It was particularly unacceptable for

---

[4] *Ibid.*, p. 431.

[5] B.G.M. Sundkler, *Bantu Prophets in South Africa*, Oxford University Press, 1976[2], p. 172. As recently as 1989, black Methodists from Soweto staged a demonstration at the Central Methodist Church in Johannesburg during a Sunday morning service, against racial discrimination in the church and the white chairman's handling of a black minister's transfer. (Sowetan, 13 November 1989).

[6] *Ibid.*, p. 48.

them to find that at the same time the church was an agent of the process of dehumanisation and exploitation in the religious realm. It was not strange then that blacks began to think of establishing their own church, where they could rediscover their humanity together.

The United Methodist Church

Much later, but more dramatic and tantamount to an "ecclesiastical disaster", was the banning of the Methodist Church in the Transkei "homeland" in 1978.[7] The "prime minister" of the Transkei, Mr George Matanzima, himself a Methodist preacher, was angered by a church conference decision not to send greetings to heads of states, for he saw this as an attempt to avoid giving recognition to his "republic". Church officials tried desperately, but in vain, to dissuade him from declaring the Methodist Church an "undesirable organisation" in his territory. Deputy chairman of the Clarkebury district (which covered most of the Transkei), Rev. Paul Shone, was subsequently declared an "undesirable alien" and escorted with his family to the border post. Sixteen other ministers remained loyal to the Methodist Church and left in the wake of the formation of a new church. Rev. Sizwe Mbabane, last secretary of the Clarkebury synod, was invited to serve in a white society in Boksburg and became only the second black minister to do so. Those who remained included the district chairman, Rev. Ferrier Fikeni, who felt that the formation of a "breakaway church" was better than having no church at all. Fikeni was instrumental in drawing up a new constitution for his church which, though modelled on the South African church, did not include legislation along racial lines. While the decision to secede was hardly theological in outlook, there were evidently other deep frustrations which motivated the Transkei ministers not to remain loyal to the Methodist Church. The church was certainly no paragon of Christian virtue on the issue of race relations and the possibility of having their own church run by their own leaders, free from white domination, must have encouraged them in their course.

Formation of the Black Methodist Consultation

In spite of the Methodist Church consistently professing itself to be "one and undivided" since the advent of National Party rule in South

---

[7] *Dimension*, Newspaper of the Methodist Church, July 1978.

Africa (1948), the black experience of this unity was peripheral. For many it simply did not exist on the empirical level. White racism continued to permeate much of religious life, like a "monster", as the church was characterized by relentless discriminatory practices. Black Methodists were increasingly feeling the need to strive for freedom from ecclesiastical injustice—from "baasskap"—and were seeking recognition in a church that was rightfully "theirs". The Methodist Church was until now controlled by "white decision-makers" and the time had come for some clergy to embark on a critical programme to turn the tide. Their vision was "a church of equal representation at all levels of power sharing", where black Christians could claim "privileges and rights in God's family". The moving spirit in this new "conscientisation" was the church's youth secretary, Rev. Ernest Baartman. Ordained in 1966, Baartman had deep roots in the black consciousness movement, which was now at the height of its influence. He summoned a consultation of black Methodist ministers, to meet at St John's Methodist Church in Bloemfontein, in May 1975, to reflect on the ministry of the church from a black perspective, and, more particularly, to assess the role and contribution of black people in the leadership structures of the church. This meeting gave birth to the formation of the Black Methodist Consultation (BMC), with Baartman elected chairman and Rev. Khoza Mgojo secretary of the new organisation.

When these ministers congregated at the same venue a year later, they immediately observed that although blacks constituted the majority membership in the church (seventy five percent or more), they were carefully excluded in proportion from the decision-making courts of the church. The Methodist Church at the time composed twelve districts and the leadership of all except two was in the hands of white chairmen. In effect, this meant the perpetuation of "baasskap" on the one hand and the "dependency" syndrome on the other. Such white domination ensured that white concerns always remained primary concerns in the life of the church and that white interests were thus safeguarded by an entrenched hierarchy. Double standards, for example, in handling the transfer of a minister, produced immense feelings of insecurity among the rank and file of black ministers:

> If Minister A is white and was invited earlier into a particular circuit, and Conference feels he should be transferred to a different circuit, the normal process would be for Conference just to transfer him to where the Conference feels he would be serving the church better. But

the practice has been that the stationing committee would stop and that the chairman would go into the tedious exercise of negotiating with the man involved, pleading and exploring all kinds of possibilities of the proposed transfer, before a final decision. But, if a similar situation arises and the man happens to be black, a direct opposite process would be followed. The man involved, if he is lucky, his master and white chairman will phone him after a decision has been taken telling him that he has been transferred to circuit number so and so. Otherwise he would hear about the transfer when the chairman came back from Conference, and he will have to adjust to that decision in a very short space of time, whether he likes it or not.[8]

The Bloemfontein consultation was also "conscious of the activity of the God of History", who was instigating rapid and urgent changes in Southern Africa. As "servants of Christ", the ministers pledged themselves to work for the dismantling of all "old traditions and customs which are a reproach to the word of God" and the "elimination of racism and the structures of injustice in the life and witness of our church."[9] The Consultation was strongly of the opinion that the church should not divorce itself from political life. Some Christian leaders, it noted, were totally oblivious to "the needs of liberation that lie within the teachings of the Christian faith". Black sermons had to "germinate political consciousness, so that our people are led to take relative action in a local situation". The stationing of ministers should not be done along ethnic lines but in relation to circuit needs. Membership of the BMC was henceforth to be open to both clergy and laity. Educationally, "black awareness" was to be the starting point: "We should accept the fact that we are Black and set our goals in the pilgrimage of Blackness in relation to our Black situation". Self-

---

[8] *The Acts of Black Methodists in Southern Africa 1886–1986*, Ed. Otto Mbangula and Sidney Dube. Prepared in celebration of the Tenth Anniversary of the Black Methodist Consultation, BMC, 1986, p. 6. Black ministers therefore felt obliged and made it a common practice to be at Conference every October, to watch developments closely and overcome their "feeling of utmost helplessness in the presence of those who have power to decide your destiny and that of your children." Black ministers being moved could at least consult with their white bosses "over a cup of tea, or running after your Chairman as he is rushing to the toilet between sessions". The minister in this way could consider himself a "co-opted participant" and thus explain his transfer to his family and congregation with confidence and dignity (p. 70). In addition to this course, most of the information about the BMC has been obtained from the BMC Minute Book, which is a collection of minutes of the May and September meetings held from 1976 to 1985, with appendices, and the BMC newsletter *The Black Methodist.*

[9] Minutes, p. 7.

examination was necessary as it was agreed that blacks had been affected by the psychological oppression born out of existing structures.

In the aftermath of the 1976 Soweto uprising, the BMC met at Bloemfontein to examine the prevailing political situation and was challenged to identify "the basic causes of what is taking place in Azania these days. If Black Consciousness means anything to us, we must be emancipated psychologically and must be able to stand up straight".[10] During devotions Rev. Enos Sikakane encouraged young people to read black history and cautioned the consultation that "sometimes the enemies are within the gates and not outside". "We as Black people have to know who we are. We have been fed very long as chickens. The time is ripe for us now to fly and be on our own."[11] Chairman Ernest Baartman observed that the Methodist Church had been "very quiet, in spite of the crisis in our country" and implored members present to renew their commitment. In the discussions that followed it was noted that a person is neither a white nor a black Christian and what mattered most was the spirit of Christ dwelling within: "Our Blackness comes from God. It stretches from the wretchedness of the earth into the Trinity". It was further noted that much had to be done in relating God to the black experience. The BMC agreed to support at the forthcoming church conference the nomination of a black president in the person of Rev. Abel Hendricks. The intense consultation ended with the singing of the national anthem *Nkosi Sikeleli i'Africa*.

The BMC faced other challenges in its formative years as well. On numerous occasions the *status quo* in the church regarding the composition of circuits was questioned. While the principle of amalgamating circuits into non-racial or geographical ones was supported, black circuits were to resist being "absorbed" into white ones, as was increasingly the practice. The BMC believed the integration of circuits did not necessarily mean that people would worship together.[12] The spirituality of the Black Church was furthermore a unique contribution which blacks should not abandon nor be ashamed of: "Integration of services should not just be a coming together on Sunday services to absolve the consciences of the Whites, and it should not be furthering the Westernization of the church".[13] One of the prerequisites of

---

[10] *Ibid.*, p. 9.
[11] *Ibid.*, p. 9, 11.
[12] *Ibid.*, p. 21.
[13] *Ibid.*, p. 37.

integration was that the blacks and the whites should see each other as equals. But the question was also asked, "Are we really equal with Whites financially? If we are not, is it not true that those who are stronger financially are weak?"[14] Care had to be exercised, therefore, to avoid a situation where blacks would end up being "landed with whites whose arrogance and know-all attitudes are going to override the Black socio-cultural conditions". The main problem with integrated circuits was the predominance of white super-intendency. The BMC refused to accept the determining factor to be "seniority" in the appointment of superintendents, as this was sometimes "planned": "How many "senior" black men (in their years in the ministry) have accepted for years the superintendency of young junior Whites?"[15] The BMC was not aware of situations where whites were willing to come under black leadership. Integrated circuits would also not work if whites did not treat the question of understanding African languages as a priority. The real dilemma was that blacks were still finding themselves in "master and servant" relationships with the advent of geographical circuits.[16]

While the BMC was founded as a response to "white power arrogance" in a church that professed itself "one and undivided", its origins may also be traced to the great awakening of black people, in a period of organised black resistance and struggle. In the words of Rev. Otto Mbangula, "It reflects the wider determination of exploited and oppressed Black people not to submit to the definition and organisation of reality as articulated by a white oppressive and bourgeois exploitative elite and their culture within the South African social formation."[17] The BMC was intended as a "Black Consciousness

---

[14] *Ibid.*, p. 132 (Appendix N)

[15] *Ibid.*, p. 133.

[16] A geographical circuit would be composed of clusters of both black and white congregations. By May 1987 (see p. 7) of Minutes), the BMC felt that "the proposition about geographic circuits" was not feasible for the following reasons:
  (1) it has to be preceded by attitude changes on the part of whites, i.e. they must be prepared to meet blacks on an equal basis.
  (2) it must be preceded by an education process which will facilitate a two-way communication whereby whites will learn African languages.
  (3) difference in manner of worship, e.g. Easter Convention and revival services.
  (4) difference in nature of departments, e.g. Women's Manyano, Young Men's Guild, etc.
  (5) the existence of the Group Areas Act has an effect on a minister's place of residence.

[17] *Acts of Black Methodists*, p. 80.

formation", hence its membership was exclusively black. This was essential "because it believes that no one but black people can save themselves sincerely and wholly."[18] One of the guiding principles for the BMC black consciousness philosophy is derived from adherents' "belief in God through Jesus Christ, who has called us into being and made us to be active participants in his creation."[19] The BMC was therefore defined as a Christian organisation for the oppressed in South Africa. It was not to be seen as a "religious duplication" of any black political group. Neither was it a secret organisation, as its views were openly communicated at official Methodist courts and conferences. Funds were being solicited in accordance with standard Methodist practice and the projects like the support of black theological students were reported in the official church newspaper. The BMC was indeed born out of turmoil and the demands of a rapidly changing society, where black Christians were feeling challenged to "negotiate the unknown" and cry out to each other, "Rise up, O men of God; the world for you doth wait."

From its inception, the BMC sought actively to promote its aims and objectives among blacks throughout the connection. From initially being a male ministerial preserve, it moved swiftly to accommodate both laymen and laywomen, with particular attention given to youth work.[20] Many avenues of Christian ministry in the Methodist Church were attended to with renewed dedication and vigour, as a result of "pushing" from the BMC. Not all Methodists, though, rejoiced now that blacks "were pursuing with might their objective of being equal participants" with whites. Instead, the BMC found itself confronted by "fears and insecurity in many quarters" within the church. The "Black monster" was fast being seen as a threat to the stability of Methodism in Southern Africa. One district chairman publicly questioned the "luxury of a separate group" or "closed-shop consultation" in a situation of open dialogue. He was sharply reminded that "it is precisely whites like him, who know what is good for black people, who are

---

[18] *Black Methodists*, 1/1, p. 2.

[19] *Acts of Black Methodists*, p. 83.

[20] To the youth the BMC had special appeal. Selby Madwe found the BMC saying, "Hey, we are black, let us rise and put on a new garment. Let us shake ourselves loose from the bonds and affirm our blackness, and therefore our human beingness". Ivan Samdaan said, "We do not question the presence of whites in the Methodist Church, but what we do question is their claim to have all the rights to dominate and rule others on the basis of their skin colour" (*Black Methodist*, 1/1, p. 11).

the basic cause for the continued existence of the BMC."[21] Neither
was it true that the BMC was "the only racist organisation" in the
Methodist Church, as others implied. Blacks were not going to be
intimidated by thinly veiled threats and would continue with their
commitment to the struggle for non-racialism in the church. The BMC
remained convinced that "History will no doubt judge us as having
been full of love for the church of Christ."[22]

The single most influential area where the BMC was to make its
greatest contribution was in the development of black leadership. There
were numerous attempts at the annual conferences to nominate black
clergy to leadership positions in the church. No fewer than six active
members of the BMC were elected to the church's highest office—
President of Conference. From its formation, the BMC believed that
"the stage is now set for the equal sharing of power between Blacks
and Whites in all aspects of policy-making."[23] However, the BMC
was aware that the most important administrative court of the church
was not the conference but the district synod, and so it called on
black clergy to "demand a fair share of power at the chairmanship
level". If a district was unable to nominate a suitable black candidate
for chairmanship from within its ranks, an "outsider" (minister from
another district) should be sought.[24] The position of chairman was
vested with much power in the Methodist Church and the BMC was
convinced that black members where not being faithfully served by
white chairmen who had white interests at heart. This realization
seemed to have filtered through as well as to some whites, who noted
that the Methodist system as a whole was "white" and "western" and
"capitalist".[25] Two white chairmen eventually offered to resign their
positions "in the interest of encouraging black leadership" but were
faced with a barrage of criticism from some white Methodists. One
proved his integrity by honouring his commitment, while the other
capitulated and began entrenching himself in his position, to the
detriment of blacks.

The common practice at most Methodist synods has been to elect

---

[21] *Dimension*, August 1 and September 5, 1982. In this heated exchange the black
"fine young man" and "Christian brother" blessed with an excellent education was
cautioned to "humble himself before the Lord" by the chairman, who had made
a special effort to "reaffirm my love for my black brethren."
[22] *Minutes*, p. 127 (Appendix M).
[23] *Ibid.*, p. 5.
[24] *Ibid.*
[25] *Dimension*, March 4, 1979.

whites as chairmen and blacks as vice-chairmen. The BMC took strong exception and questioned why "it has always been our tendency to think about white brethren for high positions in the church."[26] The "uselessness" of the position of vice-chairman was raised in 1977 and the BMC agreed that blacks should not accept nominations to this position, or vote on it. In one district, the black vice-chairman refused re-election, in spite of strong pressure from his white superior.[27] In another district, the white chairman succeeded in strategically preventing his deputy's resignation, much to the dismay of the BMC. The situation has hardly been reversed over the years, despite intense caucusing and the general pattern of change sweeping the country. The Methodist Church is currently being administered by eight white and five black chairmen. Of the latter five, two have very small "mission" constituencies, one was elected on a third ballot with tight opposition from a white candidate, while another had his position momentarily "hijacked" while on leave overseas. In the ineffective position of vice-chairman, however, there are nine blacks and only four whites. This racial imbalance in a church whose majority membership is black did not pose a problem to one chairman, who believed that there "can be no more democratic system of election than that employed in the election to office in our church", and was therefore comfortable with the *status quo*.[28] These chairmen have on occasion been a "law unto themselves" and their powers were again evident when they took upon themselves the title of "bishop", instead of chairman, to the dismay of many. The BMC was therefore wise to locate the real power struggles on the district synod floor, rather than on the national conference platform.

The limited extent to which a black president is "allowed" to serve black interests, on an executive that is predominantly white, is now being questioned. In addressing the 1988 church conference, the Reverend Otto Mbangula noted that, after having a string of black presidents and a handful of black chairmen, blacks were asking "Why have things not changed? Is there anything wrong with the people we elect onto these positions. Why do they get so easily swallowed up by something?" The answer, according to him, was simple: "The fact lies in the structures they represent and have to maintain", since

---

[26] *Minutes*, p. 4.
[27] *Ibid.*, p. 28.
[28] *Dimension*, September 5, 1982.

they were designed to enhance white supremacy on the one hand
and black subordination on the other. Mbangula concluded that the
church could have a hundred black presidents but "as long as structures
are not changed real power will always remain in white hands."[29]

Did the election of blacks to certain influential positions in the church
mean that "we have won the battle", or was it merely "window-
dressing?" This was the crucial question posed by Rev. Lizo Jafta,
in the context of black theology and the future of Methodism. Jafta
believed "The first thing to be done is to evaluate the performance
of those black leaders whom the BMC has put into office". He went
on to ask: "To what extent have they been honest to black feelings?
To what extent have the aspirations of blacks in the Methodist Church
been expressed through them? To what extent has the white liberal
mentality sucked them into the white oppressive Laager? In what kind
of circles are they to be mostly found?"[30]

To venture an answer to these disturbing questions is probably
unwarranted now, but they cannot be relegated to the background
of any scenario. Jaffta's further question must therefore always be asked,
"How black are the black leaders?", if the programme of black theology
and black consciousness is to remain relevant to the BMC.

Conclusion

Does the threat of schism remain? Remotely. The Clarkebury district
in the Transkei has been reclaimed, with the fall of the Matanzima
dynasty, and so the last major secession is merely of historical
importance. The formation of the BMC carried with it the potential
to mobilize black Methodists, even to the point of seceding from the
establishment of the church. Leaders rather diverted this potential
into seeking piecemeal amelioration of the black predicament in
leadership and other related areas of church life. The BMC meeting
held in Cape Town before the October 1989 church conference,
decided to "push" for one or two ordination services to be held in
the Langa township; alternatively, requesting black ordinands to boycott
the service if the conference did not approve. Such pressure tactics
are to be welcomed in bringing the church closer to "home" and
in helping her discover her "grassroots". Yet, what is clearly lacking

---

[29] *Black Methodist*, 1989.
[30] *BMC Reports*, Tenth Anniversary Edition, 1986, p. 15.

is an overall strategy to liberate the church from being captive to its present bureaucratic framework, cultural fixation and *status quo* orientation. Current black leaders seem silently to concur that for various reasons, schism is the most viable option to transport the church into the next century. The uniformity of this perception can be gauged by the fact that, while much rhetoric about a "breakaway" or "confessing" church has been perennially echoed, no systematic attempt has been made to date by any individual or group, to explore the implications of such a move. Blacks have therefore resigned themselves to remaining within the ranks of "settler" Methodism, unlike the Tiles, Dwanes and Mokones, while increasing the tempo of their struggle for change.

The future of Methodism in Southern Africa is pregnant with possibilities, and changes on a momentous scale can be ushered in. The ideology of apartheid is slowly crumbling, as numerous discriminatory laws are being repealed in the interests of a new political dispensation. One of the world's most famous Methodists, Nelson Mandela, has been released from his political prison and is now the key player in negotiations with the government for a new South Africa. The political tide has certainly turned for the better and Methodists need no longer engage in their habitual tirade against the sins of the National Party. While the prophetic aspects of the church's mission never cease to exist, it would be a futile exercise for Christians to persist in denouncing evils that are now transitory. The more urgent task is to read the "signs of the time" and engage in concrete forms of action that anticipate the new society to be built on the ruins of apartheid. Elsewhere I have drawn attention to a variety of concerns for church involvement, including the struggles of workers, women and students.[31] The vestiges of apartheid in the church remain, and in seeking to obliterate them one faces "the very problems that would be raised by those in the political sphere who would be dismantling the system".[32] One should therefore not expect the church to become an overnight replica of the Kingdom of God on earth; rather, a pathway forward has been created through political change, and the Methodist Church can shape this change and be changed by it. This also implies

---

[31] See my "Christian Resistance to Apartheid", Skotaville, Johannesburg, 1989, pp. 171–175.

[32] Statement of presiding bishop, Stanley Mogoba, at 1989 conference, in *Dimension*, November 1989.

that the future role of the church should be located and defined in the larger context of the liberation process that will probably gain momentum in the coming years. In the light of this scenario, it is probable that the impetus for independent formation will decline even further.

ORIGINS OF THE SPIRITUAL HEALING CHURCH IN BOTSWANA

R.H. FRIESEN

Abstract

The Spiritual Healing Church, one of the 170 registered AICs in Botswana, has it roots in the charismatic revival of 1923 in which Harry Morolong of the Thaba Nchu-Bloemfontein area played a leading role. Prophet Mokaleng assumed leadership of the group which grew out of the visit of Moralong. Only in 1952 did this movement constitute itself into an independent church. This paper also discusses, *inter alia*, the reasons for establishing this church, the role of women, the organisation of the church, education and economics, and the role of the Bible and tradition in the church.

Introduction

While numerous studies have been made of individual independent churches in Africa, and especially in the Republic of South Africa, this is not true of Botswana, where one finds almost no published studies of AICs. In addition to the few published works (see bibliography), there are a fair number of unpublished studies at the University of Botswana in the form of student papers, conference proceedings, and the university's Religion in Botswana project.

For the purpose of background to this study of the Spiritual Healing Church in Botswana, it may be helpful to recall the history of Christianity in the country as a whole. This began with the interaction of early British missionaries with the *dikgosi* (leaders) of the Botswana *morafe* (nations) in the nineteenth century. Robert Moffat of the London Missionary Society made the first missionary journey into present-day Botswana in 1824, and his mission at Kuruman in South Africa greatly influenced the course of Christianity in Botswana. Because of the need for the *kgosi's* approval for all activities of the *morafe*, Christianity developed along ethnic group lines, with each group accepting the denomination of their *kgosi's* resident missionaries. Thus the Bangwato, Bangwaketse, and Bakwena followed the LMS. The Barolong were Methodist, the Bakgatla were Dutch Reformed, and the Bamalete were Lutheran. (This is not to say that every member of the *morafe* joined the church, but those who did so had only the one church to join.) This "tribal" pattern continued well into the twentieth century, until it was finally broken down by competing mission groups, the rise of independent churches and the general mobility of modern society.

There are approximately 170 registered AICs in Botswana today. A number of these originated outside the country, particularly in South Africa in the early decades of this century. More recently, splits and breakaways within Botswana itself have caused a growth in the number of churches. Many of these groups are very small, often consisting of only one congregation.

The Spiritual Healing Church, although influenced by prophet-led movements in South Africa and Lesotho, had its origin and growth entirely in Botswana, in the 1950s. The church was founded in the village of Matsiloje in north-eastern Botswana in 1952, by Prophet Jacob Mokaleng Motswaosele. The church is now under the leadership of Archbishop Israel Motswaosele, eldest son of Prophet Mokaleng, who died in 1980. The headquarters remain at Matsiloje but the largest congregations are in urban centres, particularly in Gaborone, Mahalaphy, Serowe and Francistown.

The Charismatic Revival of 1923: Forerunner of the Spiritual Healing Church

The Spiritual Healing Church, although founded in, and indigenous to Botswana, is a child of the independent church movement in the Republic of South Africa and in Lesotho. The spark which eventually gave rise to the Spiritual Healing Church was lit by a prophet of this movement, Prophet Harry Morolong, who visited the village of Matsiloje, in what was then the Bechuanaland Protectorate, in 1923.

1. The Barolong of Thaba Nchu

The Botswana of Matsiloje are members of the Barolong *morafe*, of the clan known as the Seleka Barolong. Their ancestors came to Matsiloje from the town of Thaba Nchu in South Africa early in this century.

The clan had been living at Thaba Nchu since 1833, where they had settled after years of migration and upheaval during the *Difaqane*.

Under Kgosi Moroka II (who ruled 1830–1880), Thaba Nchu became a flourishing town and enjoyed relative prosperity and stability. The Wesleyan Methodist Missionary Society established a mission among the Barolong and built churches and schools. A leadership crisis, however, succeeded the death of Moroka II. This caused the *morafe* to divide and a portion of it to emigrate to the Bechuanaland Protectorate.

The Barolong who emigrated were led by Samuel Moroka, son of Moroka II; Samuel was banished from Thaba Nchu, after the death of his rival Tshipinare in the bitter quarrel which followed Moroka's death. After some years of wandering from place to place, Samuel Moroka and his followers turned their eyes northward, to a relatively unsettled area of the Bechuanaland Protectorate known as the Tati District or the Tati Concession.

2. *Immigration to Matsiloje*

Since 1888 the Tati District had been claimed by the Tati Concession Company, a British commercial venture, although the Protectorate government did not officially recognize the company's rights over the district until 1911 (Tapela, *The Tati District*, p. 88). At that date the company was given full ownership of the land, which they hoped to sell to European settlers, mining having failed to prosper sufficiently in the district.

It was to the Tati Company that Samuel Moroka applied for permission to settle, when he moved north from the Transvaal in 1898. The company agreed to the request, but Samuel's small group found the district inhospitable and drought-prone, and experienced much hardship on their arrival.

Samuel Moroka, nevertheless, encouraged several thousand of his followers at Thaba Nchu to join him, which they did in 1916. Although the scheme of settling these people at Matsiloje seemed initially promising, disaster soon followed. Unusually cold winter weather followed by drought left Matsiloje in the condition of a refugee camp. Malaria took its toll, as did malnutrition and an epidemic of Spanish influenza in 1918. Some of the Barolong became disillusioned and returned to the union, while others went to look for work elsewhere in the Protectorate or in what was then Rhodesia.

Reduced in numbers, demoralised and poverty-stricken, Samuel Moroka's followers found their community life deteriorating rapidly by 1923. This was true despite the fact that, as Methodists, they had found support from the Methodist Church in Rhodesia, which supplied them with a minister.

Perhaps as a result of the difficulties, moral conditions deteriorated in the village, especially among the young people. Matsiloje acquired a reputation for profligacy, carousing and fights (Lesabe and Sereetsi, June 21, 1988).

3.   *Prophet Harry Morolong*

It was into this situation that a visitor arrived in Matsiloje in 1923, one who was to have a profound impact on the village. This was Prophet Harry Morolong, a resident of the Thaba Nchu-Bloemfontein area and a relative of the Barolong at Matsiloje. Morolong is thought to have come under the influence of Prophet Walter Matitta (d. 1935) of Lesotho, possibly during one of Matitta's evangelistic preaching tours through the Orange Free State in 1918 and 1921. Morolong claimed to have been instructed in a vision to go to Matsiloje to preach because the village was in such difficulty (Lesabe, June 21), 1988).

Morolong spent several weeks preaching at Methodist Church gatherings in Matsiloje. Evening prayer services were initiated, with singing, prayer and preaching. Morolong's preaching was apocalyptic in content and charismatic in style. He called on the young people of the village to prepare for the coming of God's kingdom by reforming their lives. People came in throngs to hear Morolong's preaching, and he is remembered by those who heard him as the one who "planted the Spirit" in Matsiloje (Sereetsi, June 21, 1988, and December 10, 1988).

The unusual spiritual phenomena which accompanied Morolong's preaching—violent trembling, shaking and speaking in tongues, startled his hearers and caused some to distrust his message. After Morolong returned to South Africa, some of the young people who had been influenced by his preaching continued to gather for prayer. Two weeks after Morolong's departure, many of the youth in these meetings began to have experiences of being filled with or touched by the Holy Spirit and to exhibit phenomena similar to those of Prophet Morolong— shaking, speaking in tongues and praying in the Spirit.

The prayer meetings continued to be held for the next three years. They consisted of singing, Scripture reading, prayer, preaching and prophetic messages revealed by the Spirit. The participants in the prayer movement were teenagers and a few older young people, all from Methodist Church families. They were led by several of the young men of the village, including Jacob Motswaosele, Jacob Lesaba and Esau Lesabe.

This charismatic revival had a startling effect on the village of Matsiloje. The wild behaviour of the young people ceased. Kgosi Moroka, the church leaders and the parents sought for an explanation; some said that the children of the village were possessed by demons. After consulting several church leaders, Moroka gave permission for the prayer meetings to continue, under the supervision of the two local Methodist evangelists, Jeremiah Tshose and Paul Segopa (I Motswaosele, October 26, 1987). The meetings became more sporadic over the years as the young people went to work in South Africa, returning infrequently to Matsiloje. The movement eventually died out altogether in Matsiloje, at least in its original form.

Prophet Mokaleng (1900–1980)

1. *Early Life*

One of the participants in the Matsiloje revival of 1923 was a young man named Jacob Mokgwetsi Motswaosele, later to be known as Prophet Mokaleng, founder and head of the Spiritual Healing Church.

Jacob Motswaosele (better known by his nickname "Mokaleng") was born in 1900, in Thaba Nchu in the Orange Free State. His parents, Israel and Diole Motswaosele, moved with the family to Matsiloje in the 1916 migration. Shortly after their arrival, Mokaleng's parents died in the tragic epidemics which took so many lives. For a time, Mokaleng lived with relatives and worked as a herdsman. He never received any formal education (I. Motswaosele, October 26 and 27, 1987).

When Harry Morolong began his meetings in 1923, Mokaleng attended them and soon became a leader in the group. In 1926 he left Matsiloje to look for work in the Union of South Africa. On his annual or semi-annual visits home, the prayer meetings were resumed, but ceased in his absence (J. Sereetsi, June 21, 1988).

In 1928, Mokaleng was married to Martha Tshose of Matsiloje. Two sons and three daughters were born to them. At that time the family were members of the Methodist Church, but in South Africa Mokaleng encountered and eventually joined the St John's Apostolic Faith Mission of Mma Christinah Nku, probably in 1948 or 1949 (B. Moilwa, April 26, 1990).

In 1949, Jacob Mokaleng felt the call of the Holy Spirit to prophesy. He had several visions in which he was instructed to return to Matsiloje permanently. In this spiritual crisis he sought the counsel of Mma Nku and was told to obey this call. She told him, "You have been ordered to go to Bechuanaland and to serve the people there. You have been given the country of Bechuanaland." (I. Motswaosele, October 26, 1987; J. Motswaosele, February 4, 1990).

In 1949, Mokaleng and his family returned permanently to Matsiloje, where prayer meetings were quickly resumed. Mokaleng was filled with the Spirit and began to prophesy. People began to come to him for prayers and healing, and within a year Mokaleng was conducting a full-time prayer ministry, with healing as its central focus. (Healing had not been part of the earlier prayer meetings.)

The years 1950 and 1952 were stirring ones in Matsiloje. Large groups of people from all over the Protectorate, and beyond, gathered at Matsiloje. Each day the prophet (as Mokaleng soon came to be called) led outdoor prayer services in the morning and again in the afternoon or evening.

A great number of ill, crippled, and blind people went to the prophet for healing; he was also sought out by people with special problems, e.g. those who were unemployed or who could not have children. Mentally ill people were brought for healing. People who had lost touch with a relative who had gone to South Africa asked the prophet to pray for that person's return or "to call him back".

Prophet Mokaleng eventually had some small buildings constructed near the site of the present church, in which people could stay and the sick be treated. A large shelter was put up in which prayer services could be held. Here, crowds of people sat patiently and quietly on the ground, awaiting their turn for consultation and prayer. In his healing ministry, Mokaleng used mainly water and prayer, occasionally also salt and ashes.

Sunday services were high points of the week. They involved preaching, prayers for the sick and much singing, during which individuals were sometimes possessed by the Spirit. When Prophet Mokaleng was possessed by the Spirit, he would sing for one or two minutes, then calm down and pray (M. Kokoro, July 5, 1989).

These events in Matsiloje aroused a certain amount of curiosity and opposition on the part of the Protectorate authorities. Prophet Mokaleng was occasionally summoned to Francistown for questioning at the District Commissioner's office. But, unlike some leaders of African independent churches, Mokaleng was never arrested, flogged or imprisoned for his activities. The *morafe* authorities seem to have been tolerant from the beginning. Samuel Moroka had died and his nephew, who succeeded him, did not interfere in the prayer and healing services.

2. *Founding of the Spiritual Healing Church*

The new religious movement, sparked by the revival of 1923 and continued in the prayer and healing ministry of Prophet Mokaleng, eventually separated from the Methodist Church and the St John's Apostolic Faith Mission, in which it had been nurtured, and a new church was born. This took place in 1952.

Starting a new church had not been the prophet's intention; he wanted to pray for people, heal them and send them back to their own churches. A number of his followers, however, urged him to begin an independent church. Because Mokaleng was looked on as a dissident, those who went to him also were looked down on and ostracised in their home churches.

On October 10, 1952, a resolution to establish an independent church was taken by the prophet and a few followers. Mokaleng chose the name "Apostolic United Faith Coloured Church" for the new denomination. (The name of the church was to undergo several changes before reaching its present form). Following the practice of the "apostolic" family of churches in South Africa, the new group instituted believers' baptism by immersion as the means of joining the church. Prophet Harry Moroleng was invited to return to the village to perform the first baptisms, which took place on April 6, 1953, in the Ramokgwebane River.

In 1955, Prophet Mokaleng began construction of a church building in Matsiloje. Harry Moraleng was again invited to return to speak at the opening of this building. In his speech he pointed out that although the work of the Holy Spirit began there in 1923, it was only now with the dedication of this building that the progress of that work could be seen (J. Sereetsi, June 21, 1988).

3. *Spiritual Gifts and Ministry*

Prophet Mokaleng was a man of powerful charisma. His spiritual gifts were widely recognized, and foremost among them the gift of healing. Several examples will illustrate the experiences of healing.

I was attracted to this church by the power of prayer shown by the prophet. My fiance went to the prophet for healing in 1950 and I went to see her several times during her stay in Matsiloje. When I went, I was suspicious of what was taking place, but I returned home convinced. A woman who was completely crippled was brought and the prophet healed her with blessed water. This and many other instances convinced me of the prophet's abilities (T.L. Molake, June 22, 1988).

Mokaleng performed many miracles, mostly using just prayer. In 1952 my wife was ill and I took her to Matsiloje for healing. At that time she had been lying helpless for seven days. The prophet said, "You will see that faith will heal. After we have sung three songs, the sick one will rise". She did! I was amazed. The prophet had not even prayed for her yet. We returned home after two days and my wife had no recurrence of the illness (P.A. Wright, August 17, 1989).

As a teenager I worked for Mokaleng, helping him in treatment of the sick. I saw many people healed in startling ways—bones straightened, the blind able to see. He did many miracles in front of my own eyes. Mokaleng used a variety of methods—usually prayer, but not always. He sometimes used water, salt, ashes, or mud. One crippled man was there for three weeks before he was healed. Suddenly one day the prophet told those supporting this man as he entered the church to let go of him. They feared he would fall—but suddenly he could walk, and started to sing happily. I saw such things not once but many, many times (B. Moilwa, November 23, 1989).

Mokaleng also sometimes diagnosed a person as needing surgery and sent him/her to a hospital for medical treatment.

A second spiritual gift for which Mokaleng was widely acclaimed was the gift of "sight": the ability to diagnose the cause of an illness, to divine a person's motives or past experiences, to interpret dreams and visions, and to foretell future events. In the words of one of his followers, "Mokaleng liked people very much, and could prophesy what kind of people were coming to him" (M. Gaorutwe, July 9, 1989).

Prophet Mokaleng was also known as a powerful preacher who could hold the awestruck attention of a huge crowd. He preached from the Bible; although he could not read, others read the Bible to him and he memorized portions of it, especially from the Old Testament prophets.

Prophet Mokaleng is remembered as a man of great authority, imposing stature, and of very powerful, commanding personality. At the same time, he was a very kind person who helped many people. "Mokaleng was a simple man, gifted with power from God" (B. Rantsudu, May 19, 1989).

Prophet Mokaleng continued to live in Matsiloje all of his life, but as time passed and religious freedom increased, he began travelling to other parts of Botswana and also to Namibia, where he was very popular among the Herero people.

Prophet Mokaleng died on January 25, 1980, in a hospital in Pretoria. The funeral took place at Matsiloje on February 9. A large tombstone, dedicated at Easter 1987, has two biblical texts on it: 2 Timothy 4:7–8 and Hebrews 11:4.

Development of the Spiritual Healing Church

1. *Growth of the Church*

The foregoing serves as a background to the actual growth and spread of the church, as has taken place since 1952.

Prior to Independence in 1966, the church experienced great difficulty in expanding outside of the Tati District, where they enjoyed a fair degree of freedom. Thus although Mokaleng's church in Matsiloje was permitted to exist by Kgosi Tshabadira Moroka, no other branches were allowed by *dikgosi* in other places. Even small prayer meetings of the prophet's followers were frowned upon, although such groups did in fact meet clandestinely (and sometimes fairly openly) at several locations outside of Matsiloje.

The experience of the Spiritual Healing Church between 1952 and 1966 was in some ways that of an underground church. Many people were baptised and joined the church at Matsiloje, where they enjoyed a remarkable degree of freedom. But such freedom did not exist for them when they returned to their homes in other parts of the Protectorate. The small prayer groups which they started later grew into fully-fledged congregations.

Since Independence, the church has grown to its present size of 28 congregations. A constitution was adopted in 1972 and formal leadership patterns adopted. Unlike many independent churches, the Spiritual Healing Church emphasises the importance of church buildings and expects each congregation to construct a building for themselves as soon as this is at all possible. Each congregation is expected to be self-reliant and only seek partial help from the wider denomination in financing their building.

Formal theological education has not been a part of leadership training in the Spiritual Healing Church, with the exception of the prophet's eldest son, Israel Motswaosele, who studied at the Morija

Bible Training Institute in Lesotho from 1963 until 1966. Upon his return, he opened an official branch congregation or mission station in the newly-designated capital city, Gabarone, in 1966.

2. *Role of Women*

Women have been active in the Spiritual Healing Church since its beginning. They have not become a part of the formal hierarchical leadership, but their freedom to express their views has increased over the years.

One exception in terms of formal leadership is the fact that women may be deacons. The talks of women deacons is mainly that of giving treatment, such as massage or baths, to women who come to the church for healing. (Men perform similar tasks for other men.)

For women, the church means opportunities. They enjoy a high degree of independence in their women's organisation, in which men do not interfere. While they must obtain the approval of the Executive Committee for their plans, this approval is virtually always given. Many women feel that they are free, rather than oppressed, in the church and that the church relies on them a great deal. Most would agree that "women are the backbone of the church" (G. Marumo, *et al.*, April 13, 1990).

The Mothers' Union originated in the earliest days of the Spiritual Healing Church. It was organised by Martha Motswaosele, the wife of Prophet Mokaleng. Soon after the church's founding, she began gathering the women into a fellowship, similar to that in which she had previously been active in the Methodist Church. The Mothers' Union is open to all women aged nineteen or older. Unmarried mothers are accepted on an equal standing with those who are married. Their participation in the organisation or, for that matter, in the church as a whole, is not restricted. The purpose of the organisation is to provide Christian fellowship which will encourage women in the church and draw them nearer to God. This goal is pursued through weekly Sunday afternoon gatherings and through annual conferences or conventions. The Sunday afternoon "class" includes prayer, singing and preaching; three or four women may preach at each meeting. Annual conferences are both regional and national in scope. The Mothers' Union has its own bank account for the substantial amounts of money it raises for church work. The Mothers' Union is regarded (at least by the women) as "carrying" the church financially.

In 1988, Archbishop Israel Motswaosele raised the question of whether women should be ordained in the Spiritual Healing Church. The question was not raised by the women themselves, and there had been no agitation on their part for this step. After much discussion, it was decided at the national conference in August, 1990, that women would be ordained to be lay preachers, but not as evangelists or as full ministers (*baruti*). All of the women, as well as some of the men, were opposed to the ordination of women as *baruti*. They felt that it is "too early" and might be confusing and divisive to the church (G. Marumo, June 27, 1991).

Early in 1991, Archbishop Motswaosele visited the Gaborone congregation and announced that the church constitution had now been amended so as to allow women to be preachers. He then called two women to the pulpit to preach. Each spoke for about five minutes. Following this living evidence that women can preach, Motswaosele called for all women who wished to preach to come forward. Approximately thirty young women did so and the Archbishop prayed for each one individually, that she might receive the gift of preaching.

3.   *Organisation*

In 1972, Prophet Mokaleng designated his two sons, Israel and Joseph Motswaosele, to take over the leadership of the Spiritual Healing Church after his death. There was, and still is today, a clear feeling that the roles of prophet and of administrator are separate gifts to the church and should not be combined in one person. The younger brother, Joseph, was anointed by his father as a prophet while the elder, Israel, was designated as the administrator (or archbishop, as the office came to be called). This arrangement was made clear to the church membership well before the prophet's death, so that the transition after his death was smooth and did not result in the breaking up of the church, as has so often occurred in independent churches at the death of their founder.

At setting out an effective organization for the church, Israel Motswaosele consciously looked around at other churches and chose what seemed to him effective and useful. The levels of pastoral leadership were designated as follows: (1) preacher; (2) deacon; (3) evangelist; (4) minister *(moruti)*. A minister must be a mature man, preferably thirty-five years old, and must be married.

The Church's Perspective on their History

In the minds of the members of the Spiritual Healing Church, the
most important event of their history was the life and ministry of
Prophet Jacob Mokaleng Motswaosele. This central fact that Mokaleng
was a great prophet who performed miracles and founded the church
is known to each member.

When those members who are best acquainted with the church's
past view their own history, several additional themes emerge.

1.   *Sources of their Church's beliefs*

Three prophets are remembered as forerunners of the Spiritual Healing
Church : Walter Matitta, who was a great prophet in Lesotho; Harry
Morolong, who brought the new work of the Holy Spirit to Botswana;
and Christinah Nku, who recognized that Jacob Mokaleng was called
by God and commissioned him for his work in Botswana. Morolong,
in particular, is remembered because he was a personal acquaintance
who visited Matsiloje a number of times and directly affected the
founding of the church. Other than these prophetic figures, the sources
of the church's beliefs and teachings are seen as the Bible and traditions
which started long ago and are now being kept and carried on by
the church. Thus, when questioned about the source of such teachings
as divine healing, believers' baptism, and the non-use of alcohol, church
leaders may reply that these practices were adopted in order to be
more like the Bible, or that they started "very long ago". Such beliefs
are accepted as handed-down tradition, with little critical thought being
given to their sources.

2.   *Reasons for starting an Independent Church*

The spiritual reason for the founding of the church, in the minds
of its adherents, was the ostracism and "banning" which individuals
encountered in their home (mission) churches after having visited
Prophet Mokaleng at Matsiloje. People needed a church of their own;
many encouraged Mokaleng to start a new church because they were
not permitted to return to their previous churches. Thus, the church
was founded to meet the needs of these people.

3.   *Experiences of Persecution and Religious Freedom*

The church's history prior to Botswana's independence is seen as a story of persecution. Persecution was not so much at the hands of the Protectorate government as by the mission churches through pressure on the *dikgosi*. It was most severe during the early 1950s but decreased as religious pluralism spread through the country just prior to independence. The church received some recognition of its right to exist as a church during the early 1960s, while at the same time the Protectorate government ceased investigating its activities.

In the minds of some of the early leaders, the attitude of the mission churches to the independent churches has not changed greatly since 1966. There remains some uncertainty as to whether independent churches are seen as people who can pray to God and as true churches. Other leaders feel that the Spiritual Healing Church is accepted on an equal basis with other churches, citing their experiences of ecumenical cooperation in their own communities.

4. *Education and Economics*

Non-literacy and poverty are recognised as part of the church's background, but they are not seen as insurmountable obstacles. Although Prophet Mokaleng had no formal education, he was nevertheless a great prophet, gifted by God. Poverty can be overcome by personal effort and the mutual support of the congregation. One can see the progress the church has made since its founding by looking at its buildings and other visible signs of growth. Racism has been overcome, as have poverty and lack of education; the church's history has shown that Africans can found and lead their own churches, even though some Western missionaries may have doubted this.

5. *Traditional Beliefs*

The Spiritual Healing Church has not required a person to cease being an African in order to join the church. Members see themselves as retaining what is helpful and also biblical in their traditional beliefs and culture. Like the Israelites, they remember and call upon their ancestors. Their church has substituted divine healing and protection rituals for the practices of the traditional religion, calling upon God for healing and protection; their prayers thus fill the same needs as did the rituals of the traditional religion.

Interviews

Rev. Israel Motswaosele: Gaborone, October 26 and 27, 1987; Matsiloje, December 11, 1988; Matsiloje, February 3, 1990; Gaborone, April 14, 1990.
Rev. Jacob Lesabe: Francistown, June 21, 1988; Francistown, February 3, 1990.
Rev. Jacob Sereetsi: Matsiloje, June 21, 1988; Matsiloje, December 10, 1988.
Rev. T.L. Molake: Mahalapye, June 22, 1988.
Mr Bampoloki Rantsudu: Gaborone, May 19, 1989.
Rev. Moutlwatsi Kokoro: Gaborone, July 5, 1989.
Rev. Monosi Gaorutwe: Bokaa, July 9, 1989.
Rev. P. Andrew Wright: Maun, August 17, 1989.
Mrs Gopolelamang Marumo: Gaborone, October 17, 1989, Gaborone, April 3, 1990.
Rev. Benjamin Moilwa: Gaborone, November 23, 1989; Gaborone, March 19 and 21, 1990; Gaborone, April 23 and 26, 1990.

BIBLIOGRAPHY

Boschman, D., "The Conflict between New Religious Movements and the State in the Bechuanaland Protectorate Prior to 1945", Unpublished Master's thesis, Harvard Divinity School, 1989.
Byaruhanga-Akiiki, A.B.T., *Workshop on Independent Churches in Botswana*, Gaborone, University of Botswana: Religion in Botswana Project, Vol. 1 (mimeo), 1983.
Lagerwerf, L., *They Pray for You: Independent Churches and Women in Botswana* (Leiden-Utrecht: Interuniversitair Instituut voor Missiologie en Oecumenica, 1982).
Mogale, M.B.M., "Church Survey: Spiritual Healing Church in Botswana", Unpublished bachelor's degree dissertation, University of Botswana, 1989.
Ngcongo, L., "Religion and Politics in an African Chiefdom: The Mothowagae Secession Revisited", Pula, *Botswana Journal of African Studies*, 3/1 (1983): 59–78.
Tapela, H.M., "The Tati District of Botswana, 1866–1969", Unpublished Ph.D. thesis, University of Sussex, Brighton, 1976.

THE CONFLICT BETWEEN THE SPIRITUAL HEALING CHURCH AND THE AUTHORITIES BEFORE INDEPENDENCE

B. RANTSUDU

Abstract

In this paper two sources of opposition to the establishment of African Independent Churches in Botswana are identified. They are the traditional leadership and missionaries. Traditional leadership, the paper argues, was effectively used by the colonial administration to thwart the development of independent churches. In the reserves the independent churches were denied church sites and the leadership was harassed. The laws of the country did not provide for the registration of new churches. The colonial administration even allowed the traditional leaders to persecute independent churches. Perhaps all this was done as a safeguard against the development of independent churches which the colonial administration feared would cause political instability.

The paper argues that the missionaries viewed the African Independent Churches with contempt and accused them of poaching membership. There was also an outcry against the refusal of the African Independent Churches to allow their members to consult doctors and attend medical hospitals. These caused conflict between the missionaries and the leaders of African spiritual churches.

The purpose of this paper is to highlight some of the problems encountered by the Spiritual Healing Church in what was then the Bechuanaland Protectorate,[1] between 1952 and 1966.

There were some negative attitudes towards the emergence of new, non-missionary churches. The prominent agents who harboured these attitudes were the following:

(i) Traditional leaders
(ii) Leaders of missionary churches

Let us now look closely at each party and see how it encouraged a negative view of African Independent Churches. It is important to understand that both traditional leaders and missionaries were closely

---

[1] The name given to Botswana before Independence.

working together; indeed, one might say they were putting pressure on each other.

Tribal Leaders and the Spiritual Healing Church

Before Independence in 1966, the Republic of Botswana was ruled by the British as a Protectorate. The traditional rulers of Botswana were *dikgosi*,[2] leaders who were traditionally the custodians of all tribal customs and traditions. It was logical, therefore, for the British to use the services of the traditional leaders in order to effectively control Botswana. The British Administration divided the country into eight major tribal groupings or reserves.

In the reserves only missionary churches were allowed, viz. the London Missionary Society, and the Anglican, Methodist, Lutheran and Dutch Reformed Churches. The idea behind this is not clear but one may assume that the Administration saw the proliferation of Spiritual or Independent Churches as a predisposing factor to political instability within the colony.

A good example is provided by the Spiritual Healing Church, which was denied permission to build a church in the Bamangwato Reserve. The tribal leader behind this opposition was none other than Kgosi Tshekedi Khama. This was during the early 1950s. In 1959, the Spiritual Healing Church requested to be registered as an official church but was refused registration. The then Colonial Commissioner, Mr Steenkamp, said that he could only allow missionary churches since they were already registered from their mother countries. There was no law he could use to register Independent Churches.[3]

Some tribal leaders also persecuted the leaders of the Spiritual Healing Church. This was done with the full consent of the Protectorate authorities. The *dikgosi* used to send their local police to arrest and detain the leaders of spiritual churches. The arrests were usually made on Sundays while they were holding their church services.

One member of the Spiritual Healing Church, my uncle, Mr K. Samphane, tells this story:

> On the 9 July 1957, I was arrested in Mmadinare together with Mrs Kethepile Rantsudu, Mr Mokenti Lebane and two other women. Two khaki-uniformed policemen came into the church (a thatch-roofed shelter)

---

[2] Setswana name for traditional leaders.
[3] Interview: Archbishop Israel Motswaosele, 13 May 1991, Matsiloje.

while we were busy worshipping. We spent the whole week in the cell. Then my followers were each fined two rands. As a leader of *baitimokanyi*[4], I was given corporal punishment (four strokes). This was during the time when Kgosi Oteng Mphoeng was tribal leader at Mmadinare, having been sent by Kgosi Tshekedi Khama at Serowe.[5]

In 1963, my uncle was again arrested, together with some church members, one early Sunday morning. Although I was young at that time, I still remember very well that two police came into the shelter and ordered the whole congregation to stop what they referred to as "shouting". Most of the adults were taken away and spent the whole night (both men and women) in a single cell. They spent the night singing at the top of their voices. There was no chance to sleep because some buckets of cold water were deliberately poured into the cell. The following morning they appeared before the tribal authority, Oteng Mphoeng. The men were given four strokes each while the women were given a suspended sentence.

Missionaries and the Spiritual Healing Church

As we have seen, the only churches that were allowed before Independence were those led by missionaries. Because of this, these churches regarded themselves as the only legitimate congregations of God.

Anyone who belonged to a church other than a missionary one was considered to be a dissident. For instance, in 1955, Rev. Segaise of the London Missionary Society had his ordination suspended, for the simple reason that he took his ailing wife to Prophet Mokaleng for healing. (He was later ordained after being warned.)[6] The missionaries accused Prophet Mokaleng of deliberately poaching members from their registered and established churches. The healing aspect, which was not found in missionary churches, seems to have been the only reason why people went to Prophet Mokaleng.[7]

It was also alleged that Prophet Mokaleng refused to allow his church followers to seek medical examination. This was not true. He used to refer people to Dr Merriweather in Molepolole and other medical

---

[4] Setswana name for hypocrites.
[5] Interview: Keiterile Samphane, 27 June 1991, Mmandinare.
[6] Interview: Archbishop Israel Motswaosele, 27 June 1991, Francistown.
[7] Interview: Kgosi Obonetse Kakabale, 20 April 1991, Mmadinare.

centres in the country.[8] This is supported by the church's constitution, on 23 December 1974, which clearly states: "The following diseases are beyond our divine healing methods, viz. tuberculosis, asthma, venereal disease, common flu, diarrhoea, leprosy, measles, post-natal, ante-natal, and delivery." These conditions were to be referred to a qualified medical practitioner.

Most missionaries had arrived at a time when traditional healings were very prevalent. They took it for granted that Mokaleng was one of these healers.

Before I conclude, I should point out that some of the accusations made by missionary circles about African Independent Churches were valid and true. Some of these churches did indeed refuse to send people for medical examination, under the pretext that God had given them the power to heal the sick.

A leader of one such church was sentenced to an effective six month imprisonment. The man was from Southern District. His two innocent children's lives were taken by measles, after he refused to take them to a local clinic. The church was not even registered. But we must admit that western medicine cannot help a desperate person who has been bewitched or considers himself/herself to have bad luck.

One of Africa's theologians comments:

People are ill spiritually and mentally. . . . they need healing. In some mainline churches, this ministry is practised at a very low key. That is why people turn to African Independent Churches in their time of need. When they are healed they do not wish to go back to their churches. The AICs are accused of "sheep-stealing".[9]

---

[8] Interview: Serwelo, S. Tlale, 27 June 1991, Mahalapye.
[9] Paul Makhubu, *Who Are Independent Churches?*, p. 77.

SWAZI ZIONISM AND THE ROYAL POLITICS
OF THE KINGDOM

J.B. MZIZI

Abstract

This paper suggests that unique cultural elements often contributed to the making of the African Independent Churches. It asserts the uniqueness of Swazi Zionism, which operates in a geo-political setting entirely of its own and thrives by adhering to cultural elements. The main feature of Swazi Zionism is its attachment to the monarchy and the royal family. The paper describes how Zionism was introduced to the royal family in Swaziland and the role of King Sobhuza II in promoting Zionism.

Introduction

One of the fundamental concerns about a foreign religion which seeks to adapt itself in a new environment is how successful it will be in sowing seeds of unity amongst its new adherents. Religions that have in time become part and parcel of a people's culture may not normally see the preservation of unity as their main function. In such situations, religion and culture are not distinguishable, nor are they in conflict with each other. Instead, the culture owes its existence and sustainability to a religion, to the same extent as that religion cannot exist outside the culture which has shaped and continues to shape it.

The best example of a religion which grew and became the central pillar of a culture is Judaism. The definition of a Jew was not just one who venerated his ancestry as having flowed from Abraham, Isaac and Jacob. But he was supposed to be one who seriously acknowledged that *Yahweh* intervened in the history of his people, caused a dramatic emancipation from Pharaoh's Egypt and then gave the ten laws at the foot of Mount Sinai. The passage in *Deut* 6:20–25 is revealing:

> In times to come, when your son asks you, What is the meaning of the decrees and laws and customs that Yahweh our God has laid down for you?, you shall tell you son, Once we were Pharaoh's slaves in Egypt, and Yahweh brought us out of Egypt by his mighty hand. Before our eyes Yahweh worked great and terrible signs and wonders against Egypt,

against Pharaoh and all his House. And he brought us out from there to lead us into the land he swore to our fathers he would give to us. And Yahweh commanded us to observe all these laws and to fear Yahweh our God, so as to be happy forever and to live, as he has granted us to do until now. For us right living will mean this: to keep and observe all these commandments before Yahweh our God as he has directed us.

Thus, Judaism defined a Jew in all respects; his historical origin, physical existence, legal expectation, spiritual inclination, literally all that a Jew was could not be found anywhere else but in what today we conveniently call the Old Testament. Jewish nationalism was preserved in these writings. We should not however assume that Judaism existed in a perfect, competition-free society. The presence of other religions, such as Baalism, in ancient Palestine posed a real threat to the continued survival of Judaism. That is why the first commandment was important: "You shall have no other gods besides me". The onus was on the Jewish religious leaders to so teach Judaism that true Jews would not waver and give in to other religions that Judaism defined as pagan.

It is interesting to notice that whenever influential Israelites embraced a pagan religious concept or image, confusion reigned, and efforts had to be made to reestablish the purity of Yahwistic religion. A clear example of this situation is found in *I Kings* 18, where religious threats to Yahwism had become really serious during the reign of Ahab and Jezebel, in the ninth century BCE. To a considerable extent, the Baalistic worship prior to this period had been assimilated into Yahwism or practised alongside Yahwism, but Jezebel had a mission to exterminate all Yahwistic elements in her strong advocacy of the Tyrian god, Baal-Melkart. The words of Elijah, the lone Jewish prophet amongst Baal's 450 prophets, depict the people's dilemma: "How long will you go limping with two different opinions? If the Lord is God, follow him; but if Baal, then follow him". And the people did not answer him a word (*I Kings* 18:20–21).

Sociologically speaking, it would be false to claim that Judaism subsequently developed without foreign cultural elements, for in any situation of inter-cultural contact, a give-and-take situation is inevitable. However, it is beyond the scope of this paper to discuss the foreign elements that emanated from the so-called pagan religions which impinged on Israelite religion.

Africa, too, had always had its own indigenous religions—what various scholars call African Traditional Religions. These religions were as varied as the African ethnic groupings. Scholars such as John Mbiti, while acknowledging the presence of ethnic religions, were prone to aggregate the ethnic religious experiences and then calling the result African Religion or African Philosophy. There may be a serious danger with such generalization because it assumes that at the core, African people are the same. If a scholar of African Religions begins from that premise, he or she is more than likely to confuse issues and fail to differentiate between particular African cultures.

I should not be construed as supporting the Bantustan philosophy developed in the heyday of Apartheid South Africa. When the Afrikaner over-emphasized that Zulus were not Xhosas and should therefore be taken to where they belonged in order to rule themselves, the motive was not the cultural preservation of Zulu nationalism but economic considerations resulting from the 1913 Land Act. Bantustans were created to serve as labour reservoirs for the so-called White South Africa. But the fact remains that Zulu culture is not necessarily African culture. Yoruba culture in West Africa is not African Culture. Ethnic cultures are subsets of the vast African Culture.

As a student of New Religious Movements and African Indigenous Churches, I have frequently noticed the unique cultural elements that shape an African Indigenous Church. H.W. Turner (1976 : 13–14) emphasises that the newness in a religious movement takes its shape both from the religious nature and the historical reality in which it emerges. He argues that what is essential in the historical circumstance is the result of the contact the primal society had with the much more powerful and sophisticated society and its religion. Turner's definition is thus:

> a new religious movement . . . refers to a new development arising in the course of the interaction of a tribal or primal society and its religion with one of the more powerful and substantial departure from the classical religious traditions of both the cultures concerned, in order to find renewal by reworking the contributing traditions into a different religious system.

Zionism is thus as unique in any geographical locale as the primal culture and the type of Christian or Muslim influence that interacted with that primal culture. (It should be noted, however, that no documentation exists on African independency in Muslim countries). We may further assert that Zulu Zionism has fundamental differences from Swazi Zionism, even though, in terms of the cultural heritage, there are many commonalities between the two nations. This is expected to be true of any form of African Zionism elsewhere in Africa. But it is true again that in any given culture, there may be more than one strand of Zionism owing to the reasons for the emergence of each form of Zionism. For example, following Sundkler's definition of a Zionist Movement, namely, that it is a movement concerned with healing and has such characteristics as speaking in tongues, etc., one sees that Swaziland has two basic types. The first group are the White Gown Zionists, some of whom are monogamous, others polygamous. They carry wooden crosses and generally do not take Bibles into their churches. The preacher reads scripture verses but he may preach without regard to the context of the scripture he has read. Prayers for the sick are predominant. These churches usually have South African connections, due to either historical origin or ecclesiastical control.

The second group are the Red Gown Zionists. It should be pointed out that "Red Gown" is a nickname. In fact, they do not want to be called Zionists—they call themselves "EMAJERICO". From my studies, I believe it is legitimate to classify them under the Zionist type, even though they are more nativistic in approach and less interested in the Bible than the White Gown Zionists. In terms of preserving Swazi nationalism and the cultural ethos, the Red Gowns are leading. Their founder Bishop Eliyas Melika Vilakati, is one of the key players in the national Ncwala Ceremony. One of the basic theologies he propounds is that the dead should, under no circumstances, be forgotten. He derives his theological position from nature, Swazi Traditional Religion and the nocturnal visitations he enjoys from old Hebrew ancestors such as Abraham, Jacob, Jeremiah and John the Baptist. Sometimes, Vilakati claims, the late King George of England visits him too.

The point we are attempting to drive home is that Swazi Zionism is unique. It operates in a unique geo-political setting and has to thrive by observing and upholding all the cultural elements necessary for its survival. The main characteristic of Swazi Zionism is its closeness to the Monarchy and the Royal Family. This has historical reasons which we shall discuss in the following section.

The Advent of Zionism in Swaziland

The name of Johanna Asiyena Nxumalo features prominently in any discussion on how Zionism spread from South Africa to Swaziland. A daughter of Vanyana Nxumalo, she was born in the early 1890s and trained as a teacher at the Inanda Teacher Training School in Natal. Johanna was a sister to King Sobhuza II's mother. While teaching at the Groenvlei School near Wakkerstroom, Johanna came into contact with Daniel Nkonyane's Christian Catholic Apostolic Holy Spirit Church in Zion and was baptised in 1913.

Following her baptism, Johanna became a vigorous preacher with gifts of prophecy and praying for the sick. Her father and brother Benjamin were very supportive of her exploits. They encouraged her a great deal to plant Zionism in Swaziland. Sundkler (1976 : 209) records an interesting recollection by Johanna's husband, after she had died:

> She prophesied and prayed for the sick and for barren women in order that they might get children. With the sick she would see how they could be healed. Yes, she had the spirit to a high degree . . . Yes, it was this Johanna Nxumalo who prophesied with veils, and then followed it up with sticks. She led people, using both sticks and veils, following those who taught them the function of these. Yes, she trusted that the sticks would help the sick.

The role of Johanna was therefore important for two reasons. First, her proximity to the Royal Family meant that she could easily spread the Zionist gospel without going through the sometimes tedious royal protocol. Through her, Zionism could more easily reach the Queen Regent and other influential members of the Royal Family than could the missionary gospel which was already more than thirty years old.

Secondly, because of her affiliation to the Nkonyanes, it was Johanna who introduced the Nkonyanes to the Royal Family. Although Zulu by nationality, the Nkonyanes claimed that they had originated in Swaziland. An act of healing was conducted on the Queen Regent Labotsibeni, after she had suffered a terrible loss of sight. Daniel Nkonyane was summoned to pray for her and it is recorded that the Queen was so impressed that she said: "Never shall I abandon a church that has helped me thus."

Those words by the Queen Regent were prophetic for indeed now, nearly eighty years later, it seems the Zionist course will never be abandoned by the Swazi Royalty.

After King Sobhuza II was installed, Daniel Nkonyane came to
meet him. Dlamini (1976 : 9) records:

> When Daniel Nkonyane came to Swaziland from Charlestown, he was
> received at Embikwakhe by Prince Mboko who then introduced him
> to King Sobhuza II at Lobamba Royal Residence. In their meeting,
> he laid hands on the King and thereafter gave him *litfusi*, a rod which
> had gone through ritual blessing. Daniel advised him to have it stuck
> upright whenever he was presiding on a national occasion. The rod
> was meant as a protection for the nation. . . .

The period 1920–1935 witnessed a steady growth and consolidation
of Zionism in Swaziland. Even though the King was supposed to
be non-denominational, it is clear that he was naturally attracted to
the Zionist course. It is important at this stage to discuss briefly the
cultural tensions that existed in the country, emanating from the clash
between the primal Swazi culture and the British imperial culture
with its Western form of Christianity.

The Role of Sobhuza II in Cultural Unity

Apart from the pressing problem of the land question, featuring high
on the young King's agenda was the need to preserve the culture
of the Swazis. This had to be done at the top for obvious reasons.
Westernism and the Christian influence had struck. The missionaries
preached a Christianity that attacked the culture of the people and
many traditions and customs were severely discouraged in the name
of the God of the Bible.

Alongside the Christian missionary was the colonial settler community, which looked down on the culture of the Swazis. The colonialist
wanted to replace the Swazi culture with the so-called civilised Western
culture. Thus, the missionary and the colonial settler were dedicated
partners in their mission to destroy the culture of the Swazis. The
irony was, however, that the colonial official A.G. Marwick had left
all matters traditional in the hands of King Sobhuza II. Indeed, this
was a blessing in disguise.

The missionaries worked fairly well with fewer clashes among
themselves. This was evidenced in 1911, when they met to agree on
the partitioning of the Kingdom into spheres of ecclesiastical influence.
Kusel (1976 : 79) records:

> At the meeting a resolution was passed indicative of the desire to secure
> the spread of the gospel throughout the country and to allocate areas

for the different churches. They passed a motion as follows: That an understanding be accepted, that no work be undertaken by any society within the effective range of an effectively occupied mission station, but that each religious body be entitled to minister to its converts.

The passing of this polity agreement was indicative of the desire to maintain cordial working relations among the missionaries. It was not until 1929 that the Swaziland Missionary Conference was established. This Conference did not welcome Swazi clergymen and clearly distanced itself from churches of the Ethiopian and Zionist types. The Conference leaders worked in very close co-operation with the British Colonial Administration. To all their annual general meetings, a representative of the colonial administration would be invited as an important guest speaker.

It is clear that at this stage Sobhuza II and his people could not see any godliness in the missionary. The partnership the missionary had with the colonialist led to an unconscious rejection of the gospel of the missionaries and favour was extended to the African clergy. The extent of the polarization of the Swazi society as a result of Western Christianity may be the subject of another paper.

In the early 1930s, an attempt to destroy Zionism brought Zionists even much closer to the Monarchy. A.G. Marwick, having been persuaded supposedly by the missionaries and his own colonial government, wanted to ban Zionism under the pretext that it was a society for witches, because they worshipped in the silence of the night. Before doing this, Marwick approached Sobhuza II to express his opinion on this move. The Swazi King advised that Marwick should leave the matter to him.

Sobhuza II had to use all his power to win Swazi support for his campaign to preserve the culture of the Swazis. He had already embarked on establishing Swazi National Schools to counteract the teachings of the fast proliferating Mission Schools. Students were allowed to dress traditionally when attending the Swazi National Schools and cultural lessons were taught. Now was the King's golden opportunity to marshal the fragmented Zionist population under his care. Indeed, a meeting called in 1937 under the gum trees near Lobamba Royal Residence, was a tremendous success. It was that meeting which gave birth to what Sundkler has called The Good Friday Movement, organised by the League of African Churches. Membership to the League was open to all Zionist and Ethiopian Churches.

The aims and objects of the League are recorded in the constitution as follows:

i.   to create a federation of all African Churches, fellowship of such churches in Jesus Christ, brotherhood among African Christians.
ii. to protect its members.
iii. to open branches or stations in all areas falling under its juris-diction.
iv. to raise funds for the Federation.

The Royal presence in the League cannot be doubted. The General Executive Council, according to the Constitution, should have a national representative appointed by the Paramount Chief (title of the Swazi King given by the British). Minutes of the Executive Council of 3 March 1958 record that the *Ingwenyama* (King) had ruled that a certain Mr B.B. Shongwe should prepare his financial report as the NGWENYAMA felt that it was on account of the absence of such a report that various church members were apparently dwindling.

It is clear, therefore, that Sobhuza II had to promote and consolidate Swazi nationalism using all available avenues, including the Zionist and Ethiopian factors. The circumstances of the 1920s and 30s dictated that such a move was necessary. The calendar of national events in Swaziland is interesting to observe. From mid-November to late December or early January there is the *Ncwala* season (Feast of the first fruits); in March/April there is Good Friday; in late August—early September there is the Reed Dance. None of these national activities is less important than the others. Christians, mainly of the Zionist persuasion, attend and participate in all of them without any apology.

The Zionist—Royalty relationship is of a give-and-take type. Historically, the Zionists see the Royalty as the reason for their continued existence, otherwise A.G. Marwick would have banned them. Culturally, the Royalty sees Zionism as an important partner in cultural preservation. In this respect, Zionist churches, because of their tolerance of cultural elements, are closer to the heart of the Swazi central socio-political institution, namely, the Royal Family.

A plethora of questions regarding the contemporary need for this relationship always worry one's mind. There are two aspects to the issue. The history of the 1930s is past; Swaziland has been a sovereign state since 1968; and there can be no Marwick to ban Zionism. So why do the Zionists feel so attached to the Royalty? Our answer to this question can only be speculative.

Probably the closeness the Zionists have enjoyed with the Royalty has given them some sense of power and spiritual elation or elitism. This is noticeable in the announcements by the Presiding Bishop of the League, whenever he summons Christians to the Good Friday, Ascension Day and National prayers. A senior prince always accompanies this Bishop and he usually sings songs that depict national unity. *(Izimvu ziyamazi umalusi wazo*—The Sheep know their shepherd; and *Wamemeza uHezekia Wathi Mathambo Hlanganani*—Ezekiel prophesied at the valley of the dry bones).

The Royal spiritual advisers and councillors are drawn from the League of African Churches. These spiritual councillors are also responsible for settling disputes between League members on behalf of the King. The siSwati name for them is *Sifuba seNkosi*, meaning the chest of His Majesty.

No doubt, the spiritual promotion felt by the leadership of the League makes them assert Zionism as something of a State Church. In this connection, one recalls that in the early 1930s Rev. Stephen Macimbela and Rev Andreas Zwane attempted to amalgamate their movements, after declaring them autonomous from the control of the Nkonyanes. They called this new church "The Swazi Christian Church in Zion of South Africa". The constitution of this church, which was adopted on 16 February 1942, defines the amalgamation as being composed of all sects of the Zionist Movement within the borders of Swaziland. The headquarters of the Swazi Christian Church and League of African Churches was Lobamba (the main Royal Residence). The name of this amalgamated church obviously suggests a "Swazisation" of Zionism, an effort clearly coinciding with Sobhuza II's efforts towards the cultural re-awakening of his people.

Whereas the Marwick incident was responsible for the unity of the Zionists around the King, the Royalty also obviously feels a sense of comfort in having this large group of Christians around itself. Most of the historical churches condemn certain important institutions that are pivotal to the Royal heritage, e.g. ancestor veneration, polygamy, consulting traditional healers, "forced" marriages, etc. The Swazi Christian Church in Zion states its position towards traditional healing and healers clearly in article 8 of its constitution.

> The Church does not touch any sort of medicine, but does not interfere when   relatives consult medical practitioners recognised by the State. We believe in the laying on of hands, and praying for our sick.

On the subject of discipline, the constitution records that "this church is a monogamous body, and any member found guilty of adultery or breaking any of the Ten Commandments shall be excommunicated by the Deacons' Court . . . No strong drink is allowed, and any member found guilty of drunkenness from any strong drink or Kaffir Beer, or the use of Leaven, or the use of pork shall be dealt with by the Deacons' Court."

Despite these strong measures, the Swazi Christian Church in Zion is clearly tolerant, especially when the Royalty inevitably does these things.

Briefly, some of the advantages of the Zionist-Royalty connection are:

1. The re-living and commemoration of the A.C. Marwick incident of the 1930s;
2. The provision of acceptable spiritual counselling to the Royalty;
3. The preservation of the basic tenets of Swazi Zionism around the Royalty;
4. The provision of a mechanism for settling disputes in a Christian court as opposed to a public court of law;
5. The continued assurance of Christian allegiance to the Head of State;

Important disadvantages can be identified as well:

1. The Zionist monopoly in counselling the Royalty may be resented by the other Churches;
2. The Zionists may find themselves blessing every cultural institution, sometimes compromising the message of the Bible;
3. The Zionists may be manipulated by the State to always pray for peace instead of realistically addressing the causes of instability;
4. The leadership may find it difficult to distinguish between doing God's work and doing the King's work. There may be a conflict of spiritual allegiance in this respect.

The most disturbing aspect of the League of African Churches is its failure to change leadership according to its constitution. The document makes it perfectly clear that office bearers shall hold office for a period of five years. Our investigations have revealed that there was a deliberate effort by the past President to conceal the League's constitution. As a result of this concealment, most of the activities, including elections, of the League were conducted unconstitutionally.

It should be acknowledged that the constitution of the League was patterned after the Western model of such associations. It is expressed in the English language and, in our opinion, it is well written. But the way it records how the business of the League is to be carried out, or even the composition of the executive council, is absolutely foreign to the Swazi. One can safely assume that the main input into the constitution must have come from members of the Ethiopian Churches such as J.J. Nquku who became the first Secretary General. Very little or no contribution could have been expected from Zionist leaders, most of whom were hardly educated.

The tendency, therefore, is to do things the Swazi way. Those in the leadership do not see themselves as representatives of the people. They consider themselves as appointees of His Majesty. That is exactly why change of leadership remains a remote possibility, even at this stage. A clear example of such intransigence is how the present League President was appointed. He had been Vice-President for a short while after the death of Rev. Mncina. President Matsebula passed away in 1989 and Bishop Zitha became his automatic replacement. He was introduced to the Royalty as the successor, without going through a democratic process where the League members would have elected a President of their own choice.

Concluding Remarks

Readers of this paper may wonder why we have said nothing about healing as the primary element in the survival of Swazi Zionism. Healing plays an important function only at local congregational level. At the national level, the concerns are with paying allegiance to the King and showing undivided support for the *status quo*. In one sense, the paper has dealt with post-healing unifying forces, which appear to be less Christian and more culture-centric. There is no traceable theology behind the founding and early formation of the League. The reasons were purely cultural at a time when this was very important for Sobhuza II.

In order to continue maintaining its close ties with the Royalty, Swazi Zionism has developed a sort of right-wing theology, i.e. a theology that clearly supports the *status quo*. We have suggested some dangers to this kind of relationship. So long as Swazi Zionism maintains such a close relationship with the Royalty, we doubt if it can fulfil the prophetic function of the church. Another concern is the annual repetition of one and the same thing, noticeable mainly during Good

Fridays. The monotony is clearly disturbing and smacks of profound conservatism and spiritual stagnation. The church is supposed to be a dynamic institution, with the ability and propensity to meet new social demands as the spirit leads. The post-healing Swazi Zionism has shifted from spiritual leadership and dynamism to the rigmarole of Royal protocol and culture-centric concerns.

BIBLIOGRAPHY

Cazziol, R.J., "Zionist Churches in Swaziland", M.A. Thesis, University of Natal, 1988.
Cazziol, R.J., "Church co-operation in Swaziland: A test for Western Church presence in Africa", Thesis, Evangelical Church of Berlin—Berlin-West, 1976.
Dlamini, T.L.L., "The Christian Catholic Apostolic Holy Spirit Church in Zion: Its Development, Life and Worship", M.A. Thesis, University of Botswana and Swaziland, 1976.
Sundkler, B., *Zulu Zion and some Swazi Zionists* (Oxford University Press, 1976).
Fogelquist, A., "The Red-Dressed Zionists: Symbols of Power in a Swazi Independent Church" (Uppsala Research Reports, 1987).
Turner, H.W., *Religious Innovation in Africa* (Boston: G.K. Hall, 1979).
"The Approach to Africa's Religious Movements." *African Perspectives* 2, 1976.

Primary Sources

Constitution of the Swazi Christian Church in Zion of South Africa.
Constitution of the Federation of African Churches in Swaziland.
Minutes of the Swazi Christian Church in Zion of South Africa of 24 November 1940.
Minutes of the League Committee Meeting of 3 March 1958.

RELIGIOUS INDEPENDENCY IN THE CENTRAL REGION OF MALAWI

C.M. PAUW

Abstract

For various reasons the African Independent Churches initially did not find a strong foothold in the Central Region of Malawi. Some of the explanations suggested for the absence of secessionist tendency in this region are the absence of multiple missions, sound biblical and doctrinal teaching, a centralised authority structure, and the particular cultural and religious background of the people of the Central Region. This paper indicates how independency first appeared in the form of church movements from outside this region, but after 1970 the tide turned and new movements started asserting themselves. Today a large number of people claim adherence to independent churches.

Introduction

The death of David Livingstone in 1873 was the immediate cause of the first permanent mission to Malawi, if the abortive attempt of the Universities' Mission to Central Africa in 1861 is not taken into account. The Livingstonia Mission of the Free Church of Scotland entered the field in 1875, followed a year later by the Blantyre Mission of the established Church of Scotland. In due course the former established its sphere of work in what is today the Northern Region of Malawi, while the latter spread out over most of the Southern Region. With the Central Region still unoccupied, the Dutch Reformed Church in South Africa established its Mission there in 1889. At about the same time, the Roman Catholic Church began work in various areas. The UMCA which had returned to the scene some years earlier, initially extended its sphere of work mostly around the southern and western Lake Shore area. Several smaller missions, including Seventh Day Adventists, the South Africa General Mission (later to become the Africa Evangelical Fellowship) as well as a number of Industrial Missions, had also appeared on the scene by the turn of the century. Out of the work of the Scottish and Dutch missions the largest Protestant church in the country, the Church of Central Africa, Presbyterian came into being during the 1920s, while several other Protestant missions worked closely together through the Consultative Board of Federated Missions (cf. Pauw 1980 : 17–43).

Twenty-five years after the coming of Christian missions to Malawi, the first independent church appeared on the scene when John Chilembwe set up the Providence Industrial Mission 1900 (Shepperson and Price 1958; for extensive documentation on Chilembwe and the 1915 uprising, see Chakanza 1990 : 95–106). Less than a decade later, the Watchtower movement had gained a foothold, especially in the Northern Region (McCracken 1977 : 184, 189, 201–208), while the late 1920s saw several secessions from the Livingstonia Presbytery in the North, notably the African National Church and the Black Man's Church in Africa, the latter a union of three breakaway groups (McCracken 1977 : 273–276). Meanwhile, the African Methodist Episcopal Church was introduced into the country in 1924, the same period during which several Zionist and Apostolic groups began to appear as well (Parratt 1979 : 192–195).

What is interesting about the advent of independency in Malawi is the fact that while it became firmly established in the Northern and Southern Regions of the country, matters took a different course in the Central Region. That also explains why almost all publications concerning independency have to date dealt with the other two regions, while very little has been written about the Central Region.

Absence of secessionist tendencies in the Central Region

As already noted, Christian missions have been active in the Central Region for almost as long as in the other two regions, thus it would be natural to assume that independency would have manifested itself on a comparable scale. And yet, excluding one district, namely that of Ntcheu, there is hardly a single instance where a church was formed by way of secession from an existing mission church. While being part of the Central Region administratively, the Ntcheu district belongs, geographically speaking, more closely to the Southern Region. Ecclesiastically, at least in terms of the CCAP, most of it falls within the sphere of the Blantyre Synod. It also falls within the sphere of a number of smaller missions, of which several originated in the activities of Joseph Booth, whose influence was instrumental in the formation and rise of a considerable number of independent churches (Chakanza 1987 : 135–145).

As far as the rest of the Central Region is concerned, the main missions were the Dutch Reformed Church Mission (Nkhoma Mission) and the Roman Catholic Missions. In the Nkhota-Kota district along the Lake Shore, the field was mainly occupied by the UMCA. It is generally noted that very few secessions take place from within the ranks of the Roman Catholic Missions, and this is also true of Malawi (Linden 1974, 180–182; cf. also Chakanza 1982 : 151–158).

The remarkable fact is that in the case of the main Protestant mission, namely the Nkhoma Mission, there is also hardly a single secession of any significance. The annotated list of 135 Independent Churches in Malawi, drawn up by J.C. Chakanza in 1983, appears to contain perhaps only one or two examples. In one case, an ex-evangelist of the DRCM returned in 1974 from working in Zimbabwe. Together with some helpers from Zimbabwe, he introduced a branch of the Free Methodist Church (Chakanza 1983 : 47). American missionaries subsequently became involved with the work but the original founder soon clashed with them and he left to form, in due course, several other churches and "missions". In another case, a former member of Nkhoma CCAP was involved in establishing a Zionist church (Chakanza 1983 : 65) but it would appear that this was not a direct secession from the CCAP, but rather from another Zionist group which he had formerly joined (*ibid* : 64). In the 1960s, two small secessions took place from Nkhoma Synod, both involving ministers who had come under discipline. One found the First Presbyterian Church in the Mchinhi district but, according to an official of the Nkhoma Synod, nothing is known about this church today. The other broke away with a group of followers at Mlanda Mission in the Dedza district, but the breach was subsequently largely healed.

What are the reasons for the relative absence of this form of independency? Very few secessions have taken place also within the Blantyre Synod. Parratt suggests that in the latter case the reason for the absence of major schisms lies in the fact that there were other options open to independent spirits, notably the various movements initiated by Booth (Parratt 1979 : 200). But in the Central Region such options were absent.

In the case of the Livingstonia Mission, McCracken (1977 : 187–

188) suggests four main factors leading to the early secessions: lengthy apprenticeship and instruction of converts prior to admission to church membership; compulsory education and literacy before converts were accepted for baptism; financial demands made upon church members; and a strict administrative policy in which the missionaries maintained firm control. Yet, by and large, the same policies were followed by Nkhoma. The period of catechetical instruction was even longer (to this day a minimum of two and a half years training is required, longer than in the other CCAP Synods), compulsory school attendance, ability to read and possession of a catechism and at least a portion of the Scriptures were laid down in 1903 as requirements for baptism by the Council of Congregations. Similarly, in view of the ideal of a self-supporting church, much emphasis was placed on contributions in kind and in money by church members, and those who did not contribute were regularly reprimanded. If Livingstonia Mission was excessively cautious in granting authority to Malawian ministers (McCracken 1977 : 197), Nkhoma was as cautious, if not more cautious. Yet few signs of radical reaction ever appeared. In fact, when opposition to missionary control finally came to a head in the early 1960s, it did not come from the ministers but from teachers acting under the Nkhoma Synod Teachers Association (Pauw 1980 : 375–380). We shall return to this issue later.

David Barrett developed a scale for measuring the incidence of independency in any given tribal group (1968 : 108–115). In terms of this Tribal *Zeitgeist* scale, it was possible to positively identify a large number of factors facilitating independency in the Central Region by the time Malawi itself became independent in the mid sixties. Barrett identified twelve, the same number he identified for the Tumbuka in the north (1968 : 310, 311). This included the size of the tribal population; the presence of polygamy and the ancestor cult; the length of time the missions had been present, as well as the number of missionaries working in the area; Scriptures in the vernacular (portions before 1900, New Testament by 1907, whole Bible by 1923); a low percentage of Muslims; a relatively high percentage of Protestants and Catholics; as well as the existence of independency in physically adjoining tribes. Moreover, an incumbent mission of the Reformed tradition was another factor, identified by Barrett elsewhere as contributing to independency (1971 : 155). It is of interest to note that in the north the Tumbuka New Testament plus some Old Testament portions became available in 1911 and in subsequent years, but that the whole Bible was published only in 1957.

What then would be the reason for this state of affairs? Without going into detailed argument about each, I would venture to put forward the following suggestions.

a) *Absence of multiple missions*

The fact that the Nkhoma Mission was virtually the only Protestant Mission in the Central Region means that there was an absence of competing missions and that only one Protestant church body came into existence. In combination with other factors, this should be regarded as a major reason for the relative absence of independency.

b) *Mission policies followed by Nkhoma*

In a number of respects the Nkhoma Mission followed the same policies as those followed in Livingstonia. However, there were also marked differences. The first lay in the educational policies developed by the Nkhoma missionaries (for a more detailed exposition of these policies see Pauw 1980 : 151–183; cf. also Lamba 1984). After initially closely cooperating with Livingstonia Mission, the Nkhoma missionaries soon determined to avoid what they saw as the pitfalls and difficulties of providing an extremely high level of education for a select few, at an early stage in the development of the church and of the country. They rather chose a policy of seeking to provide education to the masses on as wide a level as possible. A basic ability to read and write, and especially to read the Scriptures, was an important aim. Higher training was provided to those who were employed by the Mission to teach and train their fellow Malawians. The level of this higher training was gradually raised, in order to keep up the growing needs for higher education in the church and in the country. From around 1940, greater emphasis began to be placed on higher education as such. But the result of this approach, especially in the early years, was that the first generation of church leaders were not as highly educated as were their counterparts in the north.

In the case of Livingstonia, candidates who had been trained for the ministry had to undergo an extremely long period of probationship, which was a further factor in the earliest secessions. In the case of Nkhoma, it was somewhat different. Once candidates were trained for the ministry, there was little further delay in ordaining them (Pauw 1980 : 258–260, 308f). Nevertheless, the road leading to ordination was a long one: First, a careful selection was made of candidates to be trained as teachers. Then, after some years of service, the most promising ones would be chosen to be trained as evangelists. Finally, from amongst the senior evangelists, the most suitable men would be chosen to receive further training as ministers. Due to this process of selection, the men who eventually reached the most senior position of ordained ministers (the first three men were ordained in 1925), were proven men, dedicated and committed, and regarded as people who would render "faithful" service to the Church and the Mission. Under these circumstances they were not likely to experience as easily the frustrations of their counterparts in the North or, at least, would be prepared to submit for a longer time to the authority of the missionaries. From 1943 onwards, this process was discontinued and people were henceforth permitted to apply directly for admission to the training course (Pauw 1980 : 309). Although this brought about change, the impact was not felt for quite some time.

Another factor was the emphasis placed on forming a strong and stable Christian family by, on the one hand, paying much attention to work amongst women and girls and, on the other hand, seeking ways to ensure the minimum disruption of family life through migrant labour. Rather than train men in skills which would force them to go and practise elsewhere in the service of the white man much emphasis was placed on developing entrepreneurship and skills which could be practised locally. Especially during the second and third decades of the century, this Mission developed a massive program of agricultural and industrial training at the level of village industries (cf. Pauw 1980 : 190–199), to such an extent that the Phelps-Stokes Commission, which toured African countries in 1924, could report that, in respect of agricultural training and village industries, Nkhoma Mission "has not its superior in all the Nyasaland schools visited by the Commission" (Jones 1924 : 212).

This emphasis, together with the application of the Reformed ethical principle of honest, hard work, produced a kind of "ethos" and a kind of "peasant" church, emphasising, so to speak, the "Bible and the plough" in such a way that Christianity came closer to the grassroots level of people's lives. This concentration on the grassroots affairs of people must be regarded as a factor contributing to the relative lack of independency in the Central Region.

c)   *Theological and ecclesiastical emphasis*

The first emphasis that can be mentioned here is that on sound doctrinal and Biblical teaching. The long catechetical training, while being a possible factor in discouraging people, should also be regarded as a positive factor in grounding people in the faith. Added to this, there was an emphasis on Bible reading and Bible study. To promote this, an annual Bible reading and sermon guide, *Mlozo,* has been in production for almost 60 years for use by individuals, school teachers, Bible study groups, elders and preachers. Together with the catechetical training, this approach, no doubt, served to provide a firm base for doctrinal and Biblical knowledge and to lessen the possibility of people being lured away into the teachings of *mipatuko* (sects).

Coupled to this is the kind of concept that developed concerning the church. On the one hand, there was less of an emphasis on the "Free" church concept, on individualism and on the primacy of individual conscience than was noted by McCracken (1977 : 277f) as having played a role in the Livingstonia secessions of the late twenties. On the other hand, the Dutch brand of Reformed Presbyterianism introduced by the Nkhoma missionaries tended towards a more centralised authoritarianism. This can be illustrated in two respects. First, the position of the missionary and later, especially, the Superintendent of the Mission was in due course merely transferred to the parish minister and in particular to the General Secretary of the Synod. Thus, when the Nkhoma Synod took over full responsibility and authority for the work in 1962, the General Secretary, as the secretary or clerk of the Synod soon came to be called, not only was given immediate occupancy of the former Superintendent's house, but soon became a very powerful and influential figure in the Synod. Although his appointment never became a permanent one, as was the case in the other two CCAP synods in the country, he nevertheless not only served as the official spokesman of the Synod, occupying the post in a full capacity, but also could exercise, albeit unofficially, a considerable degree of executive authority (cf. Pauw 1980 : 393f). It is only recently that the Synod has rectified this position. Secondly, and coupled to this, the church tended to become rather centralised in its manner of exercising authority. Synodocratic elements surfaced from time to time and there was a tendency to present overtures on even the most trivial matters to Synod, merely because presbyteries or congregations did not wish to make their own decisions, but wanted the authoritative backing of a synodical decision. To be able to say *Sinodi akuti* (the Synod says) carried much more weight.

Such a form of centralised authority structure in some ways resembles that found within the Roman Catholic Church. This made it less palatable for people to consider breaking with the church while dissidents could also be quickly and effectively dealt with.

On the other hand, the Presbyterian system of church rule, and the way elders and deacons have been made responsible for local wards, has largely provided scope for individual leadership and exercising of various forms of ministry. It has been established that as many as 95% of the church members listen to an elder preaching on a Sunday while many see the minister only once in three months when they come for Holy Communion (Pauw 1980 : 291). Otherwise, for all practical purposes, and in all matters of pastoral duties, the local elder is in effect the pastor, virtually exercising a kind of tent-making ministry.

d) *Cultural background*

A factor which played a wide role in promoting religious independency is the fact that Christian Missions have in many respects failed to deal effectively with a variety of issues related to the cultural and religious background of African peoples. Yet, certain elements within traditional society appear to have played a role in actually countering the growth of independency in the Central Region.

One such factor is the prevalence of a secret society called *Nyau*. Throughout Chewa society, both in Malawi and in Mozambique, as well as in the Eastern Province of Zambia, the occurrence of *Nyau* has been noted (cf. Schoffeleers 1976). It is not found amongst the Tumbuka peoples of northern Malawi, and it is uncommon amongst the Nyanja and other peoples of the Southern Region. In the Central Region, *Nyau* remains very much alive even to this day. Even though in recent decades, a popularised form has come to the fore, in which dance troupes perform before the public, the real thing still prevails and is a strong force for retaining certain aspects of traditional culture and religion. It is therefore not surprising that with the advent of Christianity *Nyau* soon came to the fore as a powerful opposition to the new religion. Wherever *Nyau* had greater influence, the progress of Christianity was notably slower. By the 1920s it had become such an issue that both the Dutch Reformed (Pauw 1980 : 331f) and the Roman Catholic Missions (Linden 1972 : 252–273), especially in the Lilongwe and Dedza areas, were constantly at issue with the supporters of *Nyau* (cf. Linden 1975 : 30–44). Even the Board of Federated Missions took the matter up on occasion with the Colonial Government, in order to try and obtain a ban on the movement. *Nyau* proved to be a conservative force, protecting Chewa culture from foreign intrusion and seeking to counter the disruptive effects Christianity was having upon tribal society. It offered particular resistance to mission schools (cf. Linden 1974 : 79–80; Schoffeleers 1972 : 252–276).

The conflict between *Nyau* and Christianity created such a degree of polarisation that there was little scope for something in between. A person was either a committed church member or entirely on the side of *Nyau* and traditional religion. In this sense, the *Nyau* issue must be regarded as a factor inhibiting independency.

In the sphere of sickness and disease, Independent Churches often step into the vacuum created by the inability of mainline churches to provide people with adequate answers. An interesting phenomenon has developed in the Central Region, notably in certain districts such as Mchinji, where the traditional healer was not been replaced by the prophet healer of the Independent Church, but by individuals who claim healing powers and exercise their talents. Some do so even while remaining church members. In some respects their methods are similar to those of traditional healers, but they have also introduced Christian elements, such as praying to God for blessing and healing and reading certain portions from the Scripture, before proceeding to diagnose or treat a disease.

Often these individuals are women. Gilibeta, who is regarded by some as the best healer in the country at present, is a good example. In 1982 she was reported to be married, with three children and in her mid-forties (Kwapulani 1982). Her husband and two females assist her and she practises on Wednesdays and Sundays, the days on which a spirit from God known as the spirit of Gilibeta, a healer spirit, takes possession of her. She offers prayers to God, "our Father in heaven". She makes use of various roots and herbs which her husband collects, and patients pay fees. She has a "hospital" with dormitory wards, where patients can stay until they are healed. In some cases, they stay even for three or four weeks. The local denominations, the African National Church (of which she apparently was once a member), the CCAP and the Roman Catholic Church evidently find little to condemn for they take no action on their members who consult her. Although she begins and ends her divinations with Bible reading and prayers, the gatherings are not church services. As an example, the following prayer for a healed patient is quoted: "Father in heaven, this man became deranged and moved about in the forest like an animal. By the power of your trees (herbal medicines) . . . the madness has left. I commit him to you so that the spirits *(ziwanda)* will not return."

The fact that this phenomenon is found particularly in the Mchinji District, which borders on the Eastern Province of Zambia, may be an indication that influence from a movement known in Zambia as the Church of the Spirits *(Mpingu was Mizimu)* is beginning to spread to Malawi. This movement, akin to the Mutumwa churches described by Dillon-Malone (1983, 1985, 1987), is already, according to informants, well established in the Eastern Province. Possessed people appear to claim that they belong to their own church, called the Church of the Spirits (cf. Kwapulani 1982 : 145).

There are also several other women who practise in the district, one of whom is Maria, a Roman Catholic member whose husband is a Sunday School teacher. She was healed from spirit diseases and is now possessed by the spirits of the Virgin Mary and John the Baptist. When a healing session is about to begin, she asks first for a hymn to be sung and for several passages of Scripture to be read. Thereafter, the spirits take possession of her and she begins divining. The Catholic Church questions her activities, but leaves her alone. Once she was taken and prayed for, but she merely became spirit possessed and nothing was effected (personal interview with J.C. Chakanza).

The presence of this type of healers in the community must also be regarded as a factor in the lower incidence of independency in the Central Region, since they provide for certain needs of the community otherwise catered for by the independent churches.

Other possible factors within Chewa society which may play a role in this respect, such as certain tribal characteristics, social cohesiveness and the role that men are able to play in the church within the wider context of a matriarchal society, require further investigation.

Independency in the Central Region

While little evidence exists in the Central Region of the occurrence of independency in the form of schism and secession from mainline churches, this does not mean that independency as such has been totally non-existent. The phenomenon has been present in the region for a long time, but then almost exclusively in the form of movements and churches introduced from elsewhere, mostly from within Malawi, but also from outside, usually by migrants returning from Zimbabwe or South Africa.

Reference has already been made to the African Methodist Episcopal

Church, started at Kasungu by Hanock Msokera Phiri in 1924, a year after Kasungu mission had been handed over by Livingstonia to the Dutch Reformed Church Mission. By 1940, branches of the Providence Industrial Mission had been established in the Lilongwe and Dedza districts and a secession had already taken place in the form of the Achewa Providence Industrial Church. Both the PIM and the AMEC became well established, gained sizeable membership and in due course were accepted as members of the Christian Council of Malawi. To date none other of the so-called Independent Churches has been admitted to the Christian Council, although several have applied from time to time.

During the 1940s, small Zionist groups began to appear here and there, followed by a few Apostolic churches. Small branches of several of the churches which had originated in the Northern Region were gradually introduced into the Central Region. This included the Last Church of God and his Christ (mostly in the Kasungu area), the Blackman's Church and the African National Church, started by Paddy Nyasulu and others and introduced into the Lilongwe area in 1938. Secessions have repeatedly taken place. So, for example, the African National Church split into two as did the African Abraham Church and the African International Church, both claiming to be the original church founded in 1929. The African Yakobo Church and the African Emmanuel Church, which had both seceded from the African National Church in the north, were also introduced. A few secessions from the Ethiopian Universal Church (also known as the Ancestors Church and given the nicknames *Zoipa Chitani*—"do the bad things") are also found.

Thus, it is true to say that African Independent Churches of various types did gain a presence in the Central Region although none had a very high profile, membership was relatively low and they were mostly ignored by the large mission churches. Individual members did leave the latter to join the AIC, mostly persons who had been disciplined on account of charges of beer drinking or polygamy, but this was the exception rather than the rule. No significant breakaways are known and they were seldom, if ever, regarded as a threat.

The turning tide

The situation described above remained more or less the position until around the 1970s. But the decades after political independence were also decades of change on the church scene. A large number of new missions and missionaries, mostly from the United States, entered the country during the 1960s and thereafter. As a result, new churches were established in many areas throughout the country. This not only broke the relative monopoly of the CCAP, but promoted the concept and possibility of multiple church formation. A secondary effect, most conspicuous amongst Pentecostal type churches, was a tendency for internal divisions to take place. The result has been the formation of several African-led independent churches within the Pentecostal tradition.

The influx of a variety of new churches and missions from within the "evangelical" tradition, as well as the prevalence of an evangelistic tradition within the Nkhoma Synod of the CCAP, furthermore facilitated the formation of a variety of fellowship groups, revival teams and evangelistic bands. While some, particularly those operating within the Nkhoma Synod, have remained in the church, others reveal a tendency to evolve into self-proclaimed autonomous churches, often showing Pentecostal or charismatic characteristics.

Moreover it has become clear that the older Independent African Churches, such as a variety of Zionist and Apostolic churches, the Africa International Church and particularly the African Abraham Church, have gained in stature and influence during the post-independence era. This has become even more pronounced during the past decade. Not only have many new groups come into existence, but their numerical adherence has, by all indications, increased remarkably. Official statistics do not exist on church adherence, but inquiries made in various areas have brought to light the fact that in some cases, virtually whole villages have joined African Independent Churches. Random questioning of people around the countryside has created the impression that in certain rural areas more people claim adherence to an Independent Church than to mainline churches. In large towns, as well as in Lilongwe city, Independent Churches are well represented. The vast Kawale township in Lilongwe has proved to be a veritable breeding ground for new groups.

These observations, based on research undertaken in the Central Region during 1990, make it clear that not only is a silent revolution in process, but that the fifth and final phase in Barrett's *Zeitgeist* scale of independence has undoubtedly now been reached though somewhat belatedly. Independency has become a factor of increasing significance in the Central Region, something of which serious note will have to be taken in future.

BIBLIOGRAPHY

Barrett, D.B., *Schism and renewal in Africa* (Oxford/London, 1968 (a)).

Barrett, D.B., "Interdisciplinary theories of religion and African indepen-dency", in D.B. Barrett (ed.): *African initiatives of religion* (Nairobi: East African Publishers, 1971, pp. 146–159).

Chakanza, J.C., "Religious independency in Malawi: The Catholic Church, a negative case", *Afer* 24/3 June 1982, pp. 151–158.

Chakanza, J.C., "An annotated list of Independent Churches in Malawi 1900–1981" (Department of Religious Studies, Chancellor College, Zomba, 1983).

Chakanza, J.C., "Religious independency in Southern Malawi", in Shank D.A., *Ministry of missions to African Independent Churches* (Elkhart: Mennonite Board, 1987, pp. 134–155).

Chakanza, J.C., "New religious movements in Malawi: a bibliographical review", in A.F. Walls and W.R. Shenk (eds.), *Exploring New Religious Movements* (Elkhart: Mission Focus, 1990, pp. 95–106).

Dillon-Malone C., "The Mutumwa churches of Zambia: An indigenous African religious preaching movement", *Journal of Religion in Africa* XIV/3 1983, pp. 204–222.

Dillon-Malone C., "The Mutumwa Church of Peter Mulenga Part I", *Journal of Religion in Africa* XV/2 1985, pp. 122–139.

Dillon-Malone C., "The Mutumwa Church of Peter Mulenga Part II", *Journal of Religion in Africa* XVII/I 1987, pp. 2–31.

Kwapulani, A.M., "Spirit possession in the religious history of Mchinji District, Central Malawi", History seminar papers, Chancellor College, Zomba, 1982.

Lamba, I.C., "The Cape Dutch Reformed Church Mission in Malawi. A preliminary historical examination of its educational philosophy and application, 1889–1991". *History of Education Quarterly*, Fall 1984, pp. 373–392.

Linden, I., See Schoffeleers and Linden, 1972.

Linden, I., *Catholics, peasants and Chewa resistance in Nyasaland, 1890–1939* (London: Heinemann, 1974).

Linden, I., "Chewa initiation rites and Nyau societies. The use of religious institutions in local politics in Mua", in T.O. Ranger and Weller (eds.), *Themes in the Christian history of Central Africa* (London: Heinemann, 1975).

Parratt, J., "Religious independency in Nyasaland—a typology of origins", African Studies 38/2 (1979) pp. 183–200.

Pauw, C.M., "Mission and Church in Malawi, The history of the Nkhoma Synod of the Church of Central Africa, Presbyterian 1889–1962", DTh dissertation, University of Stellenbosch, 1980.

Ranger, T.O. and Kimambo I.N. (eds.), *The historical study of African religion* (London: Heinemann, 1972).

Schoffeleers, J.M., "The Nyau: our present understanding", *Society of Malawi Journal* 29/1976, pp. 56–68.

Schoffeleers, J.M. and Linden, I., "The resistance of Nyau societies to the Roman Catholic missions in Colonial Malawi", in Ranger, T.O., and Kimambo, I.N., (eds.), *The historical study of African religion* (London: Heinemann, 1972, pp. 252–273).

Shepperson G. and Price, T., *Independent African, John Chilembwe and the origins, setting and significance of the Nyasaland Native Rising of 1915* (Edinburgh: Edinburgh University Press, 1958).

BLACK CHURCHES IN THE UNITED STATES AND SOUTH AFRICA: SIMILARITIES AND DIFFERENCES

J.E. KUNNIE

Abstract

Comparing the contexts of the United States of America with that of South Africa, the writer argues that an interplay of social and economic forces in the religious expression of the black people has resulted in the emergence and growth of black churches.

In looking at the origin of the black church in the USA the paper notes that racial discrimination which was practised by the whites against the blacks, resulted in a rebellion and a quest for ecclesiastical freedom by the blacks. The movement for ecclesiastical and theological autonomy among the blacks in South Africa was also prompted by white racial and social domination. The immediate outcome of this was the emergence of Ethiopian church movements. Charismatic fervour, however, led to the emergence of Zionist and Pentecostal church movements.

The writer accepts the complex nature of the black religious traditions of the USA and of South Africa, but holds that the commonalities outnumber the differences. The author concludes that both traditions have played a role in political liberation and independence from white domination, and that it would be advisable to initiate interaction and interchange between the black religious communities of these two continents.

Introduction

Religious expression, as the sociologist Emile Durkheim asserts, is the product of the interplay of various social and economic forces in certain historical epochs. The phenomena of black churches both in the United States and South Africa are not exempt from this presupposition, essentially the historical contexts of slavery and racism in the case of the former, and colonialism and racial domination in the instance of the latter. Interestingly, as I will elucidate in this paper, there are some striking parallels in the experiences of these churches amongst any two oppressed communities of colour in the world, specifically, of any two African communities around the globe. These two peoples have prodigiously similar histories, including the spawning of Christian churches on American and African soils and resulting in that historic institution in the United States known as the black church, and the indigenous African independent churches in South Africa.

The Black Church in the United States

The black church has historically been the most important institution in the social lives of African people in the United States, ever since its conception as the "invisible institution" born during the era of chattel slavery in America. Albert Raboteau, the African American scholar confirms this point when he states in the preface to his classic work, *Slave Religion: The "Invisible Institution in the Antebellum South"*:

> an agency of social control, a source of economic cooperation, an arena for political activity, a sponsor of education, and a refuge in a hostile white world, the black church has been historically the social centre of Afro-American life.[1]

The roots of the black church in the United States are found in the resistance of African people to chattel slavery, initiated by English colonialists and slave merchants who were bent on building a commercial base in North America, on the backs of African peoples stolen from the shores of west and central Africa in the early part of the seventeenth century. The black church, as it was originally conceived, emerged as a liberation movement of African peoples in the United States to extricate themselves from the manacles of chattel slavery imposed by white slave masters in the northern coastal towns and southern plantations. Gayraud Wilmore, the African American religious scholar and theologian contends:

> The independent church movement amongst blacks, during and following the period of the revolutionary war, must be regarded as the prime expression of resistance of slavery—in every sense *the first black freedom movement.*[2]

The church was the site where the contradictions of racism and racial discrimination, practised by whites against blacks, surfaced and were confronted openly. Wilmore opines in this regard:

---

[1] Preface, *Slave Religion*, (New York: Oxford University Press, 1978).

[2] G. Wilmore, *Black Religion and Black Radicalism*, (Maryknoll, New York: Orbis Books, 1982), p. 78.

The movement therefore could pass as representing the more or less legitimate desire of the slaves to have a place of their own in which to worship God. But it was, in fact, a form of rebellion against the most accessible and vulnerable expression of white oppression and institutional racism in the nation: the American churches.[3]

It was in the "invisible institution" fomented by the African slaves, unseen and undetected by the so-called Christian slave masters, that the antecedent of the radical black churches resided. The enslaved men and women of African descent improvised and evolved their one theology of black freedom, during their "secret meetings" which spoke of emancipation from slavery, and "stealing away" to a land beyond the Jordan, leading eventually to the independent "underground" black church. Raboteau says:

> But the religious experience of the slaves was by no means fully contained in the visible structure of the institutional church. From the abundant testimony of fugitive and freed slaves, it is clear that the slave community had an external religious life of its own, hidden from the eyes of the master. In the secrecy of the quarters and the seclusion of the brush arbors ("hush harbors"), the slaves made Christianity truly their own.[4] ... as the core of the slaves' religion was a private place, represented by the cabin room, the overturned pot, the "praying" ground, and the "hush harbor". This place the slave kept his own. For no matter how religious the master might be, the slave knew that the master's religion did not contravene prayers for his slaves' freedom in this world.[5]

One of the principal factors that led to the fiery spirit of rebellion and the quest for ecclesiastical freedom during the aeon of slavery, was the fact that "slave code gave associations a great deal of control over black churches."[6] Whilst the institutions of slavery persisted, it became extremely difficult, almost impossible, for African slave converts to enjoy any level of autonomy and independence. Hence the subsequent splits, especially amongst members of the Baptist communities. The first separate black church was founded "between 1773 and 1775 in Silver Bluff, South Carolina, across the Savannah River from Georgia."[7] Many black preachers emerged subsequently and, despite legislative

---

[3] Wilmore, p. 78.
[4] Raboteau, p. 212.
[5] *Ibid.*, p. 219.
[6] Raboteau, p. 79.
[7] *Ibid.*, p. 139.

prohibitions, continued to organise black Christian communities. One such church was the African Baptist Church of Williamsburg, which thrived, notwithstanding opposition from racist white churches. There were also black churches which were born through separation from white churches. One such was the Gillfield Baptist Church of Petersburg, Virginia, which split from the Gillfield Church,[8] as it then was, when members joined with black Baptists in Philadelphia who had already separated from a conservative white congregation in 1809.[9]

The most well-known of church schisms along racial lines in the USA was the formation of the African Methodist Episcopal Church in 1816. In 1787, Richard Allen and Absalom Jones walked out of St George's Methodist Episcopal Church in Philadelphia one Sunday morning, after being summoned to sit up in the gallery where "black people are supposed to be seated". In the AME Church, Richard Allen retained the Methodist polity of the Methodist Episcopal Church, but expanded the theology, with an emphasis on the pride in Africanity and on the gospel of freedom and equality. It was the AME church, under the leadership of Bishop Henry McNeal Turner, who travelled to South Africa in 1898, which began to establish ties with African Christians in South Africa and mediated through the leadership of people like Mangena Mokone, a Wesleyan Methodist, and later James Dwane to form the AME church in South Africa. Dwane spoke of African nationalism and self-government in 1896, principles which appealed to Bishop Turner, so that by 1898, there were 10,800 AME church members in South Africa. Interspersed with the formation of Ethiopianism, which sought to unite Africans across ethnic lines, and opposed segregation, was the articulation of a disposition of African nationhood and sovereignty, which sent tremors of fear into the hearts of zealous and imposing white missionaries.

The AME church in the USA, today renowned for its emphasis on education, literacy and self-upliftment of African people, is an important symbol of the potency of black ecclesiastical self-government and the power of black religions to empower oppressed people for freedom. Its kinship with black people in South Africa is a significant link of religio-political solidarity, vital for the consolidation of black social power.

---

[8] *Ibid.*, p. 132–143.
[9] Wilmore, p. 79.

It would be remiss of me to omit the radical role that the Christian faith assumed in the resistance to the tyrannical institution of slavery in the USA. In 1800, Gabriel Prosser, a devout Bible student, maintained that God had called him to be a liberator of the African people, likening his people to the Hebrew slaves. He led an armed insurrection, after which 35 slaves were consequently hanged. Subsequently, in 1822, Denmark Vessry, an active member of a black congregation which had split from a white Methodist church in 1817, was inspired by biblical teaching and launched an attack on white slave masters, resulting in his execution. So too, in 1831, Nat Turner, a charismatic religious leader, organised a major slave revolt, viewing himself as being called to do "some good purpose in the hands of the Almighty"[10], to break the shackles of his fellow slaves. He was executed for the attack and revolt. Yet again, the fiery spirit of liberation infused the spirituality of the black church, inspired and galvanised such church activists, lending credence to the fact of the radicalisation both of the black church and black religion.

The feeling of being excluded and denied fundamental privileges by the black Methodists in white churches in New York City, led to the formation of the African Methodist Episcopal Zion (AMEZ) church in 1820, in New York. James Varick, the first superintendent, became a major figure in the expansion of the AMEZ church.[11] The AMEZ church was deeply involved in the struggle for freedom from slavery, with its congregation functioning as important points of respite in the underground railroad, sparked by such heroes and heroines as Frederick Douglas, Catherine Harris, Harriet Tubman, Thomas Jones, and Sojourner Truth.

Yet another important development in the evolution of the black religious communities in the United States was the burgeoning of black Pentecostalism in the latter part of the nineteenth and the early twentieth century. The central figure responsible for its growth and flourishing was William Seymour (1870–1922), a son of former slaves from Centerville, Louisiana.[12] It emerged from the "context of the brokenness

---

[10] George Eaton Simpson, *Black Religions in the New World* (New York: Columbia University Press, 1978), p. 223.

[11] Wilmore, p. 85.

[12] Ian MacRobert, *The Black Roots and White Racism of Early Pentecostalism in the USA*, (London: Macmillan, 1988) p. xii.

of black existence"[13], incorporating black symbols and music into its liturgy and influenced by a strong charismatic flavour, with accent on the power and gifts of the spirit.[14] The Pentecostal revival in Los Angeles in 1905, making L.A. the Pentecostal capital of the world, was in the main a black motivated movement, in which white, Mexican, Asian, and workers of all colours came together. Sadly and tragically, the pathology of white racism as demonstrated by white mainline Pentecostals, rejected the Pentecostal revival, prompting a bifurcation of the movement into separate black and white churches. Contrary to the general impressions conveyed by many white scholars in black religions, black Pentecostalism was not a chimerical, sedate and other-worldly experience. Leonard Lovett argues:

> It may be categorically stated that black Pentecostalism emerged out of the context of the brokenness of black existence . . . Their holistic view of religion had its roots in African religion.[15]

The emphasis on the inspiration of the Holy Spirit, as recounted in the first chapter of Acts in the Bible, did not diminish the motivation and zeal for freedom from racism on the part of black Pentecostalism. The endeavours by the National Black Evangelical Association, formed by Herbert Daughtry, an activist minister in the New York area, in attempting to relate the spirituality of black evangelicals to concrete socio-political and existential material reality, is one piece of evidence that substantiates the integrated understanding of many Pentecostalists of the recent past as far as the relevance of religion to socio-political transformation is concerned.[16]

The black caucuses found in predominantly white churches, like Black Presbyterian United, Black Methodists for Church Renewal, Black Episcopalians, and the African American Caucus within the Lutheran Church, can also be viewed as extensions of the black church, though the influence that these have had on the black community is somewhat marginal owing to small numbers. Yet, as one beholds the contemporary black church, one sadly notes the destruction of its original character as a liberation community, at least, in the main. Gayraud Wilmore describes it as the "deradicalisation of the black

---

[13] Cited by Leonard Lovett in *ibid.*
[14] *Ibid.*, p. 2.
[15] *Ibid.*, p. 9.
[16] *Black Religion and Black Radicalism*, ed. G. Wilmore and J. Cone (New York: Orbis Press, 1979) p. 97.

church". James Cone, the pioneer of black theology in the USA, and
a former minister of the AME church, laments the deterioration and
decline of the black churches in the USA in the 80s and 90s, as
its role in the struggle for liberation and the realization of a vision
of social justice, political freedom and economic quality has become
seriously compromised.[17] The black church rode on the crest of the
radical wave of change in the 60s, when it was immersed and deeply
involved in socio-political struggle; today, there is evidence of a collapse
from that wave to a nadir of despair, hopelessness and irrelevance.
The black churches can no longer claim to be at the cutting edge
of American society, as the leading protagonists of radical structural
change, as part of the mission to the oppressed free.

The Black Churches (Indigenous African Churches) in South Africa

According to the latest statistics, there are over six thousand indigenous
independent churches in South Africa,[18] with a combined membership
of over 9 million people. We are thus referring to the largest group
of Christians in South Africa, and one of the fastest growing on the
sub continent. Patently, it is impossible to describe the formation of
the majority of these churches within the purview of this paper. I
will thus attempt to furnish a sketch of some of the principal independent churches, including the Zionist, Nazarite and Ethiopian
churches under which many splinter churches have emerged.

The independent churches basically resulted from the attempt by
the black Christians to wrest ecclesiastical and theological autonomy
from the white mission churches.[19] They have been criticised both
by the so-called left wing for being "apolitical" and by the so-called
right wing for being too "political". Both sectors reflect a lack of
understanding for the complexity of the plethora of African Independent Churches in South Africa, the sprouting of which was a
response to the deprivation and alienation induced in black people
by the apartheid system. According to the work by Bengt Sundkler,
Bantu Prophets in South Africa, the AIC tended generally to emerge in

---

[17] See Cone's Critique in *For My People* (New York: Orbis Press, 1984) pp. 83–
84.

[18] Information compiled from Department of Information statistics, by G.C.
Oosthuizen, 1991.

[19] Martin West, *Bishops and Prophets in a Black City* (Cape Town: David Philip) 1975,
p. 1.

urban settings, and as a result of socio-economic stresses,[20] caused particularly by fragmentation in black family life, lack of decent and adequate health care and the sense of personal isolation evoked by a socio-political dispensation which denied black people their fundamental humanity. The AIC were also spawned in direct response to the irrelevance and detachment of European theologies, practices and doctrines, as they existed especially in areas of material well being and spiritual fulfilment, to the immateriality of black life. The white mission churches were inept at striking a responsive chord in the African breast.

The fist of the AIC was the Ethiopian church, conceived in the Witwatersrand region in 1892. An important figure was Nehemiah Tile who, because of his Thembu nationalistic outlook, was viewed with suspicion by the Wesleyan Mission Church.[21] Tile formed the Tembu Church with Ngangelizwe, chief of the nation as ecclesiastical head. Another Wesleyan minister, Mangena Mokone, was another who resigned from the Wesleyan Methodist Church, to lead the Ethiopian Church. *Psalm* 68:31, which states, ". . . And Ethiopia shall stretch forth her hands unto God" represents the Biblical text upon which this contention was based. Ethiopia symbolises "the whole of Africa, a free black Africa, liberated from colonial overlordship, and to be led by the Africans themselves."[22] Dwane was yet another figure of significance who, amidst his tensions and dissent with the AME church, formed by African American Henry Turner, established the Order of Ethiopia. The Ethiopian church was characterised by a nationalistic political fervour, articulating the slogan "Africa for the Africans", which the AME church did not warmly embrace. P.J. Mzimba, originally of the United Free Church of Scotland, founded the African Presbyterian Church in 1898. Mzimba, like Dwane and Mokone, had also been exposed to educational philosophies and institutions in the United States (including W.E.B. Du Bois and Booker T. Washington's Tuskegee Institute), a factor which certainly had some influence in their determination to become self-reliant and autonomous from the white mission churches. The issue of ecclesiastical leadership such as the position of bishop being denied to black people in the

---

[20] Cited in West, p. 6.
[21] Sundkler, *Bantu Prophets in South Africa*, p. 28.
[22] Sundkler, *Zulu Zion and Swazi Zionists* (London: Oxford University Press, 1976) p. 15.

churches also caused dissatisfaction among black members of the white mission churches.

The Congregational Church split into the Zulu Congregational Church, founded in 1896, and the African Congregational Church of 1917. The Zulu Uprising, led by Bambhata in 1906, sparked by the poll tax introduced for Africans by the white colonial regime. After Samungu Shibe, the leader of this church died, two other churches emerged: the "Baptist" in 1918, and the "Shaka Zulu Church", with strong nationalistic sentiments.

The African Faith Healing Church, as its name suggests, places primordial stress on healing and the power of the Spirit, as in Zionist churches. G. Mruyana was another Zulu Congregational preacher who, owing to white racist control, left and formed his own church which later also split after his death.

In the 1960s, the Zionist churches, according to Sundkler numbered some 2000 in South Africa.[23] They were characterised by a strong charismatic fervour, with social and political aspirations. Zion represents a movement of the African Spirit, the *Ama-Ziyoni*, a place where African people are able to transcend the humiliation of their material existence under apartheid, accompanied by a historical link to the city of Zion in Illinois, USA, with influences from Rev. J.A. Dowie of Zion City, Illinois. The Zionist churches include the Africa Zion Baptist Church, the Holy Catholic Apostolic Church in Zion of South Africa, the Holy Spirit Jerusalem Church in Zion, the Jerusalem Apostolic Kuphiliswa Church in Zion, the Star Nazarite Church in Zion of Sabbath and the Zion Apostolic Swaziland Church of South Africa.[24]

The teaching of the Zionist churches focuses on "divine healing", "immersion in the true God" and the imminent return of the Lord.[25] The emphasis on the Pentecostal quality, the inspiration of the Holy Spirit, is also axiological in Zionist theology and worship. Speaking in tongues, purification rites and taboos are also practised. Some of the important black figures who assumed leadership in Zionist churches are Paulo Mabilitsa (the Christian Apostolic Church in Zion); Daniel Nkonyana (Christian Catholic Apostolic Holy Spirit Church in Zion); J.R. Philip (the Holy Catholic Apostolic Church in Zion); Elios Mahluya (Zion Apostolic Church of South Africa), and Fred Luthuli (Seventh

---

[23] Sundkler, *Zulu Zion*, p. 15.
[24] *Ibid.*
[25] Sundkler, *Bantu Prophets*, p. 48.

Day Adventists). The Nazarite churches also warrant mention—inspired by the founder and prophet, Isaiah Shembe, who was baptised by Rev. W.M. Leshega of the African Nakime Baptist Church in 1906. Faith healing, drumming and other purification rites are central in the practice of the Nazarites. Succession of the leaders is also significant—generally the son assumes the position of leader once the father dies.

Sundkler makes an interesting distinction between the "Ethiopian" and the "Zionist" branches among the AIC. The Ethiopian churches reflect a strong Africanist outlook, having seceded from white mission churches owing to the latter's white control and racism. Their call is "Africa for the Africans", a rejection of white colonial domination of Africa; yet their hermeneutical methods generally adhere to Protestant missionary biblical hermeneutics. The accent on rank and ritual is another important characteristic of these churches. Ethiopianism serves as a revolving philosophical point for members.

The Zionist churches, on the other hand, as has been mentioned, represent a movement which has incorporated nativistic healing practices and purification rites, concomitant with prayer and influence by the Holy Spirit. Immersion baptism, physical restoration and spiritual rejuvenation are key practices of the Zionist church. Even though they are independent from mission churches, they have generally been less politically involved, in comparison with the Ethiopian church, although many Zionist churches are now assuming an outlook that is more characteristic of the Ethiopian churches.

Of late, the AIC have been organised into the Council of African Independent Churches (CAIC) and have also joined the South African Council of Churches (SACC). The African Spiritual Council of the AIC and the African Spiritual Churches Association (ASCA) published a document on August 16, 1989, to distance themselves from people like Bishop Mokoena and Archbishop Masiya, leaders of the conservative Reformed Independent Churches Association (RICA), which has aligned itself with the De Klerk regime. The ASCA also adopted a progressive position, calling for the continuance of sanctions against apartheid, the linking of the ANC (African National Congress) and the PAC (Pan African Congress), the removal of troops from the townships, and a total rejection of alignment with the "oppressive apartheid regime."[26] This statement serves as a rebuff to the contention

---

[26] *Crisis News*, December 1989, p. 7.

by some critics of the AIC that the AIC are totally apolitical and divorced from the struggle for socio-political independence.

Similarities and Differences between the Black Churches in the USA and the Black Independent Churches in South Africa

1. Both church organisations/communities emerged in response to the virulent racism of white Christianity; to slavery and Jim Crow segregation in the USA and to white missionary colonialism and political, economic, and social domination in South Africa.
2. Both churches were sparked off by the attempt by struggling black people to "be themselves", to wield ecclesiastical autonomy and self-determination, to be part of an institution which black people could own, control and manage, entirely on their own.
3. Both churches were characterised by a strong spirit of Africanity and pride in blackness. The AME churches, for example, spoke of the beauty of blackness (God is a Negro—in the words of Bishop Harry McNeal Turner). The principles of black consciousness featured in both these communities—African in the AME church was not an incidental term and a sense of Pan-Africanism prevailed amongst them.
4. Both churches reflected a strong political outlook, specifically with the objective of freedom. They were both rooted in the struggle for emancipation. In the USA, the black churches were born out of the struggle for racial justice and for liberation initially from slavery and later from social injustice, as evidenced by the vigorous activism during the sixties. The Independent Churches were also politically orientated—"Africa for the Africans" was the one desire, along with evocation of Ethiopianism as the symbol of blackness and a sign of yearning for the freeing of the entire African continent from European colonial conquest. (The Bulhoek Rebellion of 1921, led by Enoch Mgijima, is one example of such resistance to white colonial domination). In this regard, there is a fusion and synthesis of religious and political dimensions in the outlook of black churches both in the USA and South Africa. There is no dichotomy of the spheres of religion and politics, nor of personal faith and society (at least in the foundational faith of both church communities). Sadly, there appears to be a growing detachment from involvement in the struggle for socio-political transformation amongst sizeable sectors of black churches in the USA and amongst the indigenous

churches in South Africa, which suggests a distancing on the part of these communities from their provenance of social protest.[27]

5. Both churches emerged in response to concrete material and social needs induced by racial and religio-cultural oppression. The vicious nature of colonialism, slavery and capitalism produced family fragmentation, individual alienation, physical exploitation, social deprivation and psychological frustration. The vacuum of addressing these existential needs was filled by the spawning of the black churches—for the purpose of self-elevation and self-affirmation, providing a sense of self-esteem for peoples reduced to eviscerated beings by the toll of psycho-social degradation. It is germane to note here that the black churches in both the USA and South Africa were essentially constituted by persons from the working class and sub-working class sectors. It was people from the bottom-most strata of American and South African societies that joined the ranks of the black and indigenous churches.

6. Both black churches incorporated the ingredients of dynamic black African cultures, modified and re-shaped in various forms. The utilisation of song, spirit evocation, spirit possession, musical improvisation, polyrhythmic harmonisation, hand-clapping, foot-stamping and singing, water baptism and even drumming signified the manner in which these cultural elements were integrated into the worship and theology of these black religious communities. The pivotal role of the spirituals in the black churches in the USA is evidence of the carry-over of the African cultural freedom tradition. The articulation and oratory skills of the black preacher are elements which are also extant in both church traditions. In this sense, the fluidity of culture serves as an instrument of liberation, concomitantly functioning to preserve the historic identity of these black communities. The pride in black culture and its adaptability and resilience in serving as a bulwark to counter the machinations of racial oppression and colonialism have been vital for the tenacity of black religious faith, in both the United States and South Africa. Axiological within this praxis of faith, of course, has been the primordial emphasis placed on the inspiration by the Holy Spirit, that force which provides healing to the sick, sustenance to the downtrodden, and power to the preacher to proclaim the Word.

---

[27] Refer, for example, to a letter to the *Johannesburg Star* of July 22, 1991, which clearly states that the Zionist Churches are strictly apolitical.

7.   The central role that women play in the black churches in the
     USA and in the indigenous churches in South Africa, must be
     underscored in the identification of the similarities of these two
     religious communities. The African Methodist Episcopal Church
     (AME) and the black Baptist Churches testify to this important
     observation. Women constitute the backbone of the black churches
     in the USA, at times making up 75% of the congregational
     membership. Even though most clergy in the black churches are
     male, the people that literally conduct the daily activities of the
     church are often overwhelmingly female.

Amongst the African Independent Churches in South Africa, women's
Manyanos are examples of organizations where women exercise religious
leadership. In the Ethiopian church, women's "leadership runs on
parallel lines to that of the men."[28] The Apostolic Mission Church
of South Africa was led by Minister Lucy Mofokeng, the only female
superintendent of a black church in South Africa. Even though women's
leadership in these churches has not attained parity with that of men,
the situation is far more conducive for women's upliftment and
integration in religious activities, than it is in the white mission churches.
The active participation of women is to the fore in the life, worship
and ministry of all indigenous black churches, especially in areas of
healing, music and community support.

8.   Though these black churches have historically fought for freedom
     in this world and differ sharply from the oppressor white churches,
     they nevertheless retained much of the doctrine of the white
     churches, for example, on sin, salvation, the Trinity, etc. Biblical
     interpretations among the AME for instance, are similar to those
     of white Methodist Churches in the USA. Among the Ethiopian
     Churches, "church organisation and Bible interpretations are
     largely copied from the patterns of the Protestant Mission Churches
     from which they have seceded . . ."[29] The Bible assumes primordial
     significance in the theologies of these respective black churches
     in the United States and South Africa. Thus, elements of the
     polity of some of the white churches have been retained in some
     of the black churches.

9.   The call to ministry of clergy persons in the black churches in

---

[28] Sundkler, *Bantu Prophets in South Africa*, p. 141.
[29] *Ibid.*, p. 54.

both the USA and South Africa is generally verified by the power of the Holy Spirit to inspire such persons to preach and teach, with secondary emphasis on formal academic training as a vital precondition to ministry. It is only of late that these churches have begun to develop educational institutions which could train and equip black ministers with formalised academic preparation for ministry.

If there is such a host of similarities between the black churches in the USA and in South Africa, are there any differences? There are a few variances which distinguish these strikingly similar black churches.

The first difference is that there is not the proliferation of black churches in the USA that there is in South Africa (over 6000 according to latest figures). In the South African situation, black churches sprout through the insight of charismatic leaders, after the death of a church figure, or in the aftermath of prophecies, visions and dreams by staunchly religious figures. Personality differences and schisms provoked by incompatible interpretations of Scripture have also spawned indigenous churches.

Secondly, there are certain religio-cultural differences, inevitably so, owing to the differences in geographical and historical context. Black churches in the USA are the result of the history of slavery, racism and oppression, and represent what is mainly, by far, an urban phenomenon, since large pockets of the black populace reside in the inner city. In South Africa, the indigenous churches are both urban and rural. In addition, the latter are generally inclined towards utility of natural elements and places. The Indian Ocean, off the coast of Natal, is important for purification rituals, as is the hill *Ekuphakameni*, to the Nazarite church. This kind of attachment to places close to nature has not been evinced in the theology and praxis in the faith of black churches in the USA. Water and rituals using water, for example, do not assume the preponderant role in black churches, in the USA, that they do amongst many indigenous churches in South Africa.

Thirdly and finally, there appears to be a more profound sense of collective empowerment amongst many indigenous black churches in South Africa, in contrast to the aura of individual atomisation extant amongst many black communities in the USA. The rugged individualism promoted by the capitalist landscape of the American ethos inevitably influences the outlook of black churches, albeit on a more limited scale than in the white churches. Indigenous African cultural expression, with its emphasis on collectivisation and communal cooperation, aided by the vagaries of indigenous language, has helped to preserve the spirit of togetherness amongst many indigenous churches in South Africa. Such expression would vary, of course, according to location, political context and circumstances.

Conclusion

It is evident from this excursion through black religious communities in the USA and in South Africa, complex as they respectively are, that there are issues which are intrinsic to both, and that the commonalities overwhelmingly outnumber the variances. They both represent some of the fastest growing segments of the universal Christian Church in the world today and both have been protagonists in the struggle for political liberation and national independence from white domination. It is high time that greater levels of interaction and interchange were initiated between these dynamic black religious communities in the USA and in South Africa.

BIBLIOGRAPHY

Cone, J., *For my People*, New York, Orbis Press, 1979.
Crisis News, 1989.
MacRobert, I., *The Black Roots and White Racism of Early Pentecostalism in the U.S.A.*, London, MacMillan, 1988.
Raboteau, A., *Slave Religion*, New York, Oxford University Press, 1978.
Simpson, G.E., *Black Religions in the New World*, New York, Columbia University Press, 1978.
Sundkler, B.G.M., *Bantu Prophets in South Africa*, London, Oxford University Press, 1961.
Sundkler, B.G.M., *Zulu Zion and Swazi Zionists*, London, Oxford University Press, 1976.
West, M., *Bishops and Prophets in a Black City*, Cape Town, David Philip, 1975.
Wilmore, G., *Black Religion and Black Radicalism*, New York, Orbis Books, 1982.
Wilmore, G. and Cone, J., (eds.), *Black Religion and Black Radicalism*, New York, Orbis Press, 1979.

SECTION B

VALUES AND ETHOS

MUSIC AND POWER IN TRADITIONAL ZULU SOCIETY: THE SOCIAL ROLE OF AMAHUBO SONGS

M. XULU

Abstract

This paper describes *amahubo* songs and Zulu socio-religious music which form the cement of social and religious thought. Furthermore, all performance contexts of *amahubo* songs are underlined by the felt presence of the ancestors. Zulu people perform *amahubo* songs in order to attain power to live. At the same time these songs are the power behind the Zulu identity. They define life as the Zulu people perceive it, therefore, they are also part of the Zulu socio-cultural re-awakening which includes the search for traditional roots. These songs seek to maintain a living bond among the living, but also between the living and the ancestors, and between God and people.

Introduction

One of the current trends in ethnomusicological[1] studies is the study of the role and status of individual song items and genres within their social contexts. Societies create musical genres which serve specific social needs. The social role and status of that specific genre becomes a central issue, sometimes even surpassing the organisation of sound patterns. However, in most cases what becomes evident is that in societies where a song type or genre has a specific social function, the organisation of sounds patterns corresponds to the concepts and ideals which the song serves. If this is to be taken any further, it means that sound directions serve not only an abstract aesthetic musical purpose, but they also serve a concrete social purpose. The rise and fall of a melody is not only an aesthetic occurrence to be admired on its own, but it is more a social realisation of specific ideals, mostly understood and communicated by the insiders of the given culture.

The study of the social role and status of specific song types and genres serves the purpose of revealing how and even why a given

---

[1] Ethnomusicology is the study of music in society. Cultural contexts underlying the music are studied, and the views of the insiders of the cultures being studied are considered.

society makes such music. It also serves the purpose of understanding the dynamics of a given society, more so because most traditional societies outside Western society use oral symbols, of which music is one, to mediate between themselves and the super humans.

A study of the social role and status of specific song types and genres can best be carried out where the broadest possible definition of music is given. Alan Merriam's model of the definition of music in terms of concepts, behaviour and sound is becoming the most valuable in ethnomusicology.[2] Its focal point is that it strives towards a universal definition of music while at the same time not overlooking the fact that different societies conceive music and related issues rather differently. Definitions of music given by different societies are rather more specific to the role and status of music within its specific societies. Different societies have their own specific concepts of music. They display specific behavioural patterns towards making music and in response to music, and they order their musical sound patterns in a specified manner determined by the commonly held concepts and related behaviour. Merriam's model has been applied in the present study.

Amahubo Songs

The most common definition of *amahubo* songs is that of ceremonial music.[3] *Amahubo* are associated with the ceremony. This definition is acceptable to the insiders of traditional Zulu culture. However, unless the definition is explained further it does not serve much purpose. The nature of the Zulu ceremony has to be defined. The ideas underlying the Zulu ceremony have to be clarified.

Ideas underlying *amahubo* songs exist in oral form. They are ideas which have been passed from one generation to another in oral form. What is more, unless we give a more elaborated definition of the Zulu ceremony, we may be tempted to think that these underlying ideas, because they are seldom mentioned verbally in public, are secret

---

[2] A.P. Merriam in *The Anthropology of Music*, elaborates his model of defining music in terms of concepts, behaviour and sound. This leads to the broadest possible definition of music, as against music being defined in terms of sound only, as occurs in Western thought.

[3] This is much the case in existing literature. Doke and Vilakazi in their *English—Zulu Dictionary* also underline this definition.

ideas. The truth is that they are not secret ideas. They are public ideas because a Zulu ceremony is a public event.

A Zulu ceremony is by and large a religious event. It is a physical manifestation of all the philosophies and philosophical ideas held in the Zulu religious system. A Zulu ceremony is more a live enactment of the ideas that keep Zulu society going; ideas which define Zulu society.

The most fundamental ideas in the Zulu religious belief system are the issues of individual and collective identity. From the cradle to the grave, and beyond, a Zulu person is constantly confronted with situations which define his or her individual identity only in relation to other people. He is constantly made to understand the role and status of others in his own life; that without the participation of others in his life and his participation in other people's lives, his life is meaningless. The commonly cited proverb: "Umuntu ngumuntu ngabantu", meaning, one is human because other human beings are participating in his life and he is participating in theirs, is more than its face value. It forms the basis of Zulu society.

The Zulu individual also learns of life as a continual attempt to understand the real meaning of community. The Zulu concept of community views community as a continual social intercourse among the living themselves, and between the living and the ancestors and the living and the not yet born. The cycle of the living, the ancestors and the not yet born forms the basis of Zulu thought on community. In addition understanding of God and his role is essential. Thus the normality of Zulu society is only achieved when the social bond among the living, and between the living, the ancestors and the not yet born is alive and demonstrable. Thus, the rites and the ceremonies are meant to achieve this end. Power, so essential to life is only attainable in the context where rites and ceremonies flourish and sound human relations are maintained.

At this point let us return to our definition of *amahubo* songs. What is clear here is that we are not attempting to give a dictionary definition, as it were. Ours is a contextual definition, taking the view of the insiders as the ultimate view.[4]

In *Amahubo* performance there is no concept of musical specialisation.

---

[4] Alan Merriam in *The Anthropology of Music* elaborates on the significance of the insiders view.

People who perform *amahubo* are not regarded as specialising musicians. In fact, ideally every Zulu person has to sing and dance[5] *amahubo* songs at some stage in his or her life. What then are *amahubo* songs? Briefly, *amahubo* songs are Zulu socio-religious music defining the universally[6] held socio-religious principles and forming the cement of social and religious thought. They are music for the realisation of ideals pertaining to unity, patriotism, loyalty, royalty, dignity and in fact anything else that clearly defines the idea of a Zulu personality. They are music for power.

Talking about power, we have to clearly understand the Zulu concept of power. Power here can also mean physical, social and spiritual—religious strength. The traditional Zulu interpretation of life is that it is a series of challenges and perilous moments. Unless one attains power to face the challenges of life, one ceases to live, even if one does not die physically. For the Zulu life is a cycle which has been set in motion since the very first Zulu people emerged from the reed. Thus, the Zulu myth of origin forms part of the Zulu definition of power. One does not attain power on one's own. Power is bestowed on one by others. Because the Zulu concept of living goes far beyond mere breathing and attainment of material possessions (which is sometimes not an issue) the role of other people, God, the ancestors, the not yet born and the environment is always highlighted as the most essential for the individual to attain his or her status as a human being. Thus, to live, in Zulu thought, is to be engaged in a process of a constant search for meaning of the issues that confront people on a daily basis and to draw relations between these issues on one hand and underlying ideas and events on the other.

Amahubo songs and social power

All performance contexts of *amahubo* songs are underlined by the felt presence of ancestors. It is not unusual for people to announce having been with ancestors during *amahubo* performance. The living do not sing and dance *amahubo* songs for the ancestors, but they do so with the ancestors. This is the most distinguishing factor in Zulu religious thought, in that the higher bodies at some stage mix and celebrate with the living. This is not worship. It is co-existence.

---

[5] In Zulu thought singing incorporates dance.
[6] Universally held here, refers to the context of Zulu society.

There are two types of ideas which are seldom discussed, verbally, in Zulu society. These are common knowledge and the highly valued ideas. In most cases such issues are sung and danced. Underlying this practice is the mystic power of music as a force which clarifies and relates issues which cannot otherwise be done. Music in Zulu thought is the symbolic revelation of life. It unites people by visually presenting the commonness of purpose and oneness in life. Music, more than any other activity, defines life. Thus, ideas which are too common or too complicated to be discussed verbally are sung and danced to make them even more clear. This means that to sing and dance is to engage in a process of defining and re-defining life.

In this context religious ideas and ideas about community and human relations are often sung and danced. *Amahubo* songs are the actual singing and dancing of both common knowledge and highly valued ideas. The song genre of *amahubo* acts as a storage, in which great ideas are preserved. Thus, the actual singing and dancing of *amahubo* songs in an elaboration on fundamental ideas. In this way *amahubo* songs form the lifeline of society. They are the rallying point to which society constantly refers when life has to be defined and re-defined. Singing and dancing in the Zulu value system are all transmitted through *amahubo* songs.

When *amahubo* songs are performed in a wedding, which is a rite of passage, or war, which is a rite of transformation, the aim is to invite ancestors to bestow power on the newly-weds or the warriors, and for the ancestors actually to participate in the emerging state, be it war or married life. In the case of war, ancestors are actually believed to partake of the fighting so that a Zulu army of one thousand men may carry ancestral power which gives them the strength of several thousands more men. The actual participation of ancestors in the life of every Zulu individual means that each Zulu individual is guarded by at least one ancestor as he walks around. It also means that a Zulu person possesses his own individual power, plus that of the ancestors combined with power derived from communal living.

It is significant to note that the Zulu people perform *amahubo* songs in order to attain power which allows them to live. Thus, the role of *amahubo* songs is that of music for socio-religious power. Their social status is that they are highly valued and respected. Children and other people who may not be in a position to understand the underlying meanings behind *amahubo* songs are not allowed to perform them. This is done for the fear of ancestral anger and its consequences.

The anger of other people over such an act may also disturb social tranquillity. Abuse of *amahubo* is resented because of the negative consequences this may have.

We pointed out earlier that *amahubo* songs are the power behind the Zulu identity. The philosophy of *ubuZulu* which elaborates the concept of the Zulu personality is part of the social knowledge that is embedded in *amahubo* songs. In this context *amahubo* songs are music for identity. Of course, the Zulu identity is what keeps the Zulu nation going. When a clan or region sings its own *ihubo* song it is proclaiming its identity. The same applies when national *amahubo* songs are sung. One other factor of course is that power, identity and definition of life cannot be separated. *Amahubo* songs serve the purpose of demonstrably making these issues real and common for all to witness and understand. It is the accessibility of music and its ability to diffuse divisions and class formations that make *amahubo* songs the rallying point for the formation of a coherent Zulu society.

It is also significant to note that even the actual organisation of sound patterns in *amahubo* songs comprises social knowledge. Those who, through multiple ritualisation (elders for example), have attained socio-religious power assume the leading voice in a call-and-response framework. Nationally, only the Prime Minister (Undunankulu) always does the leading. The leading voice symbolises initiative and socio-religious leadership, as well as the assertion and maintenance of power and authority. It can also be an acceptance of political authority. For the chorus of thousands to come in and respond to such a musical call symbolises acceptance of leadership, power and authority as well as satisfaction and support for the leadership that is taking the musical initiative. Thus in Zulu society those who lead people in various fields of life are also prolific musicians. It is not surprising that in all Zulu national ceremonies Inkosi Mangosuthu Buthelezi and Prince Gideon do most of the leading during the singing of *amahubo* songs. This is due to their social, political and religious positions. The present King is still too young to give such a musical lead.

Amahubo are the ultimate form of socio-musical expression in Zulu thought. It is after a series of rites, when one fully understands the dynamics of life and is, therefore, not likely to abuse power, that a person is socially permitted to perform *amahubo* songs. Thus, to participate in *amahubo* performance is not only to partake of a musical aesthetic exercise, it is also to make a social statement in which one acknowledges the contributions that society has made in moulding one into a human being, as well as to display one's understanding of being. It is also to display one's understanding of life while consolidating this with that of others, making life wholesome and meaningful. To perform is to express gratefulness to society, while making life meaningful for all. Thus, besides religious reasons, this is another reason for compulsive presence by all concerned people in musical events where *amahubo* songs are performed. To be absent is to do disservice to society.

Conclusion

We have here given a social contextualised definition of *amahubo* songs in our quest to understand their role and status in traditional Zulu society. What becomes apparent is that a discussion of *amahubo* songs touches on many issues, sometimes conflicting issues, but which underlie the performance of *amahubo* songs. It is because *amahubo* songs are the rallying point of society that an attempt to discuss any aspect of them invariably touches on many issues. The most fundamental issue pertaining to *amahubo* songs is that they define life as the Zulu people perceive it. They are performed in contexts where power is sought to maintain a lively social bond among the living, between the living and the ancestors and between the living, the ancestors and the not yet born; as well as between all these, God and the environment. *Amahubo* songs are also music for identity. Their performance contexts are marked by the wearing of traditional regalia (including weaponry), which is the enactment of the scene of the origins of man. The Zulu myth of origin underlines this. In Zulu thought *amahubo* songs generate power which is the lifeline of society.

It is also significant to note that modern Zulu musical styles namely: *sicathamiya, maskanda, mbhaqanqa*, written choral music, wedding songs and independent church singing are increasingly revitalising *amahubo* song ideas as part of the Zulu socio-cultural re-awakening which includes the search for traditional roots. Thus, *amahubo* are not the music of the past only; they are also part of the present and the future and they appear in many forms, some traditional, others modern and syncretic.

BIBLIOGRAPHY

Berglund, A., *Zulu Thought patterns and Symbolism* (Claremont: David Philip Publishers (Pty) Ltd, 1976).

Blacking, J., "The value of Music in Human Experience" in: *Yearbook of the International Folk Music Council*, Vol. 1, pp. 33–71, 1969.

Bloch, M., "Symbols, song, dance and features of articulation: Is Religion an extreme form of Traditional Authority?" *Archives Europeans des Sociologie* XV:I, pp. 555–81.

Doke, C., et al. (Comps.) *Zulu—English Dictionary* (Johannesburg: Witwatersrand University Press, 1958).

Merriam, A.P., *The Anthropology of Music* (Chicago: Northwestern University Press, 1964).

Nettl, B., *The Study of Ethnomusicology* (London: Collier McMillan Publishers, 1964).

Xulu, M.K., "The Ritual Significance of the Ihubo Song in a Zulu wedding", Unpublished M.Mus. thesis, University of Natal, Durban, 1989.

HIEROPHANIES: A HERMENEUTIC PARADIGM FOR UNDERSTANDING ZIONIST RITUAL

S.W.D. DUBE

Abstract

The paper deals with the Zionist Church movement and its ritual as a context for hierophanies which provide a hermeneutic paradigm. For a better understanding of this premise the paper provides a functional definition of hermeneutics. The paper then goes on to focus on the meaning and interpretation of symbolism in the Zionist Church movement. Attention is paid to the following symbols: water, umoya (spirit), candles, celestial bodies, the Zionist staff, different colours, and communality. The paper suggests that Zionist religious practice derives from the African worldview and the life-centredness of African religiosity. The writer concludes that the symbols which are used in Zionist ritual are a text which cannot be ignored in the process of interpreting and understanding Zionism.

Introduction

The scope of this paper is of a limited nature. It focuses on the Zionist Church movement, which is defined as a religious typology. "Zionist" is defined conservatively. Sundkler's broad outline provides a point of departure for the definition used in this essay. For Sundkler, Zionists, as organisations in the independent church . . .

> . . . call themselves by some of the words "Zion", "Apostolic", "Pentecostal", "Faith" . . . The leaders and followers of these churches refer to themselves as ama-Ziyoni, Zionists . . . Ideologically, they claim to emanate from the Mount of Zion in Jerusalem. Theologically, the Zionists are now a syncretistic Bantu movement with healing, speaking with tongues, purification rites, and taboos as the main expressions of their faith (1961 : 54–55).

Zionist ritual is characterised by, among other things, symbolism. The term *hierophanies* is pivotal in this essay in that hierophanies are evidence of a "manifestation" of the bond between man and the sacred. In hierophanies a reality which is the "wholly other" is revealed. Zionist rituals are underpinned by a symbolic character which highlights supernatural values and realities.

This paper begins with a discussion of hermeneutics. This provides a context within which the meaning of Zionist ritual could be deciphered and interpreted. The paper goes on to trace the African roots of Zionist ritual. The idea here is to ascertain the extent to which the continuity of African religious consciousness is represented in Zionist rituals. A major part of the paper deals with symbolism in the Zionist Church. This discussion seeks not only to illustrate that humans have an immediate sense of the symbolic, but also to unveil the meaning of the symbols in Zionist ritual. A brief conclusion at the end of the paper points to the significance of symbols as a useful dimension for the interpretation of Zionist religious activities.

Hermeneutics

It is perhaps appropriate to point out at the onset that an exhaustive definition of hermeneutics is beyond the scope of this paper. Hirsch (1976 : 1) suggests that implicit in hermeneutics is meaning and significance. Pivotal to this explanation is the notion that a text has a verbal meaning and a suggestion that it is possible to "know" or arrive, through interpretation, at the ultimate truth explained in the text. In hermeneutics, therefore, according to Hirsch, one contends with deciphering the meaning of a text and at the same time that meaning is related to a context which is beyond the meaning. In a religious situation, this is possible because human life bears witness to some supernatural presence. Hermeneutics raises questions relating to the underlying presuppositions regarding supernatural presence.

For Carl Braaten (1966 : 131), hermeneutics reflects on how a word or event may be understood and become existentially meaningful in a given context (situation). The idea here is that hermeneutics is the medium through which a text can be "heard". Carl Braaten concedes, however, that this notion suggests two fundamental questions on which the task of hermeneutics pivots, viz. "how is the text to be understood?" and "how does understanding itself occur?"

Ricoeur (1967 : 348) suggests that symbols give us meaning and, for those who dare, understanding can be derived from a symbol. At the same time a symbol gives rise to thought. What Ricoeur is saying here is that a symbol occasions thought by providing something to think about. Accordingly

> ... there exists nowhere a symbolic language without hermeneutics; wherever a man dreams or raves, another man arises to give an

interpretation; what was already discourse, even if incoherent, is brought into coherent discourses by hermeneutics (Ricoeur 1987 : 350).

I have quoted Ricoeur here to show that in hermeneutics the two basic considerations, viz. meaning and interpretation, are knotted together. On the one hand, hermeneutics seeks to decipher the meaning represented in a symbol whilst, on the other, it endeavours to understand the symbol itself.

Ricoeur's suggestion that "every symbol is finally a hierophany" is helpful (1967 : 356). It is in this sense that symbols manifest a bond between man and the sacred. This is particularly significant because this paper wants to suggest that Zionist symbols are a hermeneutic paradigm. On this basis it is possible, starting from symbols, to elaborate on the Zionist existential concepts which find expression in ritual.

The Life-centredness of Zionist activities and its expression in Ritual

The whole question of the emergence and the development of the Zionist Church movement is outside the scope of this paper. What is significant, though, is the need to underline that the Zionist Church movement is, by definition, an African indigenous movement. Consequently, religious consciousness, which is of African origin and flavour, characterises the activities of the Zionist Church movement.

African religion is, first and foremost, a search for life. Whilst this is true of African traditional religion, it is equally true of the Zionist church movement. The Zionists employ, among other things, a rich symbolism in their search for life. The significance of such symbols can be traced to the African context of the Zionist church.

There is a recognition that African life is lived at different levels. There is, for example, the level of human existence and the transhuman level of the cosmos. It is in symbols that this truth finds expression (Eliade 1959 : 6, 167). It is in symbols that the "obligatory and the desirable" are represented. Consequently, substances used to typify or represent or recall something, by possession of analogous qualities or by association in fact or thought, e.g. those used in Zionist ritual, give expression to certain spiritual truths (Turner 1967 : 19; Martin 1975 : 156).

Zuesse (1979 : 242) suggests a basis for a useful understanding of continuity between African religious consciousness and Zionist ritual practice:

> The African who self-consciously and humbly bends sweating in the
> brilliant sunlight, over some "medicines" and dirt mounds at the edge
> of his field to invoke the ancestors and God, is not just praying for
> the maintenance of his family and field. In the deepest level of himself,
> he is praying for the preservation of the entire astonishing fruit-bearing
> reality he moves in and knows so well, from the celestial spirits to the
> textures of the wild grasses in his fingers.

I have quoted Zeusse at length here in order to illustrate the extent
of African understanding of life and how this pivots on the interplay
between human life and cosmic order. A notion of the divine order
underscores any understanding of the resultant totality or whole. The
upshot of this understanding is the notion that the sanctity of the
universe is better expressed in ritual and especially in the symbolic
significance of ritual objects. This whole notion underpins African
spirituality. It is essential to emphasise also that the universe is seen
as self-regenerating, i.e. independently of human action. It behoves
humanity, therefore, to solicit this quality of the universe, not only
to identify with the universe, but also to benefit from the universe's
continual self-regenerating quality.

The foregoing background is helpful in understanding Zionist
symbolic action, which has been extensively documented (Kiernan,
1977 (a), 1979). Spontaneous prayer meetings on the trains, to and
from the centres of employment, are attempts at "sanctifying" the
world in which Zionists live. Prayer meetings, where Zionists seem
to "suffocate" themselves in small township rooms, as they hold their
regular services, are ritual actions which emphasise African spirituality.

Symbolism in the Zionist Church Movement

Our main concern in this paper revolves around the meaning and
interpretation of symbolism. This task is illuminated by Eliade (1959;
101) who suggests that: ". . . the most important function of religious
symbolism . . . is its capacity for expressing paradoxical situations, or
certain structures of ultimate reality, otherwise quite inexpressible."

Symbolism in Zionist ritual expresses the unity of the psycho-spiritual
and physical realms of human existence (Martin, 1975 : 158). In Zion
this is achieved through the harnessing of symbolic ritual objects, e.g.
water, coloured vestments and candles.

The use of water in Zionist ritual has long been of interest and
has been extensively documented (Kiernan, 1972; Sundkler, 1961;
Williams, 1982). Water is used either as solvent (e.g. in *isiwasho*), or

as a medicament or for the purposes of baptism. Research done by
Kiernan (1978) shows that mystical illness produces a state of "heat".
Water has a cooling effect which neutralises the state of "heat". When
water is used in the form of *isiwasho*, especially as an emetic, it removes
mystical illness. Sundkler (1961 : 211) attributes a purificatory function
to water. He arrives at this conclusion when he sees *isiwasho* as a
wide term embracing purgatives and enemas. It is important to note,
however, that water is a symbol. Its efficacy depends on the blessing
of the supernatural. Martin rightly observes that without faith and
prayer water is useless (1975 : 158). The use of water is in keeping
with the understanding of life. Water renews life and ensures health
(Kiernan, 1978, 30).

The notion of the unity of the cosmos is obvious in the use of
water especially as *isiwasho*. Rain falls from above. As it does so, it
passes through the air (*umoya*). On the ground, it mixes with substance
from the physical environment. Water is a life-giving force, which
renews animal and plant life. It is a medium which ensures a suitable
adjustment of the human body to its environment.

When Zionists travel with babies, for instance, they take with them
isiwasho from their local area. On arrival at another place, *isiwasho*
is mixed with local water and given to the baby to drink. This strengthens
the baby against any mystical attacks of illness.

Water plays a very important part in the ritual of baptism. Adult
baptism has the effect of purifying a convert. On baptism, the convert
turns away from his or her evil ways (Dubb 1976 : 125, 130). The
tendency of some people to have several triune immersions during
their lifetime must be viewed against the belief that water has supernatural power (Sundkler 1961 : 209). Water in the sea, waterfalls, rivers,
etc., is either moving, deep or clear. These characteristics are believed
to result from supernatural presence in the water.

In Zion, water "serves as a visible and a tangible sign of purification
and strengthening" (Ndiokwere 1981 : 110). Through prayer, the latent
life-giving qualities in water are activated. The use of water in Zion
gives and revives spiritual force and power, which are essential for
good health and participation in life-enhancing activities.

The management of *umoya* in the work of Zion cannot be over-
emphasised. Becoming a Zionist brings an accession of power (*amandla*)
and of *umoya* (Kiernan 1978 : 29). It is *umoya* which makes believers
speak with tongues (Sundkler 1961 : 247). The *umoya* which the Zionist
manages is the Holy Spirit, "who inspires, reveals and fills with power

and spiritual gifts" (Ndiokwere 1981 : 90). Kiernan (1972 : 200) identifies *umoya* with movement, e.g. of air and breath. In *umoya*, therefore,
there is symbolism of air and wind, whose purpose is to cool or neutralise
"hot" or dangerous states. It is in *umoya's* association with power
(amandla) that I find its relevance to the African concept of life. Vilakazi
(1962 : 87), writing about the Zulu understanding of the spirit as an
aspect of man's being, maintains:

> The spirit, breath or air . . . *umoya*, is the vital force of the body . . .
> This spirit . . . also gives strength. A tired person halts in his exertion
> to "take air" . . . *athathe umoya*, which is the same as "to take strength".

Umoya therefore plays an important part in keeping a Zionist a fully
participating member of the band. *Umoya* is the force that keeps a
Zionist going. A person's involvement in Zion is naturally dependent
on his state of *umoya*.

The highest stage in an individual's development is reached when
an individual becomes a member of the community of spirits. As a
spirit, he works as *umoya*, influencing the living members of his group,
irrespective of the size of the group and the physical location of the
members of the group. This power to influence is made possible by
the fact that the spirit shares in the life-giving powers of the Supreme
Being. The Zionist *umoya* is a foretaste of life in the spirit world, with
its life-enhancing and life-promoting relationships. It is precisely for
this reason that, once a Zionist is filled with *umoya*, he is able to reveal
hidden things and to warn against impending danger. The Zionist
management of *umoya* enables them to fight against the evil spirits
and illness which are a threat to life-affirming relationships.

In Zionist ritual, candles find symbolic significance (Kiernan 1972 : 211,
212). Candles represent fire and light. Fire is associated with power
and strength. The burning candle, therefore, symbolises the presence
and the activity of the Spirit who gives power. It is especially because
of their association with light that candles play an important role in
Zionist ritual. Kiernan (1972 : 214) rightly states: "The candle, once
blessed, becomes mystically empowered to dispel the works of darkness
and to protect a person against evil spirits and their debilitating effects."

Candles are lit from the time the service starts. The lighting of
candles is accompanied by singing, e.g.

Mazokhelwe izibani	Let the lamps be lit
Kush' iNkosi yamakhosi	Says the king of kings

Candles play an important role in healing services. They are used to represent individuals who are faced with the danger of mystical attack. When children are "purified", candles are used to "light up" their lives. When a house is strengthened against witchcraft *(ilungiswa)*, candles are buried at specific points around the house. Candles used in this way are allowed to burn for a short time before they are put out. Red candles are often used for this purpose. When they are buried in the ground, the burnt side is made to face downwards or away from the house. The idea is that any mystical attack intended for the house or its inmates will be turned away or attracted to the burnt ends of the buried candles.

The symbolism of light is, therefore, portrayed in the use of candles in Zion. Good things of life, good health and good fortune are all associated with light (Ngubane 1977 : 115). The opposite of light is darkness and mystical illness *(umnyama)*. The success of an individual's messenger *(isithunywa)* depends on the availability of light. Moreover, the sun, which is associated with human activity and the light of day, has a life-giving quality to all living things.

Some Zionist groups use the stars and the moon as symbols. These celestial bodies are also associated with light, especially in darkness. The morning star heralds the rising of the sun. The stars and the moon light up the day at night. The appearance of the Pleiads inaugurates the revival of life and the hoeing season. This time is particularly important because the plants, which lose their leaves or greenness in winter, start to show signs of life, and animals which hibernate in winter begin to appear. The use of these symbols, therefore, indicates an inter-relationship between man's life and the natural phenomena. This symbolism makes the cosmos a paradigmatic image of human existence (Eliade 1959b : 165).

The Zionist staff is another ritual object which is surrounded by symbolic significance. The staff is seen as a weapon, a reed and a herding-stick. It is in this sense that it symbolises the mystical power of: ". . . warding off attack, driving out spirits, cooling dangerous states, inculcating order and control within the community" (Kiernan 1979 : 19).

The staff in Zionist standing symbolises a pillar *(insika)*. As a pillar it gives support to an individual's "spiritual framework" (Kiernan 1979 : 15). The strength and power *(amandla)* of an individual in Zion will largely depend on this support. The idea finds support in a Zulu saying *"insika iwile"*. This is said of a hungry person. In this case it conveys the idea that there is a loss of power and that danger is imminent.

Zionist colour symbolism has attracted a lot of attention (Sundkler, 1961; Kiernan, 1971; Williams, 1982, amongst others). Most of the documentation in this area centres on colour symbolism with regard to healing and the treatment of diseases. Kiernan (1972) and Williams (1982), amongst others, draw from Ngubane's (1977) discussion of colour symbolism in Zulu traditional medical practice. Ngubane found that Zulu traditional healing practice makes use of the following colours: black *(mnyama)*, green/blue *(luhlaza)*,[1] red *(bomvu)*, yellow *(phuzi)* and white *(mhlophe)*. Black and red medicines remove mystical illness. These medicines are heated because they are meant to expel from the body substances which cause "heat". White medicines, which are meant to restore the balance of the body, are not cooked. Yellow forms a bridge between the use of black medicines and white medicines. The same can also be said of red medicines or the colour red, especially if it is associated with the blood of a sacrificial animal.

Consequently, Kiernan (1972) and Williams (1982) see the use of Zionist colours as parallel to the use of colours in Zulu traditional medical practice. They argue that blue/green and red are used in the same way and for the same purpose as the black medicines, whilst the use of yellow and white corresponds to the use of white medicines.

The problem with the available documentation on colour symbolism is that there is a tendency to give the impression that the use of colour in Zion is a response to a pathological state. The effect of this notion is to present a limited symbolic significance of the colours used in Zion, especially blue and green. Our contention is that health is not a state of restored equilibrium, it is a dynamic phenomenon. The notion of life involves the idea of becoming. It is for this reason that Zionist colours must be seen as life-affirming; not only do they restore health, but, very importantly, they help to "increase" the Zionist by conferring power on him.

It is important to view Zionist colours against Turner's assertion that "the physical acts as a vehicle for spiritual power" (1977 : 32). Zionist colours sacralise human life. Water, for instance, which is regarded as *luhlaza*, plays an important part in Zionist ritual. The vegetation, the sea the sky are all *luhlaza*. In the first instance, *luhlaza*

---

[1] Both blue and green have one term in Zulu, viz. *luhlaza*. To distinguish between shades of luhlaza they use the following explanations: *luhlaza njenge-sibhakabhaka* i.e. blue like the sky; and *luhlaza njengotshani* i.e. green like grass. When the ideophone *cwe* is used with *luhlaza* (*luhlaza cwe*), it is meant to emphasise clearness, e.g. of water.

(blue/green) is associated with natural and therefore "powerful" phenomena, or phenomena endowed with "power". The "power" inherent in these natural phenomena moves to other substances of a similar kind, i.e. like attracts the like. Lightning or heaven (*izulu*), for example, is believed to be attracted by dark green or bright colours. The ideas that such colours also have the power to attract. Further, green vegetation, water and the clear blue sky are associated with summer, when all living things are renewed and revived. Summer is the time also when there is an increase in life, e.g. through propagation and procreation.

The point, therefore, is that the colour *luhlaza* is associated with the supernatural and its life-giving and life-renewing qualities. The use of *luhlaza* seeks to symbolise unity between human beings and the cosmos because: "man is akin to nature, [is] a child of Mother Earth and brother to the plants and animals which have their own spiritual existence and place in the universe" (Turner 1977 : 30).

Apart from symbolism, the unity of divine creation, *luhlaza* is meant to "capture" or attract cosmic power so that it may sacralise human life. The use of the colour "white" *(mhlope)* is widespread among Zionist groups. White forms an important aspect of the church uniform. It emphasises, amongst other things, the Christian character of Zion. The idea is that through the blood of Jesus everything was made pure and whiteness symbolises this quality. In African thinking, whiteness stands for purity and goodness. It is therefore identified with light and associated with the day, and everything that daytime implies. Good health and good fortune belong in the category of whiteness. White candles are used, for example, whenever prayers and rituals aimed at procuring good fortune are conducted. Consequently, ritual purity, freedom from misfortune, spiritual clarity i.e. undisturbed and unimpaired communion with the supernatural, are all associated with whiteness; whiteness also represents health, strength, harmony, blessing and continuity (Turner 1967 : 57). The use of white suggests an idea of attracting the life-affirming nature of the cosmos, which is represented by the white colour.

Yellow is another colour that is often used in combination with others, by Zionists. Yellow is associated with the colour of the light yellow, coarse pumpkin *(iphuzi)*. In a sense, the use of yellow suggests an intermediate stage which is not an end in itself. It suggests the potentiality of a further development which could yield desired results. Consequently, yellow is often used by trainee healers or convalescing patients. Yellow, therefore, is identified with rebirth and regeneration. *Iphuzi*, as an item of vegetation, is associated with the cosmic order.

Red is another colour which is used in combination with others. Red stands for twilight and, therefore, symbolises a transitional stage from darkness to light. In this sense it is used in the same symbolic way as yellow. Red can also be used to stave off danger, as when a house or a homestead is fortified *(iginiswa or ilungiswa)* against mystical attacks. The use of candles in Zion often emphasises protection against mystical dangers. When the Zionists have cause to communicate with the spirits they often prescribe a sacrifice.[2] Here the blood of the sacrificial animal has symbolic importance.

I have laboured the whole issue of colour symbolism in Zion because the Zionist colours often identify the Zion community. Zionist colours provide a visible and a noticeable sign of this alternative community. The uniforms, office vestments, flags and weapons (staves) are all colourful. These colours are not arbitrarily chosen, but are revealed in dreams, in visions and during services. They are visible sign of compliance with the dictates of the supernatural. In addition to ordinary uniforms and vestments, the sashes, cords and head or arm bands are all designed in "revealed" colours. This puts emphasis on the point made earlier, viz. that Zionist colours sacralise human life and provide for the unity of the cosmic prayer. The prescribed colour combinations add to the meaning and being of an individual. They virtually change his status and increase his being.

The items of dress and colour combinations are unique to the wearer and user. When one speaks of *umzayoni* or *isayoni* (a Zionist), the notion of the being of the individual is invoked. It is for this reason that some Zionists dress up a dead person in his Zionist regalia. This underlines, in the first place, that the regalia are an important and inseparable aspect of his being and, secondly that an individual's life does not come to an end when physical death occurs.

The stars and the moon are, amongst others, important celestial bodies used by the Zionists. Different colour combinations are used to make these symbols, which are sewn on items of dress, flags, etc. They are associated with light in the darkness of night. The stars, especially the morning star and the Pleiads, are seen as forerunners of good things. The morning star appears at dawn to inaugurate a

---

[2] Sacrifice is often referred to as the "spilling of blood" *(ukuchitha igazi)*.

new day. The Pleiads inaugurate a new season. The phases of the moon bring about new seasons and are associated with changes in human and animal productivity. The use of these symbols in Zion emphasises man's affinity with nature and the fact that man's source of life and destiny are the same as that of natural phenomena.

The apparent emphasis on symbolism in the work of Zion underlines the whole attitude towards life. Life as a process of becoming makes people at one stage or the other vulnerable to mystical attacks. The free traffic in medicine in the urban areas makes life even more dangerous. What people require is symbolic treatment. The importance of symbolic treatment lies in that it is not abandoned when desired results are not obtained. This explains why many rituals, e.g. triune immersion, are not a one-time affair in Zion. Throughout his lifetime an individual requires "power", and symbolism goes a long way towards meeting this requirement.

The symbolic nature of commensality cannot be over-emphasized. Zionist commensality takes three forms, namely, the celebration of the Eucharist, the main meal taken prior to dispersal and *ilathi* (Kiernan, 1972, 382; Williams, 1982).

Details concerning the organisation and administration of the different aspects of commensality fall outside the scope of this paper. What is important here is to point out that commensality is a life-affirming symbolism. The Eucharist *(isithebe, umthendeleko or isidlo seNkosi)*, for instance, is performed occasionally. Kiernan gives an outline of the Eucharist service which involves the following: "a ritual washing of feet, sacralising of bread and then 'wine' . . . and . . . a distribution of the sacred elements to communicants" (1972 : 382; 1980 : 129). The Eucharist is charged with power. Only the confirmed ("full members") may partake of the Eucharist. Before people partake of the Eucharist they prepare themselves through fasting and prayer and, above all, by restoring and normalising relationships with their fellowmen. It is a common thing for people who have had quarrels to stay away from the Eucharist. The washing of the feet symbolises the desire to serve, which is an important aspect of community. The elements which are used symbolise the body and blood of Jesus Christ (cf John 13).

It is important, however, to note that in some Zionist groups the emphasis is on the "numinous" nature of the sacralised elements. Once such elements are sacralised, they symbolise the source of *umoya* (spirit). The Eucharist renews and increases *umoya*. It is for this reason that Africans will want to be confirmed so that they may not only partake of the Eucharist *per se*, but also share in the symbolic commensality which is portrayed in the Eucharist.

The *ilathi* is another aspect of commensality. In some cases it replaces what Kiernan calls the mean of dispersal. *Ilathi* is a service of thanksgiving for the blessings of life. The idea is to share one's good fortune with brothers and sisters in the spiritual family. The service is characterised by, amongst other things, a table full of refreshments and an animal which is prayed over and ritually killed. The type of animal used for this purpose depends on the means that the organiser of the *lathi* has. It is important to note that in most cases *lathi* is prophesied or revealed in a dream or in a vision. When members of the congregation partake of the refreshments which are provided, it is believed that the "messengers of heaven" are also present to partake of the *ilathi service*. Unlike the Eucharist, the *ilathi* refreshments are enjoyed by everybody who is present.

The meal of dispersal is "a substantial meal provided for each participant" (Kiernan 1972 : 386). This meal underlines the communal nature of the Zionist band. It brings out the qualities of African generosity and resourcefulness. The host provides the food for the visitors. For large assemblies, several bands join hands in providing food for the guests. In some cases, goats are slaughtered for the occasion. The importance of the meal of dispersal lies in the fact that the host minister gets credit for the generosity of his band. This credit not only reflects on the members of his band, but also demonstrates the successful work of *umoya*, which unites his host band and makes them give generously.

Conclusion

In this paper, an attempt has been made to advocate the use of hermeneutics as a framework for an informed understanding of Zionist ritual. In order to illustrate this, it became necessary, first, to relate Zionist religious practice to African traditional religion. In the process, the life-centredness of African religiosity could not be ignored. The major part of the paper focused on the use of symbols in the Zionist church. This was done with a view to discussing their relevant meaning, in order to arrive at an appropriate interpretation.

This paper has highlighted the need to view Zionist symbols as a text. In these symbols a whole world is enshrined. This paper suggests that the hermeneutic experience and dialogue provide appropriate tools for demythologising and "re-hearing" the text.

The crucial issue raised by this presentation relates to the whole question of objectivity. Whilst no attempt was made to address the matter directly, the line of thought suggests that, whilst objectivity is an illusive concept, one must admit one's "presence and influence" on the facts. This paper argues for the need to take the context of the text seriously, if the Zionist symbols are to be deciphered meaningfully. In order to achieve this, the divide between experience and analysis of that experience must be revisited.

BIBLIOGRAPHY

Braaten, C., *History and hermeneutics* (Philadelphia: Fortress, 1966).
Dubb, A., *Community of the saved* (Johannesburg: Witwatersrand University Press, 1976).
Eliade, M. (a), "Methodological remarks on the study of religious symbolism", in: Eliade, M. and Kitagawa, J.M. (eds.), *The history of religions: essays in methodology* (Chicago: University of Chicago Press, 1959).
Eliade, M. (a), *The sacred and the profane* (New York: Harcourt Brace and World, Inc., 1959).
Hirsch, E.D., *The aims of interpretation* (Chicago: University of Chicago Press, 1976).
Kiernan, J.P., "Preachers, prophets and women in Zion: a study of leadership and social control in some Zionist sects in a South African Township", University of Manchester, Ph.D. Thesis, 1972.
Kiernan, J.P., "The work of Zion: an analysis of an African Zionist ritual", *Africa* 46, 1976, pp. 340–356.
Kiernan, J.P. (a), "Poor and puritan: an attempt to view Zionists a collective response to urban poverty", *African Studies* 36(1), 1977, pp. 31–41.
Kiernan, J.P. (b), "Public transport and private risk: Zionism and the Black commuter in South Africa", *Journal of Anthropological research*, 33, 1977, pp. 214–226.
Kiernan, J.P., "Salt water and ashes: instruments of curing among Zulu Zionists", *Journal of religion in Africa*, X (1), 1979, pp. 13–21.
Kiernan, J.P., "The weapons of Zion", *Journal of religion in Africa*, XI (2), 1980, pp. 124–126.
Martin, M.L., *Kimbangu: an African prophet and his church* (Oxford: Basil Blackwell, 1975).
Ndiokwere, N.I., *Prophecy and revelation: the role of prophets in the Independent African churches and in Biblical tradition* (London: S.P.C.K., 1981).
Ngubane, H., *Body and mind in Zulu medicine* (London: Academic Press, 1977).
Palmer, R.E., *Hermeneutics: interpretation theory in Schleiermacher, Dilthey, Hiddegger, and Gadamer* (Evanston: North Western University Press, 1969).
Ricoeur, P., *The symbolism of evil* (Translated from French by Emerson Buchanan) (Boston: Beacon Press, 1967).
Sundkler, B., *Bantu prophets in South Africa* (London: Oxford University Press, 1961).
Turner, V., *The forest symbols: aspects of Ndembu ritual* (New York: Cornell University Press, 1967).

Vilakazi, A., *Zulu Transformations* (Pietermaritzburg: University of Natal Press, 1962).

Williams, C.S., "Ritual healing and holistic medicine among the Zulu Zionists", The American University, Ph.D. Thesis, 1982.

Zuesse, E.M., *Ritual cosmos: the sanctification of life in African religions* (Ohio: Ohio University Press, 1979).

SECTION C

CHANGING PATTERNS AND SOCIO-CULTURAL EXPERIENCE

CAUSES FOR THE PROLIFERATION OF THE AFRICAN INDEPENDENT CHURCHES

S.I. MABOEA

Abstract

Eight broad categories of causes for the rise and growth of the AIC are discussed in this paper. They are the following: The need for a charismatic healing ministry, coupled with the inadequacy of the medical approach of the West, the need for self-identity that makes people feel at home, white Christianity's failure to live up to the biblical principles, unwillingness or reluctance of missionaries and mainline churches to share responsibilities with Africans, relaxation of requirements for registration of churches, the role of the Bible, and the desire of black people to hold leadership positions.

Introduction

It is always extremely difficult to distinguish a major cause or causes from the host of background factors that influenced and continue to influence, either directly or indirectly, the formation of African Independent Churches. Whereas it is a simple matter to determine which general economic, sociological or political factors are conducive to the formation of a new church, it is by no means easy to arrive at a representative theory when it comes to individual groups or their followers. For example, in the same group, the founder-leader might well have broken away from a historical church in protest against some or other church policy. Over the years, people join this new church for a variety of sociological, political or religious reasons, until eventually the original background to the formation of the church may be missed completely. Without a historically perspective of the successive factors involved, one could arrive at a mistaken theory on the group's origin.

Factors leading to secession Charismatic Healing

While the Roman Church is an Institute of Grace through its sacraments, and the Protestant Church in Africa appears as an Institute of the Word through teaching and preaching, the Independent Church of the Zionist type is an Institute of Healing. This healing message is the pivot of all church activity. "This is not a church, it is a hospital", one prophet told his congregation. The usual answer as to why a person has joined a Zionist church is: "I was ill, they prayed for me, now I am well" (Sundkler 1976 : 220). Many AIC members view healing as Christ's major purpose of mission on earth. As a result, any leader with this gift is regarded as very important in AIC circles. Faith healers are the most respected class, not only in the churches but also within the African community.

Faith healing does not take place in a vacuum; it is normally associated with a church service and it is seldom confined to sporadic incidents in the lives of individuals. Within AIC circles, the church's headquarters usually represent healing centres. They are sometimes referred to as "Hospitals", "Zion" or "Jerusalem". Think of Lekganyane and Mutundi's "Zion City" and Ntate Modise's "Jerusalem". Church refers in this sense to a place of worship. It might be in a dwelling house, or under a tree, in shacks put up for the purpose of worship, on the banks of rivers, on the sea shore, in valleys, or at other meeting places of this nature.

Once a member discovers the gift of healing, he normally starts his own church, which will specialise in faith healing. Since illness and its causes are a great threat to Africans, such a leader usually attracts a lot of followers. Methods used by the faith healers also appeal to many people. They have a tendency to lay hands on the sick. People attend their services only to be prayed for. As a result, one finds there not only members of AIC, but also people from mainline churches and others who belong to no church. In most cases, the latter, after being healed, join the church, whereas members of the historical church maintain double membership. During the day they attend and participate in their own historical churches; during the night they attend the AIC. Although the mainline churches do not always regard the AIC as real churches, they do acknowledge the AIC's ability to handle some of the problems with which historical churches cannot cope—a capacity which makes the AIC popular among the Africans.

Since, in some quarters, the AIC are regarded not as churches but as subverters of the people, many have dual church membership. People cannot easily withstand this temptation.

Many people attend African Independent/Indigenous churches not primarily to worship God, but to be prayed for. Problems for which patients regularly ask prayers include protection, security, marriage disputes, stability, barrenness, prosperity, joblessness and family problems. Most churches pray for healing in the name of Jesus and leaders inform their patients Jesus is the One who heals and that without belief in Him, they will not be healed. By reading the Bible and preaching the gospel message, the leader persuades the people to have faith in Jesus Christ and His healing power. In this way, even though many people attend AIC specifically for charismatic healing, all are first directed to Jesus Christ. Many do accept Jesus as their personal Saviour and end up joining the charismatic healer's church.

Some AIC leaders entreat members to persevere in prayer at home. During charismatic healing services the leader not only prays for the patients, he also invites the cell group leaders, the co-pastors of the same church and the intercession team to join him. The whole congregation are also requested to pray together from their seats. It is noteworthy that some church leaders admonish the patients in the strongest terms possible, to give themselves to God, since He is the one who can heal any disease. Patients are strongly warned against expecting to receive blessings from God without surrendering their lives to the Lord.

Prayer plays an essential and central role in the healing practices of the Independent Churches. Prayer is mentioned regularly and it appears to be the vehicle that brings about the healing of those who believe in Jesus Christ.

God's healing Spirit is believed to be activated by the prayers of faithful healers within the AIC. These prayers have set people free from ancestral interference and from disease associated with the ancestral powers.

In charismatic healing that follows a biblical pattern, God starts with the heart. This reflects the principle found in the Epistle of James. "Is there any sick among you? . . . confess your sins one to another, and pray one for another, that you may be healed. The effectual fervent prayer of a righteous man availeth much" (James 5 : 14–16). The procedure is to deal first with the spiritual then the physical requirements of man. In charismatic healing, the body's needs are secondary to the spiritual. Indeed, without faith, which is the spiritual aspect, there can be no healing of the body. The Holy Spirit which

God bestows on a charismatic healer, the Spirit which indeed provides healing, is given to those who have faith in Jesus Christ. Hence, many, if not all AIC leaders insist first upon faith in Jesus, for without it there is no healing.

Healing treatment is a daily practice within the AIC, integrated into the ritual activity of the church. At Zion City, the sick come every morning for a prayer meeting and to have hands laid on them by the bishop. Later in the day, patients are visited by prophetic healers who spend much time with them. Psychologically, this part of the ministry is very important. At such visits individuals feel important, discover self-identity and experience a genuine, meaningful purpose to life.

Western medical approach's failure to meet the specific needs of African people

It is generally accepted by Africans that Western medicine is inadequate for meeting certain needs and illnesses among Africans—those whose cause is normally ascribed to either ancestors or witchcraft. This belief has advantaged the multiplication and growth of the AIC. Those who approach a charismatic healer for prayer have normally failed to obtain a cure or an improvement in their disease from the clinic or hospital. Many Africans visit a hospital and a charismatic anointed healer at the same time. The relevant approach and the implication of healing by the church encourage those who are cured of their disease to become members of the church. To them, the church has given life. The church becomes a refuge because of its successful handling of both physical and psychological troubles. It addresses and meets specific needs and people feel protected, safe and well-cared for. Hence the headquarters of the church become a place of rescue. The leader listens to all the problems carefully, assuring the patient that he understands completely his or her fear and pain, which are caused by the power of the devil. He points out that the power of God is demonstrated through His love and assures the patient, through the scriptures, of Christ's personal concern. A prerequisite for cure is total surrender of all the problems to Jesus. Through the testimony of those who have already been cured through prayer, the patient feels hopeful of a real cure. Indeed, the Holy Spirit, who works through God's Holy Word and is the core driver of healing among the AIC, prepares the patient's heart and, after a prayer of faith, the patient becomes healed.

Western medical practitioners, in spite of their concern for both the physical and psychological needs of a patient, fail to probe deeply enough into the existential realities of a patient. Thus, medical doctors cannot really address the cure of a patient's illness because they cannot adequately explain the patient's real illness involving ill relationships with ancestors, evil power or witchcraft.

Since these are considered to be the root causes of a patient's unhealthy situation, what may appear to a Western doctor to be a successful medical treatment is invariably interpreted by the African patient as merely a temporary or partial solution. The real cause which might be witchcraft or an ancestral spirit, has not been dealt with effectively.

It is precisely in this field that the charismatic healers or prophets of the African Independent Churches appear to provide realistic solutions in terms of the African worldview. The Christian message preached by the AIC carries with it healing effects and blessings because the entire work is based on first winning the sick for Jesus Christ. This winning process occurs through the senior leader listening to the patient's problems, showing concern by knocking and touching the patient's shoulders, and then redirecting the patient to Jesus through the Bible. Emphasis is placed upon the role of faith in Jesus; He is the One who not only heals but is there to heal every patient who believes.

Thus, these churches stress the element of healing that is relevant to Africans with its conviction that through faith in Jesus, through the Word, the Gospel answers all man's problems. Unfortunately, until well into the twentieth century, some Western missionaries did not generally accept that Christianity in Africa would have to be different from Christianity in Europe. There were often deliberate attempts to put the lid on any distinctive developments and to channel African church life back into the stereotype patterns of the West. Little or no effort was made to try and find answers for such reactions by church leaders. There were no discussions or attempts to sort out disputes, through either dialogue or the Bible. Because of lack of insight into African culture or its effect upon the whole of life, be it sociological, political or religious, the mission churches could not contain any differences. Breakaways were then labelled sects.

In the final analysis, this lack of understanding of Africans led to the failure of the Western missionary approach to address matters which were at the centre of African life. To most Africans, the missionaries' reactions indicated either a lack of love on the part of those who brought the gospel message to them, or a paternalistic type of love which failed to care. The one who claimed to show love was not taking cognizance of the one to whom the love was directed. The result was nothing but poor communication, without effect.

Some historical churches regard the AIC not as churches but as subverters of the gospel, or sects. This is one reason for a dual membership. Some are 'mainline' church members during the day and Independent church members, even co-leaders, during the night. These people yearn for the caring and personal identity that exist within the Independent Churches but are lacking it in the historical church, with its cold, stereotyped and one-sided leadership.

> Unfortunately some of the unique elements of the gospel are not the things we really talk about. We rather teach people that christianity involves a new set of taboos. You must not drink, you must not smoke, you must not have more than one wife, etc. And so, people often have a very strange idea of what this thing christianity really is all about. (Nida 1971, *Lux Mundi* 3).

In this way, says Nida, the good news about salvation becomes the bad news. It is the inability of Westerners to address the basic need of black people which ultimately creates a favourable climate for secession. Their frustration leads them to create a platform where they can understand God within their own situation; where God will understand their problems and address them in a positive way.

Sea water is regarded as an important element in healing and the prophet may instruct that the patient be immersed in the sea several times. This is why so many AIC people undertake a trip to the sea. The AIC prophets and faith healers use the sea to perform healing, whilst they pray. This is accepted by members of the AIC, who in this way address not only physical problems, but also the psychological problems which threaten and frustrate Africans who have accepted Jesus as their Lord. Such approaches are lacking from the Western medical practitioners.

Ash is also used by the faith healers to cure diseases. It is regarded as pure and clean since it has been purified by fire.

Most of those who are cured become faithful members of the very same church and the AIC continue to grow in numbers and attract many people. Their approach to curing disease generally meets the needs and pattern of Africans, as is confirmed by the following words: "The usual answer to the question as to why a person has joined a Zionist church is: I was ill. They prayed for me. Now I am well" (Sundkler 1976 : 220).

A place to feel at home/a sense of belonging

African Independent/Indigenous Churches create a place where their members can feel at home. A strong sense of belonging and of security is important to them, and this is realised in the care the members have for one another. Prayers are said specially that the unemployed will find work, whilst those who have jobs assist in finding them employment where possible. To most Africans the metropolitan type of life, where everyone is concerned for himself, is very strange. It is against tradition and it is abnormal. In isolation people are robbed of the all-important unity and fellowship. Against this background, people join the AIC and through their concern for one another, establish a place where members can overcome the isolation, experience that natural African fellowship, enjoy recognition as a fellow human being in need; and generally through consideration, care and love, be made to feel at home. Here lies the fundamental motive for the formation of African Independent Churches.

The missionaries' approach in bringing the gospel was, for most Africans, not effective. Their way of conducting catechism classes, too, was often extremely superficial and failed to reach many facets of the African life. The influence of the movements from which these missionaries came also played a role in aggravating the communication problem. The majority of the missionaries were products of the Revival Movement in Europe or America, or Puritanism. As a result, salvation meant saving souls and many defined sin exclusively in terms of sex and pleasure. Ultimately, their teaching was basically understood as a "gospel" of do's and don'ts. Equally, the medical services offered by the mainline churches provided only a partial solution from the African viewpoint and, in some instances, only aggravated the problems. Medical personnel relied upon their medical knowledge and expertise rather than on divine intervention or their confession of faith in Jesus Christ. The "soul winning" methods included the erection of hospitals or schools and church buildings. All who wanted to serve in the hospital had to be full members of the church. Medical care was thus no more than an aid to the real work of the mission, the proclamation of the Word which would lead to the salvation of the soul. The historical churches failed to heal the bodily illness of their members because salvation to the entire man fell outside their missionary purpose. To a certain degree, the mission schools went the same way. For many years, the only purpose or erecting schools was to help people read the Bible. The mission lost sight of the fact that a general, comprehensive education would help to save the African as a whole human being.

To Africans Christianity meant something only for Sundays. It had no relevance on Monday since it was divorced from day-to-day happenings. From Monday to Saturday, life was ruled by taboos and traditional norms. Christianity failed to provide comfort to the whole life of an African.

This issue was crucial since, in the traditional African life, religion cannot be divorced from daily life and behaviour. Religion is interwoven with cultural life, social life, economic and national life. By contrast, the Christian religion, or so it appeared, was something different and apart and could be practised in isolation from other aspects of life. This state of affairs prepared the way for the rise of the African Independent Churches.

In the impersonal urban life, there is a great need for an intimate circle of friends where the individual can achieve recognition and a self-identity that makes him feel at home. The individual's church, which is also a circle of friends who care, helps him to cope with the problems of urban life in a wide sense. In a society where the individual feels crowded and insecure, the development of identity is essential. Thus, the Independent Church, with its vast hierarchy of leaders in which virtually every adult carries responsibility and occupies some sort of official position, accommodates a real need in affording members a new sense of personal worth and importance.

The need to establish a caring fellowship, brotherhood and kinship, and to acknowledge God as the source of all answers in man's life, prepared and eventually led to the rise and growth of the Independent Churches. They answered the silent, as yet inarticulated, yearning for a religion that would provide a sense of being and of feeling at home. As a result, these churches proliferated especially in comparison with the historical churches from which some of them broke away.

White Christianity's failure to live up to the Biblical principles

When the first missionaries came to South Africa and presented the gospel message of the Bible to the people of Africa, those who accepted the gospel message took it very seriously. Such individuals respected missionaries highly because of the good news that they brought to Africa. They were not afraid to pay the highest price possible, to obtain a Bible of their own. Mission work was respected, not only by the people who accepted Jesus as their Lord, but also by the kings of those times.

> So much impressed was Mpande by Schreuder's medical cure of one of his royal ailments that he at once gave the Lutheran Missionary land at Empangeni (Zululand) and permission to build a mission station there. Thus was Zululand opened to the Gospel—by the medicine bottle (Sundkler 1976 : 25–26).

In general, the missionaries and their gospel mission were readily accepted by the people of Africa. The Bible message was also accepted as a principal law and way of life while agencies of this gospel were respected because of the message they were preaching to the people.

In South Africa, the fact that Biblical standards could not be attained, even by missionaries, for the sake of the colour separation maintained by the state, caused a lot of Africans to doubt the sincerity of the missionaries. They had faith in the God of the Bible but public and private lives were dominated by the colour question which was also experienced, and still is practised within the churches. Segregation was initiated in the churches by those very people who preached love for one's neighbour but did not show that very love to those they witnessed to.

In these circumstances, Africans consulted the Bible. The law of love was there but it was not being lived up to by the missionaries. The Christian Church in South Africa was represented by missionaries who supported segregation of people on account of colour, at the cost of the Bible that their church was preaching. The concept "no equality between black and white in church or state has, in fact and in everyday practice, been accepted by many other white churches" (Sundkler 1976 : 37).

As time went on, black people were becoming gradually educated. They started to protest against these types of attitude from missionaries within the church. Africans could not understand why clergymen should behave like secular men towards other human beings. Missionaries presented what is real love, according to the Bible, something for which Africa is thankful. Through the missionaries' paternalistic approach, this very loving God seemed to Africans to be favouring the whites. In accepting the gospel message, Africans were sincere. Before the God of the Bible all people were equal, yet the one who brought these good tidings did not regard and handle his own brother in the Lord as equal. This was very strange to Africans.

When the Dutch Settlers first came to South Africa they worshipped together with their servants. During the time when there was a real language problem, the Dutch people could not utter a word in any African language and vice versa, one church service was conducted for all people of different languages. Later when slaves and servants were able to speak the Dutch language it became necessary to separate services on the basis of the colour or language. Africans were then forced to gauge the conduct of the missionaries against the scriptural norms.

The missionaries' failure to live up to the Biblical standards created a platform for succession. Although the Bible would still remain their springboard, Africans could no longer cope with the christianity of the white man, which wounded so much.

> White christianity suppresses. Western manners that control people in daily life and even before God are presented as christianity (Makhubu 1988 : 19).

African Independent Churches were thus born out of bitter experience, as a cry for spiritual liberation which had to be expressed in day-to-day life. For Africans, as mentioned earlier religion affects all facets of life. It is not just a Sunday service affair, but exists continuously throughout the seven days of the week. Within the AIC, members feel free from white domination and, at times, ridicule the whites.

On some white farms, where there is no freedom of worship, labourers are forced to attend and also join a church designed according to the taste of the farm owner. The labourers working under his supervision are not consulted on this and to some, the farmer is right. Normally, labourers join the church of the farm owner, thus being robbed of their choice of worship. Should any labourer feel offended or un-comfortable about the church his master has chosen, he might be requested to move out. Since AIC are not readily accepted as churches, being regarded rather as sects, leaders and members of one of these churches may not be allowed on some farms. AIC are viewed as mere subverters of the people. Since people need freedom of worship, close fellowship and caring, as well as a place to air their views, through prayer freely, they join or start an African Independent Church of their own.

The AIC replaced the frustration of God's people with care. They looked after members who were in trouble of any kind. They prayed and, in the name of Jesus, healing during the services the sick who came for prayer healing, be they members or not. They called upon Jesus in faith if a disease were to be cured. They shared their difficult experience. They also shared the healing power of God which strengthened those who were ill, knowing that if they could really believe in the name of Jesus, a cure would be attained. They witnessed about the power of God to intervene in their social problems, to provide jobs, to protect and bless people with prosperity. In this way, the frustrations which Africans encountered daily were released through prayer. Such church services were found only in the African Independent Churches; hence their growth.

> Some white missionaries, instead of teaching christianity, promoted and taught white civilization (Makhubu 1988 : 24).

Africans adapted to the Western culture, only to discover eventually that there was nothing left to them of their own culture. Almost everything that had to do with African culture and was unknown to missionaries was declared sinful or unbiblical. Missionaries did this out of ignorance, at times also as a quick response to problems. Interpretation of the gospel by white Christians differed greatly from how an African would interpret it. Such interpretation too, was not acceptable to Africans since it would not accommodate their culture or address it biblically.

Traditionally, when Africans worship, they sing and dance together. They have a tendency to become emotionally or spiritually involved in the service. This is not possible in the white services, where there is strict order and control by the leader, and where some spiritual people's feelings and emotions are not expressed. AIC members sing freely and as loudly as possible. Church services also last much longer than in the mainline churches. To members of the AIC, this duration is more of a blessing than anything else. The white man's lack of insight into such deep-rooted and psychological yearnings among the blacks, coupled with the failure to live up to the biblical ideals, contributed to the founding and growth of AIC.

> The uncharitable behaviour which was not in keeping with the love
> of God they proclaimed, confused the people . . . where western culture
> was being introduced as the gospel, and the culture of blacks condemned
> as evil and heathen, problems arose which couldn't be solved except
> by separation (Makhubu 1988 : 28).

*Reluctance of "mainline" churches to share responsibilities with African
ministers*

Most missionaries created the impression of being either reluctant to
share responsibilities with their African colleagues, or not prepared
to do so. This attitude some African ministers and church members
found absurd. When it persisted, those who were not happy with it
resorted to forming their own separate church. Conditions such as
these, where Africans felt they were regarded as less important, left
them puzzled and led to feelings of frustration. This continuous under-
estimation by missionaries naturally caused Africans to draw back to
search for their own human resources and dignity. Many concluded
that, to affirm their humanity and worth as people within the
community, Africans must resort to combating whatever impediment
hindered them from regaining their dignity. If an opportunity for
maintaining their own humanity was denied by the whites, then Africans
should ensure that their values, integrity and worth were maintained
among the Africans. In this way, a foundation was laid for succession.

> The church is the only avenue of self-expression open to the African,
> so that anybody who feels the urge for such expression will found his
> own church (Vilakazi, Mthethwa, Mpanza 1986 : 19).

Some missionaries' biblical emphasis caused uncertainty about the main
aim of mission work. Many, if not all of the highest positions in
the church were occupied by missionaries. Even ordained African
ministers, who were accepted by their people as true leaders of the
church, were not readily given the opportunity to hold the highest
posts in the church. The missionaries' reasons were, for example, that
Africans did not have sufficient skills or did not know how to handle
administration and supervision. Yet these issues were not discussed
with the churches or church leaders. Such behaviour hurt African
ministers and part of the church for, to them, this appeared as pure
discrimination of people on account of the colour of their skin. Officially, the church regarded all pastors as equal but when the discrimination
continued (as is still the case in some churches today) some ministers

left to form their own church with a group that understood their reasons for doing so.

Relaxation of conditions governing registration of AIC

Since many AIC leaders were not educated, most of the AIC failed to meet the requirements for registering as a church in South Africa. In a way, this barred breakaways and growth. Some of the requirements for recognition of a church were that its pastor should have completed at least eight years schooling and that his theological training was not less than three years. Before the church could be registered, it was required that the church should have existed for a considerable period and that it should have grown in size. It needed a built church and had to be financially stable.

These requirements were relaxed in 1963. The AIC leader was no longer required to have obtained Std 6, nor was it necessary to have theological training. This made it easy for people to establish their own churches and be registered straight away. Thus, founding a new church is no longer an effort. If a member differs with his church leader, he/she may easily start his/her own church. Members who agree with the reason for secession, will follow. In this way, a new church is started, emphasising largely that which caused them to differ from their original leader.

The present requirements for registration are the particulars of the founder, the date when the church was established, the number of adult members and of young people aged 16 and above. Also required is information on the number of pastors within the church, the leaders' education and training, if any, and its duration. Particulars of administration of the church including the finance must be supplied. It may also be necessary to supply names of organisations with which the church is associated, its constitution and its philosophy of ministry. Because requirements are no longer complicated, most churches are able to be recognised and secession is encouraged.

Unfortunately, there are some leaders among the AIC who encourage breakaways. Pastors who are unable to complete the registration forms are helped by others within the AIC who also broke away. They charge fees for helping with the forms that have to be sent to Pretoria. Some charge a fair fee; others a very high one. Generally they range from ± R 40–00 to R 45–00.

Due to the fact that many AIC leaders are not trained theologically, a small group of more enlightened pastors is in a position to benefit from the registration of new churches, hence encouraging unnecessary secession. As soon as all leaders strive for theological training, where they will hopefully also be taught about administration, such unnecessary breakaways will cease. Church growth is a business of every church, but it has to arise according to the scriptures rather than through human greed.

A striving to adhere to the Bible

When Africans broke away from the mission churches to form their own churches, their basic purpose was to consult the scriptures to hear what God says. Indeed, through their efforts to hear from God Himself out of the Bible, many discovered that the Word of God did not always correspond with what was brought by the missionaries. They discovered that the God of the Bible was interested in their affairs. They learned about a God who loved and a God who wanted justice and righteousness for all people. From the Bible, they heard about a God who told them to do to others as they would expect others to do to them.

They realised that not all about their culture was not good and they started to serve God within their own context. Africans were then exposed to God direct, not via Western culture. Then only did the Africans appreciate their Africanness. From the Bible, they learned to discover God as God for all people; not as one who associates himself with a certain group of people alone. Through their own way of Bible study, they realised that God loved them as they were. It was then that the leaders began to lead people as they were. The Bible taught them of the love God has for them. From the Bible, they realised that some of their culture was good and according to God's will, such as the desire to assist those who are depressed and in trouble. They even discovered the necessity of caring for one another.

These discoveries encouraged Africans to value their humanity, which they could not always feel in the mission churches. Thus, the distress they encountered in the missionary churches, which caused them to go back to the Scriptures, was a blessing in disguise. It helped them to read, hear and understand the Bible better, from their own worldview.

> To Protestant Africans, the Bible was a higher authority than the missionary. They could therefore turn their backs on the missionary

and follow the Bible fairly easily, if it seemed that the missionary's conduct and teaching conflicted with the Bible (Daneel 1987 : 90).

Cry to occupy a high position

There is a tendency among some AIC leaders to establish their own churches, to gain a high position. This type of breakaway occurs in the mission churches as well as in the AIC. In most cases, initiators of the breakaway could come from among people who are close to the priest/pastor in the church; people who are trusted by their leaders for their faithfulness and dedication to the work of God; people who assist the minister to pray for the sick—briefly, people who, in the absence of the presiding pastor, lead the church. Such people would automatically be well versed in the philosophy of the church and because of their responsibility, trusted by the congregation. It would be they to whom the church members would go for any sort of assistance, in the absence of the pastor, whether for moral or sociological advice. Also, it would be they whom the pastor would send to perform duties in the church, which he could not do personally because of other commitments.

As time goes by, some feel they could as well found their own churches, where they would occupy the same position as that of their present leader or even higher. Such an idea would be supported by the experience gained in leading the church and by the respect the church and the community have for him because of the services he renders to them as a man of God. That he would no longer be under someone else makes him feel more important and smart. After some time, such a person will establish his own church and become its highest authority, enjoying the title of pastor. For most, the philosophy of ministry, attire and methods of approach will be similar to that of the church from which the founder broke away. He might supplement or change some of the things, yet basically, his church will not differ greatly from the Mother church.

BIBLIOGRAPHY

Brock, C., *Indigenous Church Planting* (Tennessee: Broadman Press, 1981).
Daneel, M.L., *Quest for belonging* (Harare: Mambo Press, 1987).
Hammond-Tooke, W.D., "The Aetiology of Spirit in South Africa", in Oosthuizen, G.C., Edwards, S.D., Wessels, W.H., Hexham, I, *Christian religion and healing in Southern Africa* (Lewiston: The Edwin Mellen Press, 1989, pp. 43–65).

Kitshoff, M.C. (ed.), *Testimonium* (KwaDlangezwa: University of Zululand, 1983).

Makhubu, P., *Who are the Independent Churches* (Johannesburg: Skotaville, 1988).

McGavran, D.A., *Understanding Church Growth* (Grand Rapids: Eerdmans, 1983).

Mönnig, H.O., *The Pedi* (Pretoria: Van Schaik, 1955).

Nida, E.A., *Customs and Cultures* (New York: Harper, 1954).

Oosthuizen, G.C. *Religion Alive* (Johannesburg: Hodder and Stoughton, 1986).

Oosthuizen, G.C. (ed), in *Testimonium* (KwaDlangezwa: University of Zululand, 1984).

Oosthuizen, G.C., *Godsdienste van die Wêreld* (Pretoria: NG Boekhandel, 1977).

Sundkler, B.G.M., *Bantu Prophets in South Africa* (Oxford: Oxford University Press, 1961).

Taylor, J.V., *The Primal Vision* (London: S.C.M. Press, 1973).

Vilakazi, A., Mthethwa, B., Mpanza, M.B., *Shembe* (Johannesburg: Skotaville, 1986).

SOCIAL CHANGE, RESISTANCE AND THE WORLDVIEW OF A COMMUNITY IN THE TRANSKEI

J. DE WET

Abstract

The only detailed study of Zionist-Apostolic type churches in the Transkei of which I am aware, focuses on a description of Zionism as a phenomenon. That study, undertaken by H. Pretorius (1985), concerns the movement itself. I am interested, however, in Zionism as a worldview of a community; a community with a social and religio-cultural history. Worldview as corporate enterprise is seen as an ongoing process of symbolic construction and negotiation, out of which corporate identity emerges. The focus is now on the Zionist-Apostolic type worldview, as the most recent strategy of a specific community in the Transkei for negotiating identity in a particular time (historical period) and place (social context). This thesis is supported by my tracing the history of the community in terms of a significant (identity-threatening) changes in socio-cultural conditions, and corresponding changes in the community's worldview, from the late nineteenth century to the 1980s. The Babomvu worldview dominated much of this period with the Zionist-Apostolic worldview becoming popular, more recently, amongst people who previously adhered to Babomvu-ism. Two interrelated themes stand out. These are firstly, the renegotiation of worldview and identity in a changing social environment, and secondly, religio-cultural resistance to Western civilisation.

Social change experienced by the people of rural Transkei has largely been brought about by the manipulation of rural society into the broader political economy of South Africa. At a socio-cultural level this has meant the increased dominance of Western civilisation in the indigenous context.

The persistence of this process brings to mind resistance of socio-political kind associated with the nineteenth century conflict between Xhosa-speaking people of the Cape Frontier and the Colonialists, and much later the unrest in Qumbu and the Pondoland Revolt. The dominant feature, we are told by historians such as Beinart, Peires and Bundy, is the struggle over land and resources. There are, however, other less obvious forms of resistance which need consideration.

This paper focuses on resistance of a more religio-cultural kind. I am concerned with the changes of worldview of a community in rural Transkei, in the face of periods of significant social change, in order to resist and restrict Western influences in defence of an indigenous identity and with the aim of maintaining *ubuntu*.

The Babomvu worldview provided a form of religio-cultural resistance from the days of the ox-wagon to those of the pocket-calculator. Since the late 1970s, however, this worldview has disintegrated. At about the same time the Zionist-Apostolic type churches became popular amongst those who previously constituted the Babomvu community. The possibility that the decline of Babomvu-ism and the rise of "Zionism" at about the same time is more than a coincidence, is examined. It is my hypothesis that the Zionist-Apostolic worldview succeeded the Babomvu worldview, as the outcome of a continuous process of worldview renegotiation in response to the changing socio-cultural experience. This is supported by evidence which shows that the Babomvu worldview was, at lower levels of socio-cultural change, subject to renegotiation without losing its characteristic features. As the community experienced greater levels of socio-cultural change, its worldview was re-negotiated to the point where it no longer resembled the Babomvu world-view.

There are two primary sections in this paper. In the first section, I trace the changes from Babomvu worldview as the dominant worldview of the community to its disintegration and the rise of Zionist-Apostolic type world-view in the same community. In the second section, I begin to generate an explanation as to why the Babomvu adherents were attracted to a Zionist-Apostolic type worldview.

I. CHANGING WORLDVIEW

I will start by identifying the Babomvu worldview[1] and locating the Babomvu community[2]

1. *The existence of the Babomvu worldview in a particular social milieu* (Observation 1)

---

[1] I understand the term worldview in a specific way. Redfield (in: Chidester 1987) has noted that a worldview is "the way a man, in a particular society sees himself in relation to all else". A worldview shapes the way in which persons look at themselves in relation to everything else—real and ultimately real. A worldview is that perspective from which people perceive, interpret and imagine the world they experience (*ibid.*). But it is more than a way of seeing, or a way of thinking, it is a multi-dimensional network of strategies for negotiating an identity (Chidester in: *JSR* 2/1, (1989): 16). In this sense it has the comprehensive capacity to organise every aspect of human belief, action and experience.

[2] A definition of the term "community" has long been a subject of debate in the social sciences. I will use it to refer to people who share a common identity, history and worldview. By community I mean a worldview community or ideological community. The members of the community show some solidarity vis-à-vis the outside world. "When the survival of a group becomes for its members an objective opposed in their eyes to the individual objectives which they feel they have the right to pursue, one can say this group constitutes a community, or is in the process of communalisation" (Hamilton, 1989).

The Babomvu Worldview

A number of questions guide this section. These are: who uses the label "Babomvu"? Is it more than merely an academic term? Did the people identified as adhering to "Babomvu-ism" associate themselves with this term? Is there evidence that leads one to conclude that Babomvu-ism existed as a worldview?

Hunter (1961) and Mayer (1971) pay attention to the ideas and beliefs which developed among rural Blacks in the Kei River region during the nineteenth century, concerning their position in the wider South African social environment.

A "Red ideology", according to Mayer (*ibid. : 1*), was one of two responses to increased exposure by the indigenous people of the Transkei area to Western Christian civilisation with the expansionism of white colonialism. The other response was the development of a "school ideology". Mayer (*ibid*) observes that the cleavage between "Red" and "School" people took an unusually complex and enduring form. Monica Wilson (1961) supports this by saying, with regard to the so called *Abantu Babomvu* (Red People) and the *Abantu Basesikolweni* (School People), that "the cleavage has been deeper and more persistent among the Xhosa speaking than in any other community in Africa". By the 1870s there had developed two distinct rural "ideologies", namely, that of the *babomvu* and the *basesikolweni* (Davies, 1979 : 12). According to Mayer (1980 : 1), they were distinguishable up until the later 1970s, in what is today roughly the Transkei region.

The actual term *abantu babomvu* literally means those who smear themselves with red ochre; hence, the reference to red people. The community of Babomvu distanced themselves from those whom they called *Amaggoboka*, which means those who have made a hole in the fence (tradition) and allowed the Western corruptive.

The Abantu Babomvu may have used the derogatory label *Amaggoboka* but these people referred to themselves as *Abantu Basesikolweni* (The English term generally used is "school people"). The *Abantu Base-sikolweni*, in turn, referred to the *Abantu Babomvu* as "conservative", "pagan" and "backward".

School people were associated with missionary churches and schools and accepted many elements of Western culture which the Babomvu did not. Beinart and Bundy (Klein, 1980 : 312) draw attention to further differences between the *basesikolweni* and *Babomvu*, in family structure, patterns of investment and especially in patterns of consumption. These different responses to Western civilisation and whites have been described as the "equal cooperation versus exclusiveness" or "assimilation versus Black Consciousness" (Mayer, 1980). Mayer (*ibid.*) adds, however, that it is not that the adherents of the Babomvu ideology showed no signs of "acculturation", nor that school people abandoned the indigenous tradition altogether. Rather the latter positively associated themselves with Christianity and Western "civilisation", whereas, the Babomvu very cautiously accepted only such Western cultural elements as were unavoidable or obviously necessary in the wake of change beyond their control. It would, therefore, not be unfair to say the one was culturally accommodating and the other resistant.

Mayer (*ibid.* : 27) notes that broadly speaking the Transkei was the stronghold of the "Reds" (Babomvu) and the Ciskei of the School people.[3] Hammond-Tooke (1975 : 19) supports this by singling out the Babomvu people in Transkei region as people who "resisted change to a degree unprecedented in Africa".

In its prime, according to Mayer (1980 : 2) Babomvuism presented comprehensive patterns of belief, laying down precepts for most aspects of life including economic behaviour. The criteria used by Babomvu adherents for prestige-ranking involved the extent to which one resisted the white civilisation in its various forms. The Babomvu worldview dealt in ideas such as *ubuntu* (humanity) and *imbeko* (human dignity). The Babomvu way was to strive for human dignity by maintaining an identity in ways prescribed by the *iminyana* (forefathers or ancestors). One can, therefore, speak of Babomvuism as a worldview.

This worldview, which manifested itself in passive and active resistance strategies to white dependency structures, did not exist in a vacuum. It developed in a particular social milieu. I take a closer look at this now.

Some social factors which promoted the development of the Babomvu resistance worldview

The nineteenth century marked the beginning of considerable interest in the Cape Frontier as a mission field. Wesleyan missions, the Glasgow Missionary Society (which established Lovedale station and was later succeeded by the Bantu Presbyterian Church), the Moravians, the

---

[3] This is not to say that there were no Abantu Babomvu in the Ciskei/Eastern Cape area and no Abantu Basesikolweni in the Transkei.

Berlin Missionary Society (in 1836) and the Anglicans (in 1854) were some of the early pioneers. Yet, in the 1850s Calderwood (cited in Mayer 1980 : 8), a missionary in the Kei region lamented: "If we view the caffers as a nation they may be said to have refused the Gospel." Dr J.T. van der Kemp of the London Missionary Society settled among the people of chief Ngqika in 1799. He and his successor, Joseph Williams, met with little favourable response.[4]

There was a tendency among indigenous people to associate the mission endeavour with Western civilisation and with colonial power (Elphick 1981 : 294). Missionaries were in some cases government agents and were treated with much suspicion. It would be more accurate to say, however, that they were often used by both colonial authorities and Xhosa chiefs as political brokers. Faku, a prominent leader in Pondoland, is an example of one who encouraged missionaries to found stations but this was motivated by the political gains of having a mediator, the missionary.

Early missionary proselytism took place in a well-developed context of resistance. It was right in the middle of what Macmillan has called South Africa's Hundred Years' War (1799–1880). The history of the Xhosa-speaking people of the Cape Frontier during the first half of the nineteenth century is characterised by competition over land, the scarce resource, which contributed to conflict between the indigenous people and the colonial expansionists.

Furthermore, a rather well-developed politico-religious resistance tradition was established. The prophetic utterances of Nxele, Mlangeni and Nonqawuse, for example, formed the basis for mobilisation against the colonial invaders (see Peires, *Journal of African History* 20 (1979) : 51–62; *JAH* (1986) 27 : 443–61 and *JAH* 28 (1987) : 43–63; Hodgson in *RSA* 7/1, (1986) : 3–24).

Etherington (*Africa* 47 (1977) : 35) remarks on the effective and determined resistance to Christianity by the Nguni generally. In Pondoland (North Eastern Transkei) opposition to Christianity was a matter of "policy". "[C]onverts were effectively quarantined on mission stations and ceased for all practical purposes to be members of the nation" (*ibid.*).

Missionaries had to be satisfied, therefore, with making converts among what Etherington (cited in Elpich 1981 : 292) refers to as the

---

[4] Hodgson (*RSA*, 6/2, (1985) and *RSA*, 5/1, (1984)) links the indigenous prophets Nxele and Nsikana to Dr van der Kemp's missionary work.

"flotsam and jetsam" of the Cape Frontier. A considerable proportion of those living at the mission were refugees, outcasts or misfits in their communities, having found refuge in the mission station (Pauw 1975 : 21; Etherington 1978 : 74; and Elphick in Lamar and Thompson 1981 : 292). They became known as the *Basesikolweni*.

There were some black peasants, influenced by missions, who experimented with new crops and methods of production; and others, mainly Red communities, who stopped at adopting the plough and selling surplus, livestock etc. The former entered market production desiring equality in the colonial economy, the latter defended their position of minimum involvement, thus resisting even at an economic level.

This *abantu babomvu* position of resistance was, however, aided by their being economically self-sufficient. They had the ability to defend their autonomy during the early days of contact with the ideas and beliefs of the colonialist agents who sought to undermine their political and economic independence.[5] The ability of large numbers of Xhosa-speaking peasants to produce an agricultural surplus is evident in their paying taxes[6] and having sufficient over to satisfy consumer wants (Bundy, 1979/88 : 112). Even at the beginning of the gold-mining era (post-1886) a measure of economic independence was retained (*ibid.* : 113).

It would appear that the Babomvu worldview developed in a context of material independence and resistance to colonial encroachment. In effect the Babomvu community was comprehensively distancing itself from all manifestations of Western "civilisation" because it was able to do so in the mid-nineteenth century. By the early twentieth century, however, the political economy of the region had changed. One wonders what the consequences were for the worldview of the Babomvu community of the deterioration of the political and economic base of the Xhosa-speaking peasant society and their increased contact with Western "civilisation".

---

[5] The high points of black peasant production in Western and Southern Transkei were in the 1870s and 80s (Bundy, 1972) and in Pondoland in 1894 and 1910 (Beinart, 1973).

[6] The colonial government introduced a tax system which meant that the indigenous people had to find the means to pay for the taxes.

2. *Social change results in the adjustment of the Babomvu worldview*
(Observation II)

*Significant changes in the social environment and the socio-cultural experience
of the adherents*

Drought, crop failure and disease had, by the latter half of the nineteenth
century, undermined the independence of many rural communities
north east and south east of the Kei River. In the late 1890s, in
particular, the peasant economy of the Transkei was severely affected
by the sudden outbreak of the rinderpest epidemic.

> . . . the disease which destroyed 80% to 90% of the cattle in the Transkei
> and nearly as many in the Ciskei was an economic disaster: it liquidated
> much of the peasant's capital, adversely affected his credit-worthiness,
> made ploughing more difficult and transport facilities rarer and dearer.
> (Bundy 1979/88 : 120).

The immediate outcome was the impoverishment of thousands of
peasants and the forcing of many into labour migrancy.[7] The primary
intent was to earn wages in order to supplement the home economy.
Many took to labour with the short term and limited objective of
replacing their cattle. Mfenguland, Emigrant Tembuland, Gcalekaland
and northern Griqualand East were worst affected and produced very
high percentages of migrant workers (Bundy 1979/88 : 124). The
situation in Pondoland was, however, somewhat more complex, as
it has tended to be free from large-scale disease.

A closer look at how social change was introduced in this area
will reveal that other forces were at play.

Beinart (1979 : 54–62) traces the origins of labour migrancy from
Pondoland in some detail, from which it is clear that labour migrancy
came late to Pondoland. A number of factors gradually contributed
to the changing nature of the rural society in Pondoland in the early
decades of the 1900s, as its people became absorbed within the larger
capitalist economy, primarily as migrant labourers.

Numerous diseases, drought and the imposition of taxes in the late
nineteenth century had made some families indebted to traders. The

---

[7] A migrant labourer is here understood to be a person who is away from his/
her normal place of residence for two weeks or more in any one month; who contributes
to the household and who, despite his/her absence, is regarded as a member of
the family.

simultaneous arrival of labour recruiting agents in the region attracted some into migrant labour in order to reaccumulate cattle, pay debts and taxes. Nevertheless, the people of Pondoland experienced a considerably higher level of economic and social stability relative to people in the other geographical areas mentioned above.

There were signs of an increase in dependency on wage labour during the period 1910–1930. Yet, Beinart (1982 : 161) remarks that by the 1930s the economic position in Pondoland could still be favourably compared with that of many other parts of South Africa's reserves. He points out that migrancy rates were lower; the number of cattle per capita was above average; soil erosion was slight and landlessness rarer. But, in the broader politico-economic context, the people of Pondoland shared relative poverty with the other indigenous rural communities of South Africa and were subject to similar pressures.

Natural disasters did account for some pressure on the economy but more significantly, it would appear that a number of political economic moves by the colonial government served to undermine the rural people's economic independency. The Land Act of 1931 and the Native Land and Trust Act of 1936 are examples of legislation which was passed to curtail the development of cash crop farming by African peasantry. It seems that the colonial government was not unaware of the potential threat of a prosperous black agriculture to the interests of white farmers and industrialists (Bundy 1977 : 211). According to Mayer (1980) Tomlinson Rep. 1955 page 85 records state that in 1938 a scheme was introduced to subsidise ploughs, planters and cultivators for black farmers; "considerable use was made of it until it was discontinued in 1947". Cash crop production became gradually reduced to almost nothing in the Transkei and the Ciskei. The significance of this is appreciated when one takes into consideration that rural studies done in other Third World countries, with industrial centres, indicate the indirect proportionate relationship between cash crop production and migrant labour (Bundy, 1977).

The following table (Beinart, 1982 : 172) gives one an idea of the increase in labour migrancy.

TABLE

Patterns of migration from Transkei: 1896–1936
% of men absent

	Pondoland	East Griqua-land	Thembu-land	Transkei	Transkeian Territories
1896	2.5	11.4	16.5	21.9	13.4
1904	10.1	13.8	14.7	20.1	14.5
1911	9.6	14.7	16.1	23.4	16.5
1921	13.5	18.7	17.3	18.9	17.0
1936	17.1	24.7	24.4	25.7	22.8

The percentages given in each year are not always calculated on strictly comparable data. To calculate, very roughly, the percentage of "economically active" men (those between fifteen and forty five years of age) absent, figures should be multiplied two and a half times" (*ibid.*).

By the late 1930s a significant percentage of the economically active male population was engaged in labour migrancy.

Changes in the Babomvu worldview

One would think that the Babomvu worldview, which had developed in a strictly rural context and had resisted Western civilisation, would have disintegrated once its adherents experienced the urban Western context. This did not happen as such; for there is substantive evidence which indicates otherwise.

One needs to recognise that in a town with little or no income a migrant had no means to move beyond the confines of the mine compound, where his basic needs of accommodation and food were inadequately provided for. Little opportunity existed for the sampling of urban pleasures or urban tastes. Furthermore, for those coming from the Transkei, migrant labour was an *ad hoc* experience, the aim being to replace cattle lost due to some or other disaster.

If the 1960 census is anything to go by, one will soon see that the Babomvu continued to prevail among a significant percentage of rural people of the Kei region. In the Transkei, according to the same 1960 census, 48% of the indigenous people in the Transkei west of the Mzimvubu River and 77% of those east of it claimed no church affiliation.

One way to explore the effect of labour migrancy on the rural people from the Transkei is to refer once again to the *Babomvu/ Basesikolweni* differentiation.

Both the Abantu Babomvu and the Abantu Basesikolweni were drawn out of the rural socio-economic system into the broader colonial economy. They often worked in the same industries alongside one another, lived in the same mining compounds or shanty towns, travelled on the same buses to and from the city, lived on occasion as neighbours; and yet their response to industrial society, the denial of human rights and exploitation was quite different. Mayer (*ibid.*) notes that where the school way of life had disintegrated due to "the influence of urban secularism and consumerism, the popular ideologies of industrialism, the Red way of life is still surviving."[8] The Basesikolweni community had, of course, already adopted elements of Western "civilisation" and aspired to the life that the city represented. The Western experience was therefore not so much identity threatening as it was frustrating.[9] The Babomvu identity and worldview was, however, threatened by the migrant labour experience.

I will now elaborate on the manner in which migrant labour brought pressure to bear on the Babomvu community identity and worldview and the manner in which the worldview was adjusted to cope with this.

Ancestor religion and the worldview of the relatively close-knit, face to face communities revolved round the *umzi* or homestead. The *umzi* is the pivot of religious life and the continual establishing of the *umzi* in successive generations is of vital importance to religious continuity. The practice of ancestor religion revolved round the *umzi*. Sacred space within the confines of the *umzi* marked the presence of the ancestor shades. Furthermore,

> [t]here is no ancestor religious activity (ritual) unless it is initiated by a particular homestead head and unless the ritual takes place in his own homestead. The homestead head's authority in general, including

---

[8] Mayer is here referring to the 1970s.

[9] Their expectations of economic advancement and social equality with whites never materialised. Protest and resistance amongst school people took various forms, e.g. the breakaway Ethiopian-type churches were formed by school people out of frustration with the white hierarchy in the mainline churches; political organisations such as the ANC translated the political frustrations of school people into programmes of action.

his authority to call for an ancestral ritual, has been handed down to him from his agnatic forebears who are important (superhuman) objects of reference in the rituals themselves (Kuckurtz 1990 : 227).

The absence of the majority of the males for long periods, therefore, increased the danger of some not returning to establish the *umzi*, bringing extreme misfortune and chaos on the family of the offenders. Migrant labour thus threatened the religio-social order of this "small-scale" society.

What, then, prevented the disintegration of the religio-social order?

McAllister (Mayer 1980) has examined the ritual interpretation of labour migration among the Shixini of the Transkei. The Shixini[10] is a conservative traditionalist community and falls into the category *Abantu Babomvu*. It would appear that the modification of the Babomvu worldview took place to include the reality of the majority of males being absent for long periods of time.

McAllister (*ibid.*) has shown that the *umzi*, in its appearance, technology and human relations, has remained extremely conservative, and the men's participation in the capitalist secular economy has been skilfully interpreted to fit into this framework.

The adherents of the Babomvu worldview succeeded in weaving into a single coherent system of ideas two distinctly different sets of imperatives. The traditional indigenous religious practice of building up the *umzi*[11] (referred to as *ukwakha umzi*) and reproducing the homestead relations of production remained a dominant feature. The males (homestead heads and their sons) had to endure the hardships of migrant labour for the sake of the homestead. The city experience was symbolically interpreted as military service—"a rite of passage" which a young man had to undergo in order to marry, to build up the *umzi*, maintain his family and accumulate cattle. The ancestral shades' perceived interest in their descendants' migratory activities and good fortune whilst in the city was tied to the migrant labourer's obtaining cash to return and build the *umzi*. Complex "rites of

---

[10] I am unable to confirm whether they can still be regarded as Abantu Babomvu.

[11] The establishment of the *umzi* meant the reproduction of homestead social relations, e.g. the relations between parents and children, the confirming of the role of the elder menfolk (men who had retired to their homes in their early fifties). This involved ritual practices on which, for example, the sons' immediate and future welfare depended. It also meant guarding the young men's interest in land and cattle and the protection of the dignity of the women folk.

departure" and purification rites on returning are part and parcel of the ritualisation of migrant labour among the Babomvu.

McAllister (Mayer 1980 : 205ff) offers a detailed description of the various rites. Of importance is the association of the work place and the city with going to war. The rites of departure ensure safety of a man whilst away and the rites of return are standardised rites and symbolic action in order to give thanks for his safe return; through which his good standing in the community and with the ancestors is assured (*ibid.*).

One sees, thus, that the experience of the city was incorporated and subjected to the paramountcy of the *umzi*. The Babomvu labourer's working life outside the community was not meaningful nor fully "real", apart from it being a means to an end, namely, the *umzi*.

A number of examples will further demonstrate the continuity in attitude and behaviour between the rural and urban situation.

Mayer (1971 : 23f) notes that in the city the "Red People" dressed differently and kept apart from school and town people as much as possible. Care was taken in spending money on *impahla yamlungu* (things of the white people). Only that which was absolutely necessary and which benefited the *umzi* (homestead) was purchased, i.e. a form of consumer asceticism was practised. At home the Babomvu adherent's children were warned not to play with school children because they would speak of "white people's things" and it was feared that Red adolescents may become *amatshipha* (absconders) if they entertained the thought of city things too often (*ibid.*). Red people referred to the white people, not only as bearers of "new ways", but also the destroyers of Xhosa political independence and "they have continued to keep the African down". Hence, school people were viewed as "collaborators" and "sell-outs" and the Babomvu saw themselves as national resisters (*ibid.* : 31).

It would seem from the above that the Babomvu community was able to engineer religio-cultural manipulation and sustain what Mafeje (1975 : 178) refers to as "militant conservatism", so that "they saved themselves from self-alienation" (*ibid.*). The question is whether they could sustain this position in the longer term as the scaled social change increased.

3. *The disintegration of the Babomvu worldview* (Observation III)

Some Statistics

Mayer (1980 : 48f) points out that by the late 1970s the "red folk-culture" in the Ciskei and Transkei was disintegrating under the 'influences of urban secularism and consumerism, the popular ideologies of industrialism." Pauw (1975 : 49) supports this trend. Statistical evidence, further, confirms this as well as indicating the rate of change.

In 1960, according to Pauw (1975 : 37) 41,8% (48% according to Mayer 1980) of the rural Xhosa population in the Transkei could be classified as non-christian.[12] The 1970 census indicates just over 33%, using a similar classificatory code. Kritzinger (Oosthuizen 1986 : 253) notes that the non-christian composition of the black population in the Transkei in 1980 was 25%.

Two questions arise from these statistics:

1. What factors undermined the Babomvu worldview? Here I suggest one explore the social factors that promoted it and see whether there has been any change at this level in the course of time.
2. My concern with worldview analysis prompts the question: What does the renegotiated worldview of people who are no longer adherents of Babomvuism look like? What worldview options are they attracted to?

The latter question I will deal with later (see section 4, below). I now turn to the former.

The assumption, at this stage, is that there is a correlation between a high level of social change and the disintegration of the Babomvu worldview, as the BWV no longer adequately fitted the socio-cultural experience of the community. It therefore follows that I need to ascertain whether large-scale socio-cultural disturbance was experienced by the community not long before the disintegration of the BWV.

---

[12] Pauw (1975 : 37), when referring to the people of the Transkei, includes in non-christian the categories: "other" "object and no religion" and "unspecified". In the case of the Xhosa-speaking people in the Transkei I think it would be reasonable to suggest that non-christian people means Abantu babomvu, assuming that Xhosa-speaking people are deeply religious people. The same applies to Kritzinger's category "non-christian".

Significant social change in rural Transkei

There is evidence which indicates that the rural social experience which had promoted and confirmed the resistance folk-culture was significantly disturbed. The Babomvu worldview which did not articulate clear distinctions between body and mind, subject and object, fact and value, was gradually undermined by the Western epistemology which turned this socio-religious order on its head.

Due to topographical and socio-political factors, areas of the Transkei which were strongholds of Babomvu tradition were less accessible and therefore remained outside the sphere of regular and easy communication. This may have been the case up until the 1970s; however, by the 1980s it was no longer the case.

Remote rural areas were gradually exposed to urban modes of thought as systems of communication were developed. Roads and buses connected remote areas with towns and cities. Consumer commodities became more readily available, while the transistor radio brought the urban culture into the *umzi*, the centre of the Babomvu worldview. Young people in Babomvu families had begun to attend school in significantly increasing numbers as the mission schools were taken over by the local Department of Education. Scholars thus became familiar with Western concepts and social categories at school via subjects such as mathematics, geography, general science, English language, hygiene; and more subtly at the level of everyday meaning found in the new order of time and space and school etiquette. The elders began to lament the fact that they thought they were doing their best for their children by sending them to school, only to have them neglect their customary duties.

The involuntary social restructuring of the political and economic life of indigenous Xhosa speaking people of the Transkei particularly threatened the Babomvu community and their worldview. The creation of bantustan authorities (the *Bunga* or central general council) in the Transkei and the Ciskei served to undermine the agnatic political authority in a limited way, since many Babomvu communities were geographically too far removed to feel the full force of it, initially.[13]

---

[13] The Bantustanisation of areas such as the Transkei began to reorganise rural social structure. New divisions had become apparent. In particular the authoritative position of bantustan civil servants: teachers, stock inspectors, magistrates, police, district commissioners etc., undermined indigenous distinctions and social hierarchy between agnation and matrilaterality, seniority and juniority, male and female. Changes in the relations of production affected domestic relations and kin ties.

However, the *Bunga* undermined the Babomvu community social structure in another way, by pressurising rural headmen to adopt what were referred to as "Betterment Schemes".

As early as 1936, certain rural areas ("Native Reserves", later called "Bantustans", then "Homelands") proclaimed under the Native Trust and Land Acts "Betterment Areas". These areas were to be rehabilitated and made economically viable by being divided into residential areas, arable lands and grazing commonage and by implementing the "necessary conservationist measures" (De Wet, *JSAS*, 15/2 (1989): 327–328). This meant, potentially, at least, that almost all rural black families would have to move from their old, scattered residential clusters to newly demarcated residential areas. South African Government planners viewed this as optimal usage of land. The recommendations of the Tomlinson Commission indicate that the radical restructuring of the rural environment was essential for the Betterment Scheme to be successfully implemented (*ibid.*).

In the 1950s and 1960s, attempts to implement Betterment Schemes in the Transkei met with considerable resistance (see Beinart and Bundy in Klein, 1980). People of in these rural areas came to associate the schemes with loss of livestock,[14] restrictions on grazing, and reductions in the availability of arable land (McAllister, *JSAS* 15/2 (1989) : 346). Stock limitation ignored the social and religious importance of cattle.[15] Furthermore, communities that experienced the move from one kind of residential pattern to another caused considerable social disruption and loss of political control.

McAllister (*ibid.*) also argues that the view that irrigation schemes implemented in relocated areas necessarily benefitted the community is erroneous. Scattered homesteads, he notes, were historically shaped partly by the nature of the water resources. Betterment put pressure on single water points close to the settlement due to the waterpoint-people ratio being low. In the case of mechanical fault or the water becoming unsuitable for human consumption, the residents of the relocated settlement had to walk great distances to obtain water.

Betterment seemed to mean a change in the settlement pattern, an assault on the established political and territorial unit, the disappearance of old neighbourhood groups and youth structures, and the

---

[14] Culling was the method used to reduce the number of livestock per household.
[15] Cattle are considered more than capital, their added value is derived from their being an integral part of ancestor service.

undermining of the established strategies of subsistence.

McAllister (*ibid.* : 368) is convinced that Betterment Schemes in the Transkei and the Ciskei played a major part in finally destroying the "red folk-culture" as a coherent way of life. Only a few areas such as Shixini, near Willowvale, provide evidence that "rehabilitation" has been fended off and *ubuqaba* (the red way) has lingered on (*ibid.*).

A combination of extended periods in the towns and cities (experienced by some 80% of all males over the age of 16 who were engaged in migrant labour in the 1980s (McAllister, *JSAS* 15/2 (1989) : 350) and the urban influences in the rural areas seemed to exert considerable pressure on the Babomvu worldview. The tradition was unable to fit the social reality. Cultural separatism and economic asceticism became increasingly something of the past as, particularly, the young people were attracted to the urban Western culture.

The disintegration of the Babomvu worldview prompts one to ask the following questions: Did the community disintegrate as well? Has there been a rejection of what the Babomvu worldview represented and an assimilation of Western culture and religion?

In response to both these questions, it would appear that this has not been the case. I now consider the evidence.

4. *The Babomvu community's attraction to Zionist-Apostolic type churches* (Observation IV)

The Growth of Zionism in the Transkei

Sundkler (Pauw 1975 : 32) speaks of an upsurge of interest in the African Independent Churches which took place largely in the northern provinces in 1917–27. This was the rise of the Zionist type churches[16] according to Sundkler (1961 : 49). The impact of this took much longer to be felt in the Xhosa-speaking area of the Cape (Pauw 1975 : 32). Rev. A.P. Phipson (*ibid.*) remarked in the 1960s that Zionism was a recent phenomenon in the Transkei. A few Zionist Churches existed in the Transkei from about the 1930s, but Zionism as a movement only became conspicuous in the 1950s (*ibid.*; Pretorius : 1985; Kruss : 1985). Mayer (1980 : 32) points out that Zionist and Ethiopian type

---

[16] The Zionist-Apostolic type African Independent Churches are not to be confused with the Ethiopian-type African Independent Churches. Zionist-Apostolic type churches have been referred to as the African appropriation and indigenisation of Christian symbols. Ethiopian-type churches have succeeded from mission churches primarily

AICs were powerful forces in black christianity in Natal and in the Transvaal in the 1950s but only slight headway had been made in the Ciskei and the Transkei. A steady growth, however, is noted over the period 1960–1980, according to Pretorius (Oosthuizen 1985 : 156). In the 1980s, 2–5% of the population in the Ciskei and 10–15% in the Transkei belonged to the indigenous churches. There are at least 160 distinctive Zionist-Apostolic churches which form 71% of the AICs in the Transkei (*ibid.*).

The relationship between Zionist and Babomvu worldviews in the Transkei

It is noted by Pauw (1975 : 303) that Zionist members are drawn predominantly from among people of low social status, in terms of traditional as well as modern values. Pauw (*ibid.* : 49), furthermore, remarks that a substantial proportion of those joining the African Independent churches were Red people. Mayer (1980 : 32) supports this observation by stating that school people in the Transkei/Ciskei region viewed the emotionalism of Zionist Churches as possibly good enough for Red converts but not fit for school people. Church and school people were critical of the Zionists because of what they perceived to be their deviant beliefs and behaviour (Pauw 1975 : 303). Pretorius (1985 : 8) suggests that "fairly direct connections can be found between the last-ditch defences of traditional society and the appearance of tendencies toward Zionism". Unfortunately he fails to expand on this.

A number of observations have been made so far. It is appropriate to summarise these before progressing to an explanatory frame.

5. *A summary of the observations*

i)   The Babomvu resistance worldview developed during the nineteenth century in a particular social context of material independence and resistance to colonial encroachment.

ii) In the course of time, political and economic independence was undermined and labour migrancy became an everyday reality which brought about significant identity—threatening socio-cultural change. The Babomvu worldview prevailed but in a

---

on grounds of racial discrimination and oppression; they are thought to be nationalistic but otherwise very similar to the mission church pattern of worship and doctrine.

form that took into account the changes in the socio-cultural
environment.

iii) The scale of socio-cultural change continued to increase. By the
1980s the Babomvu worldview is reported to have disintegrated,
with many adherents finding a new ideological (worldview) home
in a Zionist-Apostolic type worldview.

The observations made indicate changes in the Babomvu worldview
and the adherents' attraction to the Zionist-Apostolic type worldview.
It begs some explanation. I will, therefore, offer an explanatory
mechanism which will contribute to a theoretical understanding.

The rise, adjustment and decline of the Babomvu worldview (BWV)
and the attraction of a Zionist-Apostolic type worldview can be
interpreted as the renegotiation of identity, triggered by changes in
the socio-cultural experience of its adherents. The changes were
brought about primarily by the increasing presence of Western values
and symbols in indigenous socio-cultural experience.

Reference is made to identity, worldviews and socio-cultural experience, suggesting that they are linked. But just how are they linked?

Drawing on Cumpsty's development of H.C. Rumke's model in
"The formation and expression of the individual's felt sense of reality",
I will now look at the relationship between identity, worldview and
socio-cultural experience.

The relationship between identity, worldview and socio-cultural experience

Identity is a difficult term to define. For my purposes, however, it
can be seen to be an individual's concern with the question: "Who
am I?" The answer to this question is both personal and social. Psycho-
social identity is at once a do-it-yourself enterprise and a social activity
which involves a quest for a sense of belonging.

> Identity depends on relationships. Even if it is by over-against-ness rather
> than by identification, I will require the other in order to know who
> I am. Even if I do not affirm the other, I must affirm the cosmos of
> which the other is part and seek to belong to that, if I am to develop
> an identity. Thus, the drive to establish an identity[17] is necessarily a
> drive to belong (Cumpsty : 165).

---

[17] Cumpsty (161) observes that "Human beings appear to have two basic drives.
The one is for physical survival, not just the fight against death, but including also
the quest for space and material resources necessary for realization of physical potential.
The other is for the development of identity."

Furthermore an identity depends on how an individual's participation in his/her environment has shaped it. The detail and content of identity is generated in relation to socio-cultural experience. By socio-cultural experience we mean the sum total of each individual's every experience of his/her world-out-there. This may be unique to each individual but it is very much manipulated by culture and social structure, of which he/she is a product and in part a creator.

Cumpsty (164) expresses it thus: "The awareness of individuality, of having become an ego over and against all that is non-ego, the awareness 'that I am', leads inevitably to the quest to know 'what I am' and hence to a dependence upon the world-out-there. Self-knowledge is not possible in a vacuum. Rather, it is the obverse of the question 'What is all that out there?' An individual's sense of who he/she is, therefore, shaped by his/her participation in the world-out-there. Self-image can be said to depend on how an individual perceives his/her participation in the world-out-there. It is this conscious aspect of identity which will receive more attention.

I now unpack the notion that experience of the world-out-there (WOT), in the longer term, shapes an individual's sense of WOT and therefore his/her identity. I wish to point out that the relation between elements is referred to in very cognitive terms, without denying the more affective dimension (which is not clearly distinguishable from the cognitive), primarily because the cognitive is more accessible for investigation. I therefore speak of the more cognitive level of identity, namely self-image.

What is meant by the individual's "experience of WOT" or more specifically his/her socio-cultural experience?

This involves, at the more cognitive level, a selection from the evaluation of all that confronts an individual within a particular socio-cultural context. This selection takes the form of recognising this rather than that. The evaluation thereof takes the form of attaching values to the selected raw experience. The recognition of that which confronts one in a particular context and the response to that which is recognised is culturally conditioned.

In the long run, this experience of WOT in turn alters, adds to or confirms a person's self-conception. The felt sense of who one is may be shaped by one's participation in WOT but a pool of possible symbols gives it conceptual meaning. Thus, any attempt to explain self in relation to the world draws on a pool of possible symbols. A primary source of symbols in this pool is the individual's "established" symbolised sense of WOT and any worldview (tradition) shared with others.

At a corporate level, a (tradition) community identity is conceptualised by drawing on a shared set of symbols which gives meaning to the experience of WOT (i.e. worldview).

Cumpsty's (227f) work on "Religion and Change" provides some explanatory insights which are applicable here. He argues that there is a two-way relationship between socio-cultural experience and religious tradition or what I prefer to call worldview.

The way people make sense of their life-world and all the symbols that invest meaning in this process, can and will change in order to ensure a unified worldview and a continued sense of identity. Human beings' feelings for and understanding of their life-world are in the long run distilled and verified in their socio-cultural experience (*ibid.*).

An individual's conceptualised sense of self is derived predominantly from either the socio-cultural experience or the tradition or from some combination of the two. Therefore, there needs to be a fit in the long-run between self-conceptualisation and socio-cultural experience or, in the short term, between self-understanding and the tradition, if alienated or false consciousness is to be avoided.

In a situation where people experience identity-threatening changes in their socio-cultural environment, as described in this paper, one can expect in the longer run a change in worldview, to restore or maintain a sense of belonging and integrated identity.[18]

The strategies adopted by the Babomvu community were subject to two factors, namely, the gradual pace of change and resistance to Western civilisation in defence of unified indigenous identity.[19]

I now re-trace the stages of renegotiation of identity in this community and offer an explanation drawing on this theoretical understanding.

Moving towards a theoretical understanding

In one sense, the rise of the Babomvu worldview was a response to contact, although limited initially, with colonial authorities, mission-

---

[18] In the long run there will always be moves to maintain a unified sense of the WOT and identity (Cumpsty 248).

[19] Resistance can function in two ways. 1. It is resistance to that which is perceived to be unacceptable and undesirable, and possibly even threatening. It is outward looking. 2. Resistance can also be inward looking. It is resistance for the protection of something; it is a defence mechanism.

aries and traders, and to their promotion of Western civilisation. Missionaries introduced a new set of values from another social context and promoted it as a substitute for the indigenous values, with little success. They did, however, disturb the socio-cultural context in a way that they were probably not aware of.

It challenged, possibly threatened, the presumed worldview by providing an alternative that undermined the traditional perceptions. This triggered the conscious articulation of the contemporary indigenous frame of reference amongst those that found this encroachment of "Western civilisation" unacceptable and undesirable.

It was not only the unacceptability of Western civilisation that gave rise to the Babomvu resistance worldview. A number of other factors contributed to the BWV being established.

One notices that the intruding cultural elements were introduced gradually, i.e. the pace of change was slow. The agents and institutions of Western civilisation, although present in the adherents' socio-cultural experience, were distant and infrequent. They were, thus, culturally marginal in a homestead-centred life-world.

A consequence, to some extent, of the low profile, or lack of a presence in terms of space and time, of the physical manifestations of Western civilisation[20] was the ability to engineer cultural isolation, thus neutralising the alien threat and potential socio-cultural disturbance, and confirming the religio-cultural order which was previously taken for granted.

Once political and economic independence was undermined and labour migrancy engaged in on an increasing scale, the Babomvu were exposed to an industrial environment and frame of reference.

The indigenous cultural categories shaped everyday experience in a manner that was very different from that of Western cultural categories. The Babomvu worldview did not make sharp distinctions between body and mind, subject and object, knowledge and experience, fact and value, as in Western epistemology. Western "civilisation" (in its contemporary form of industrial capitalism) makes a number of dichotomies which contradict the Babomvu cultural categories, e.g. the radical distinction between self and other, person and context, mind and body, religion and healing; a Western notion of the world that is founded upon material and not social relations; and the situation

---

[20] Physical manifestations of Western civilisation are, for example, the trading store, white farmers, hunters, merchants, missions, colonial officials.

of the person as depending upon his/her own initiative rather than a location in a total social environment.

The relative isolation of the villages, the *ad hoc* nature of the urban experience (later it was formalised in South African labour policies and influx control legislation, which meant a continuous back-and-forth shuttle between the rural and urban areas), its undesirability and other less obvious factors led to a dual social experience. The material base and socio-cultural experience in the rural village confirmed the BWV (the only institutions of Western civilisation were the scattered trading stores with their consumer commodities and the few mission stations) whilst the industrial workplace subjected the adherents to the values and institutions of Western civilisation.

The renegotiation of the Babomvu worldview in the interpretation and appropriation of the undesirable yet essential labour migrant experience, in terms of the dominant frame of reference—the homestead—enabled the BWV to maintain a sense of "ubuntu" in what otherwise was a most disturbing socio-cultural experience.

Cumpsty (*ibid.*), regarding the effect of significant changes in the socio-cultural experience on the religious tradition notes: "As one moves up the spectrum toward unacceptability, there will be moves to modify the unacceptable and then to integrate that which cannot be modified. That is, there will be moves to modify the disintegrative effects."

The process of religio-cultural, symbolic engineering, to incorporate a socially necessary, but total unacceptable, experience into a community's worldview, so as to neutralise the threat to the community identity, is referred to as containment strategy. In the case of low levels of disturbance (the pace of change is gradual), the traditional symbolic and ritual sub-sets encapsulate the intruding elements of the "incoming" culture. Containment is an appropriate strategy if the amount of foreign symbolic material admitted to the system is small. It would not, however, be appropriate if the amount of foreign material were more substantial. Other options would have to be explored.

In the course of time, Western modelled schools, social restructuring by government planners, and the radio subtly integrated Western industrial ideas and values into common-sense meanings and routine activities diffused in everyday life in the rural village. Thus was undermined the point of reference at the centre of the BWV—the traditional homestead orientation—or what Kuckurtz (*African Studies* 42/2 (1983) & 43/1 (1984)) refers to as the homestead-centred world. Once the latter worldview categories dominated the Babomvu villager's socio-cultural experience, the former could not be renegotiated in terms which made sense of Western industrial experience, without losing its characteristic form. The BWV was no longer able to contain the increasing elements of the Western culture and still retain a distinctly Babomvu frame of reference, for the two are mutually contradictory, as are the social and economic orders of which each is a reflection, in part.

At the level of individual consciousness and worldview, the co-existence of these two mutually contradictory socio-cultural orders presented a number of possible options. One was to reject the BWV entirely and to seek an identity in Western cultural terms. A second was to assert the primacy of Western techniques and concepts whilst rejecting Western Christian civilisation—an historical materialist perspective. The third option was to renegotiate the worldview in a way that addressed the concerns of the community whilst bridging, via symbolic and ritual forms, the discontinuity between the two socio-cultural experiences and their modelling of reality. I must hasten to add that I am of the opinion that none of the options resolves the contradictions presented in the modern predicament. A shift to a worldview that provided bridging symbols seems to have been the most popular.

In situations where traditions of different paradigmatic types co-exist, the development of "bridging myths" or the embracing of "bridging symbols" is a possible means of integration. The purpose of the bridging or mediating symbol[21] is to hold together, as well as can be, the irreconcilable elements. In the long term, where two sets of symbolised sense of WOT exist alongside, there may even be a move to a bridging worldview.

The renegotiation of this community's worldview, so as to adequately fit into a frame of reference, the socio-cultural experience, whilst not compromising on core issues of concern such as the emphasis on "ubuntu", was facilitated by the availability of a Zionist-Apostolic worldview which adequately took over where the BWV left off. It

---

[21] I am not sure whether the concept of a bridge is apt as it gives the impression that people move from one side to another, leaving behind one cultural system for another. This may happen at the basic non-negotiable paradigmatic level (see Cumpsty : 31f) but people carry a great deal of cultural baggage in the moving process. This is somehow lost in the bridging concept. I am thus looking for a concept that will capture the idea of a renegotiation of worldview with elements of both cultural systems. Mediation and transformation come to mind.

can be seen as a change in resistance strategy to neutralise the destructive elements in Western civilisation.[22]

The Zionist-Apostolic worldview provided a new frame of reference and religio-cultural set of symbols, which empowered its adherents to manipulate a dehumanising socio-cultural experience in a way that defended their humanity. It mediated between the discontinuities people experience, for example, between communalism and its notion of self, and a liberal capital culture that undermines this with the emphasis on individualism.[23]

A Concluding Note

The paper goes some way in addressing the question how people in a dynamic rural context, having different experiences from those in an urban township, particularly on ideological and cultural levels, have their consciousness shaped and the form of their worldview determined.

Zionism, or the Zionist-Apostolic type worldview, in the Transkei is interpreted as the most recent strategy of a specific community for negotiating identity in a particular social context. This thesis is supported by my tracing the history of the community in terms of significant (identity-threatening) changes in socio-cultural conditions and corresponding changes in the community's worldview from the late nineteenth century to the 1980s.

A number of central components are found in this paper. These can be summarised as follows:

---

[22] Glenda Kruss (1985) and Jean Comaroff (1985) argue that any serious attempt to understand the Zionist-Apostolic churches needs to interpret, in part at least, their worldview as a resistance strategy. Kruss (1985 : 124) points out that the increased forced dependency, politically and socially speaking, led to an increased level of resistance, but also a search for new and appropriate forms of resistance among farm workers, labour-tenants, reserve peasants and peasant migrants. Zionist-Apostolic churches did not arise as a significant movement in the earlier period when reserves were still available for subsistence production, because they were not a fitting religio-cultural form for struggling rural peasants retaining some access to agricultural production and continuing to draw on traditional African cultural ideological forms (*ibid*.: 201). The implication is that, once these manifestations of resistance were undermined, Zionist-Apostolic churches became a fitting religio-cultural form for these struggling, rural village people. The Zionist-Apostolic churches' creative role is seen by Kruss as a means of survival—a form of religio-cultural resistance, not dissimilar to the "traditionalists" or what I have referred to as the Babomvu community. Her analysis is that the Zionist-Apostolic churches are a latent form of resistance and struggle of a subordinated community at a cultural and ideological level.

[23] How it does this will need to be the subject of further research in the field.

i)   One notices that the Babomvu worldview was the dominant
     worldview of the community from the days of the ox-wagon to
     the pocket calculator and that by the 1980s it had largely
     disintegrated. At about the same time, Zionism became popular
     amongst people from the same community (previously adherents
     of Babomvuism). The possibility that the decline of Babomvu-
     ism and the rise of Zionism at about the same time is more
     than a coincidence is considered and explained in terms of the
     renegotiation of worldview and identity thesis.

ii) This thesis is further supported by evidence that the Babomvu
     worldview was manipulated (renegotiated) to take into account
     identity-threatening changes in the social environment experi-
     enced by the community. This suggests that as the community
     experienced greater socio-cultural change their worldview was
     renegotiated to the point where it was no longer recognisable
     as the Babomvu worldview.

iii) The community was attracted to the Zionist-Apostolic worldview,
     which was on hand, as it was an apt strategy to ensure the
     mobilisation and appropriation of symbols for the maintenance
     of an integrated identity.

iv) One other factor adds to the feasibility of this theory. This is
     the view that both Babomvuism and Zionism in the Transkei
     can be considered defence strategies against the domination of
     Western civilisation in its various forms.

This paper forms the basis of research that is in progress. It is
appropriate, therefore, to identify some possible areas for further
research.

Hodgson (*RSA* 6/2, 7/1) has detailed the manner in which the
Nxele appropriated symbolic sources of power from Western Christianity whilst retaining a strong element of resistance to Western
"civilisation". Is there other evidence which suggests a similar strategy
amongst people who did not regard themselves as *abantu basesikolweni?*
This is of interest for comparison.

McAllister describes the "ritualization of migrant labour" at a stage
when it was taking place on a grand scale in the Babomvu community.
How did the adherents of the BWV regard those who initially engaged
in migrant labour? Were they viewed as deviants? The relevance of
this lies in tracing the phaseal process of cultural transformation.

Are there signs that the loose theoretical notion of a Zionist-Apostolic type worldview is taking a more specific form, say, as the Zionist-Apostolic type church leaders collectively develop a more systematized theological frame and establish institutions for pastoral training?

What evidence is there of the manner in which the Zionist-Apostolic worldview in rural Transkei mediates between the contradictions present in the community's socio-cultural experience? What bridging symbols are prominent in the Zionist-Apostolic type worldview, shared by Zionist Church congregations in rural Transkei?

BIBLIOGRAPHY

Beinart, W., *The Political Economy of Pondoland 1860–1930* (Johannesburg: Ravan Press 1982).

Beinart, W. & Bundy, C., *Hidden Struggles in Rural South Africa* (Johannesburg: Ravan Press, 1987).

Beinart, W. & Delius, P., *Putting a plough to the ground* (Johannesburg: Ravan Press, 1978).

Berger, P., *The Sacred Canopy* (New York: Doubleday, 1969).

Berger, P., *Pyramids of Sacrife* (Harmondsworth: Penguin, 1977).

Berger, P. & Luckmann, I., *The social construction of reality* (Harmondsworth: Penguin, 1969)

Boggs, C., *Gramsci's Marxism* (London: Pluto Press, 1976).

Bundy, C., *The Rise and Fall of the South African Peasantry*, (London: Heinemann, 1979).

Chidester, D., *Patterns of Power* (Belmont: Wadsworth, 1987).

Comaroff, J., "Healing and Cultural Transformation: The Twsana of Southern Africa", *Social Science and Medicine* 15B (1981) pp. 284–314.

Comaroff, J., *Body of Power, Spirit of Resistance: The Culture and History of a South African People* (Chicago: University of Chicago Press, 1985).

Comaroff, J. & J., "Christianity and Colonialism in South Africa", *American Ethnologist* 13 (1985) pp. 1–22.

Cragg, D.G.L., "The Role of the Wesleyan Missionaries in Relations between the Mpondo and the Colonial Authorities". In: Saunders, C. & Delicourt, R.: *Beyond the Cape Frontier, Studies in the History of the Transkei and the Ciskei* (London: Longman, 1968) pp. 145–62.

Cumpsty, J.S., *A general theory of religion* (Lanham: University Press of America) 1991.

De Wet, C., *In Journal of Southern African Studies* 15/2 (1989) pp. 327f.

Elphick, R., "Africans and Christian Campaign in Southern Africa". In: Howard Lamar and Leonard Thompson (eds.), *The Frontier in History: North America and Southern Africa Compared*, (New Haven: Yale University Press) pp. 270–307.

Etherington, N., *Preachers, Peasants and politics in Southeast Africa* (London: Royal Historical Society, 1978).

Etherington, N., "The Historical Sociology of Independent Churches in South East Africa". *Journal of Religion in Africa* 10/2 (19??) pp. 108–26.

Hodgson, J., "The Faith Healer of Cancele: Some problems in analysing religious experience among black people", *Religion in Africa* 4/1 (1983) pp. 13–30.

Hodgson, J., "Ntsikana—A Precursor of Independency?" *Missionalia* ii/3 (1983) pp. 19–33.

Hodgson, J., "The Symbolic Entry Point: Removing the Veil of Structure from the Study of religious Movements". In: Oosthuizen (ed.), *Religion Alive* (Johannesburg: Hodder & Stoughton, 1986) pp. 48–67.

Hodgson, J. & Kokoali, C., "Mutual Aid Societies, Another Kind of Independency and the Church". In: Oosthuizen (ed.), *Religion Alive*, see above, pp. 138–150.

Hodgson, J., "A study of the Xhosa Prophet Nxele", Part I: *Religion in Southern Africa* 6/2 (1985) Part II: *Religion in Southern Africa*, 7(f) (1986) pp. 3–24.

Hunter, M., *Reaction to Conquest: effects of contact with Europeans on the Pondo of South Africa* (Oxford: Oxford University Press for the International African Institute, 1961).

Institute for Contextual Theology, *Speaking for Ourselves* (Braamfontein: ICT, 1985).

Kiernan, J.P., "The management of complex religious identity, The case of Zulu Zionism." *Religion in Southern Africa* 7/2 (1986).

Kiernan, J.P., "Where Zionists Draw the Line: A Study of Religious Exclusiveness in an African Township", *African Studies* 33/2 (1974) pp. 79–90.

Kiernan, J.P., "Poor and Puritan: An Attempt to view Zionist as a Collective Responses to Urban Poverty", *African Studies* 36/1 (1977) pp. 31–41.

Kiernan, J.P., "The Weapons of Zion", *Journal of Religion in Africa* 10/1 (1979) pp. 13.

Kretzschmar, L., "Christian Faith and African Culture", Paper presented at the Religious Studies Forum, UNITRA, Umtata, Unpublished, 1988.

Kruss, G., "Religion, Class and Culture—Indigenous Churches in South Africa, with special reference to Zionist-Apostolics", Unpublished Thesis, 1985.

Kuckurtz, L., "Symbol and authority in Mpondo ancestor religion", *African Studies* 42/2 pp. 113–33; and 43/1 pp. 1–17.

Leatt, J., "Astride Two Worlds: Religion and values among Black Migrant Mineworkers on South African Gold mines", *Journal of Theology for Southern Africa* 38/ (1982) pp. 59–82.

Mayer, P., *Black Villagers in an Industrial Society* (Cape Town: Oxford University Press, 1980).

Mayer, P., *Townsmen or Tribesmen* (Cape Town: Oxford University Press, 1971).

McAllister, P.A., "Work, Homestead, and the Shades: The Ritual Interpretations of Labour Migration among the Gcaleka". In: Mayer, P., see above.

McAllister, P.A., "Resistance to 'betterment' in the Transkei", *Journal of Southern African Studies* 15/2 (January 1989) pp. 346f.

Mafeje, A., "Religion, Class and Ideology in South Africa", in: Whisson and West: *Religion and Social Change in Southern Africa* (Cape Town: David Philip, 1975).

Mosala, I., "African Independent Churches: A Study in Socio-Theological Protest". In: Villa-Vicencio & De Gruchy (eds.), *Resistance and Hope* (Cape Town: David Philip, 1985) pp. 103–11.

Oosthuizen, G.C., (ed.), *Religion Alive* (Johannesburg: Hodder & Stoughton, 1986).

Odendaal, A., "African Political Mobilisation in Eastern Cape, 1880–1910", Unpublished Ph.D. Thesis, Cambridge University, 1983.

Pato, L. (ed.), "Towards an Authentic African Christianity", Paper presented at the Religious Studies Forum, UNITRA, Umtata, Unpublished, 1989.

Pauw, B.A., *The Second Generation* (Cape Town: Oxford University Press, 1973).

Pauw, B.A., *Christianity and the Xhosa Tradition* (Cape Town: Oxford University Press, 1975.)

Peires, J.B., "Nxele, Ntsikana and the Origins of the Xhosa Religious Reaction", *Journal of African History* 20/1 (1971) pp. 51–62.

Pretorius, H., "Historical trends in Transkeian Zionism", *Missionalia*, 12/1 (1984).

Pretorius, H., *Sound the trumpet of Zion: Aspects of a movement in Transkei* (Pretoria: Iswen, 1985).

Saunders, C., "Tile and the Tembu Church: Politics and independency on the Cape Frontier in the later 19th century", *Journal of African History* XI/4 (1970) pp. 553–570.

Sundkler, B.G.M., "The concepts of Christianity in African Independent Churches", *African Studies* 20/4 (1961) pp. 203–213.

Whisson, M. & West, M., *Religion and Social Change in Southern Africa* (Cape Town: David Philip, 1975).

Wolpe, H., "Theory of Internal Colonialism the South Africa Case". In: Oxaal, I., Barrett, J. & Booth, D. (eds.), *Beyond the sociology of development* (London: Routledge & Keegan Paul, 1975).

CALLED TO BE: *ISANGOMA* OR PROPHET

M.P. JOHNSON

Abstract

Using a comparative method within a single culture, the Zulu culture, this study focuses on two kinds of healers: the *isangomas* who are the traditional healer/diviners within the Zulu culture, and the prophets, the *abathandazi* or *abapropheti*, who heal within the context of one of the African Independent Churches. The data was gathered primarily from lengthy interviews with the subjects in the field, their homes or churches. The question was asked, why are some called to be *isangomas* and some to be prophets. This choice was looked at as perhaps some way to illuminate cross-cultural change from a psychological point of view. The psychology of C.G. Jung, or analytical psychology, provided the theoretical framework for the research.

Introduction

KwaZulu or Zululand, where the majority of the Zulu people live, is surrounded by and interwoven into a modern technological culture which brings about its influence in many ways such as through schools, travel, radio, television and movies as well as science, churches and religion. Yet it is estimated that well over half of all the Zulus both inside and outside the self-governing territories still observe the customs and practices of their traditional society.[1] Nevertheless, change is occurring. The two cultures that are in contact here are the Zulu culture and the modern technological culture that surrounds it. These two worlds are described by Dr Vera Bührmann as the western world which is primarily scientific, rational and ego-oriented, versus the world of the black healer, which is non-rational, intuitive and human instead of object-oriented.[2]

This research attempts to focus on cross-cultural change from a psychological point of view, using the theories of analytical psychology, or the psychology of G.C. Jung, as a framework. Two kinds of healer/ diviners within the Zulu culture are compared, the *isangomas* who are

---

[1] Bureau for Information, *South Africa 1988/99*, p. 60.
[2] Bührmann, *Living in two worlds*, p. 15.

the traditional healers within that culture, and the prophets, the *abathandazi* or *abapropheti,* who heal and divine within the context of one of the AICs. From the perspective of cultural anthropology, this would be using the comparative method within a single culture or community "to achieve generalisation through comparison of similar kinds of phenomena. It seeks to extract common denominators from a mass of variants."[3]

Both the *isangomas* and the prophets are "called" to become healers, a decision that does not come from the ego of the individual. Rather, this is a calling that comes to the healer from other sources or powers greater than the ego of the individual. From the theory of analytical psychology, the psyche has two centres. The subjective centre is the ego, what it is that one feels oneself to be in the ordinary world. The second centre of the psyche is the Self, the ordering and unifying centre of the total psyche. The mental and physical well-being of the individual always depends upon the quality of the relationship between the ego and the Self.[4] "The Self is not only the centre, but also the whole circumference which embraces both conscious and unconscious, it is the centre of this totality, just as the ego is the centre of consciousness."[5]

If one perceives the role of the prophet as a changed or modified version of the role of the *isangoma,* then whether one is called to be an *isangoma* or a prophet may illuminate how the unconscious or the Self participates or even leads the way in cross-cultural change. This would be somewhat of a challenge to the formulations of Ralph Linton (1948)[6] and Anthony Wallace 1956[7], two anthropologists who have presented important theories on a particular kind of cross-cultural change, primarily because they both emphasise the role of conscious intent, or the ego. "Revitalisation is a special form of culture change phenomena; the persons involved must perceive of their culture or a magic portion of it as unsatisfactory and must deliberately set out to reform it."[8]

---

[3] Lessa and Vogt, *Reader in comparative religion,* p. 4.
[4] Edinger, *Ego and Archetype,* p. 3.
[5] Jung, *Psychology and alchemy,* p. 41.
[6] Linton, *Nativistic movements,* pp. 230–240.
[7] Wallace, *Revitalization movements,* pp. 264–281.
[8] *Ibid.,* p. 265.

Background: Healing in the Zulu Culture

The traditional Zulu culture is a patrilineal and patrilocal society, organised around the family kraal or village (the *umzi*). The *umzi* usually consists of the headman, with his several wives and children, and other family members. The traditional homes were round beehive huts, built in a circle, with the headman's hut facing east, at the top end, overlooking the rest. In the very centre is the cattle kraal. In the cattle kraal are kept the most precious family treasures, the cattle of the village, the grain that is stored in underground pits, and the ancestor spirits. One could say that the cattle kraal is the Zulu church or temple.[9] This is where the spirits of the ancestors are thought to live; this is the place where most of the animal sacrifices take place, asking for the protection of the ancestor spirits, or thanking the ancestors for their blessings, or informing the ancestors about any major changes in the lives of their living kin, such as marriage or the birth of children.

As with most indigenous cultures, it is difficult to isolate religion as a separate thing, apart from the general texture of life. Sir Edward Tylor's minimum definition of religion was, "belief in spiritual beings."[10] There is a belief in the old, old one, *Unkulunkulu*, who made all things. "All things as well as *Unkulunkulu* sprang from a bed of reeds, everything, both animals and corn, everything coming into being with *Unkulunkulu*. He created all wild animals, cattle and game, snakes and birds, water and mountains, including the sun and the moon. . . . . He instituted the present order, gave man the *amaThongo*, or spirits of the ancestors, doctors for treating disease, and diviners. It is he who arranged that the *amaThongo* should make known their wishes in dreams, and that when a man is made ill by an *iThongo*, men shall kill a bullock and laud that spirit to make the patient recover."[11] However, psychologically, *Unkulunkulu* is not very close to the psyches of the traditional Zulus. The Zulus say, "We did not worship him though we all sprang from him."[12]

Psychologically, the Zulus are close to the spirits of their ancestors, "whom we know". The ancestors, usually the male ancestors, whose spirits live in the cattle kraal, take an ongoing interest in their living

---

[9] Krige, *The Social System of the Zulus*, p. 291.
[10] Evans-Pritchard, *Theories of primitive religion*, p. 3
[11] Krige, *The Social System of the Zulus*, p. 280.
[12] *Ibid*, p. 281.

relatives, and have the power to bring them luck, good fortune, many children, good health, the good things in life. This they will do as long as their living kin continue to remember them properly, with the proper rituals and ceremonies. Vera Bührmann has suggested that it would be more correct in this case to talk and write about ancestor reverence and ancestor remembering than ancestor worship. "They (the ancestors) are too human, and the relationship between the Black people and their ancestors is too personal. The rituals and ceremonies are not primarily to appease and propitiate the supposedly wrathful ancestors, but to learn their wishes, to be guided by their wisdom and to have communion with them."[13] Perhaps the closeness that is experienced between the Zulus and the ancestors compensates for the distance that is felt between them and the creator, *Unkulunkulu*.

The dark side of the Self is carried by the Zulu belief in witches and witchcraft, the *abathakathi*, evil-doers, the enemy of society.

> African witchcraft beliefs are related to the fact that it is held that there is no such thing as chance except in the case of most trivial events. Important events such as accidents, death, ill health, suffering and misfortune of all kinds are believed to be due to some external agency and that "it is brought on". They always question the "how" and "why" of events and often also the "who".[14]

Sorcerers, often men, can make various medicines that can cause harm, but the most feared are the witches.

> The witch, on the other hand, does not generally use material substances to work her evil, but she has some mysterious, indefinable power. Usually she is unaware that she possesses such abilities, until she is accused of being a witch. She cannot be changed or "cured"; she cannot be "separated" from or be deprived of her power; it is regarded as something innate, which can also be passed on to a daughter. . . . The women who are regarded as witches together with their victims, the bewitched, are subject to supra-personal forces and this adds to their suffering— the former by being ostracized and even killed by stoning or burning, and the latter by feeling that life is being crushed out of them and they are facing complete annihilation.[15]

---

[13] Bührmann, *Living in two worlds*, p. 27.
[14] Bührmann, *The feminine in witchcraft*, p. 144.
[15] *Ibid.*, p. 141.

Looking at this from a psychological point of view, Dr Bührmann says:

> I perceive the fantasies about and the images of the ancestors and *abathakathi* (witches and sorcerers) as expressed. . . . as projections from their unconscious, especially the cultural and collective layers. The ancestors and witch concepts are therefore archetypal. This was not a preconceived idea or theory on my part, but developed when I became aware of the power and influence of these beliefs and images or symbols.[16]

When things are going wrong, illness, prickly pains, bad luck, death in the family, infertility problems, or when a physical problem is not easily cured by the usual remedies, then a Zulu may decide to consult an *isangoma*. The *isangoma*, the traditional indigenous healer, plays a role in the traditional Zulu society that could be described as a combination of doctor, priest, family counsellor, psychologist and psychic. The *isangomas* are highly respected and somewhat feared because of their powers, and they are very much needed. They are able to restore psychological and physical balance in their patients because, in their rituals and in their ceremonies, they are able to enter the spirit world and to communicate with the Ancestor Spirits of the patient. The Ancestor Spirits of the patient or the Ancestor Spirits of the *isangoma* will tell the *isangoma* why the Ancestor Spirits are angry or disappointed with the patient. The illness, or the bad luck, or the bad dream are some of the ways that the Ancestor Spirits communicate with their living kin to get their attention. Usually the *isangoma* will tell the patient to perform some ritual or ceremony, sometimes involving an animal sacrifice, in order to appease the offended ancestor and make things right with him. Because the Ancestor Spirits have the power to protect and to punish their living kin, it is a matter of great importance to the Zulus to maintain good relationships with them. A Zulu woman said,

> *Mthetho* (the customs of the ancestors) is a mystery reaching far back in time, a continuity of important things. We live with this continuity of the codes of our clan and we are whole and protected. We believe that if we step out and break away, we incur the wrath of our ancestors and also we become as the *tsotsis*, the purposeless riff-raff that you see in the towns who prey upon the people.[17]

---

[16] Bührmann, *Living in two worlds*, p. 21.
[17] Tyrrell, *Suspicion is my name*, p. 21.

From a psychological point of view, this means that when a Zulu is in a state of psychological of physical stress, he or she turns to the unconscious (the Ancestor Spirits) for help. The *isangomas* is the mediator between the ego world of the patient and the patient's unconscious or collective unconscious. This role is somewhat analogous to the role of the Jungian analyst who assists his patients to develop a relationship between the ego and the unconscious, and he may also be a mediator between these two worlds at times.

The decision to become an *isangoma* does not come from the ego. The *isangoma* is often called to become a healer through an illness, psychological and/or physical, that is then diagnosed by a trained *isangoma as ukuthwasa*. The word *thwasa* means "the emergence of something new, e.g. a new day, new moon, new season (often spring), or a new heavenly constellation."[18] The *thwasa* condition is regarded as being due to the ancestors' calling the patient to their service. They would say that the patient is having "the power of the ancestors". The only cure for this illness is to submit to the wishes of the Ancestor Spirits. To ignore the call can mean continued illness and perhaps madness. Often the patient will be directed in dreams or in visions where he or she should go for training to become an *isangoma*. Sometimes it is to the kraal or an *isangoma* who lives many miles away from the patient's home. The training of an isangoma may take between six months and several years. The training is expensive; it requires sacrifice and money from the family of the patient to support the treatment, and the patient must live away from home for an extended period of time.

The prophet, the *abathandazi* or *abapropheti* has a somewhat similar role to the *isangoma,* within the context of one of the AICs. Many Zulus are drawn to one of these churches specifically because they need to be healed from a physical or a psychological disease. The prophet often has been called, first by being healed from an illness by another prophet within a church context, and then by receiving the Holy Spirit and special divining and healing powers as a practising member of the congregation. The prophet heals and divines through a special connection with the Holy Spirit, and is able to heal others by connecting them with the Holy Spirit, using prayer, singing, lighting candles, putting on holy robes or chords and giving the patient holy water to drink. The prophets may not receive special training for

---

[18] Bührmann, *Living in two worlds*, p. 36.

their healing and divining roles. Some say that further training is not necessary if the Holy Spirit works through them. Successful and powerful prophets are very important for the popularity and success of the individual churches that they attend because their healing services are much in demand.

The AIC movement has been variously described and documented. Bengt G.M. Sundkler, who wrote *Bantu Prophets in South Africa* (1948) considered his book to be a study of the problem of Separatism, and concluded that "these churches are a disease in the Christian body, and are bridges back to paganism."[19] Absolom Vilakazi, a Zulu scholar, takes a different point of view: "In Africa in general, and in South Africa in particular, the Christian church is going through a new form of reformation—as far-reaching in its results as was the Protestant Reformation of the fifteenth and sixteenth centuries. This is the African Reformation, in which the peoples of Africa are breaking away from white Mission Churches."[20]

Many of the AICs (African Independent Churches) are small, with fifty to sixty members, while others have as many as 200,000 members, such as the Church of the Nazarites or the Shembe Church *(Isonto LamaNazaretha)*, founded by Isaiah Shembe in 1911. Shembe, who had had contact with the Baptist Mission Churches, founded his own church on the basis of his dreams and visions. Eighty percent of the AICs have the word "Zion" in their church name, such as, the Holy Sabbath Zion Church of South Africa, or the Foundation Divine Christian Catholic Church in Zion, or The Church of the Kingdom of God in Zion. This church movement, or reformation, or revitalisation movement, has grown from 1950, when there were 800 denominations and one million members, representing nine percent of the black population, to 4000 denominations in 1985 and 8,500,000 members, representing thirty-five percent of the black population of South Africa.[21]

The Research Method

The data for this study was gathered over four years, 1987–1990, during the months of July and August. A pilot study of field questionnaires in 1987 was followed by interviews in 1988–89. The research

---

[19] Vilakazi, *Shembe*, p. 3.
[20] *Ibid*, p. 1.
[21] Bureau for Information, *South Africa 1988/89*, p. 618.

team consisted of an interviewer, a technical assistant working with
tape recorders and cameras, and a guide and translator who is fluent
in English and Zulu. Essentially the methodology of the study of the
healers was a clinical approach. The healers were interviewed in their
homes in their churches. This was a lengthy interview, beginning with
a structured set of some ten questions concerning their personal history
and the development of their interests and talents as healers. The
second half of the interview consisted of more open-ended questions
that allowed the interviewer to develop themes and questions that
emerged in the process of the interview. The interviews were generally
from one hour to two hours in length. The taped interviews were
then transcribed and translated into English for later analysis. When
possible, two different translators of the interview data were used,
in order to cross-check the validity of the translations.

The majority of the subjects came from the townships around the
port city of Durban, such as KwaMashu; and some came from more
rural areas near Empangeni and Ladysmith. In the experience of the
research team, the healers were generally welcoming in receiving us
into their homes and their churches, and participated with genuine
interest in the research. One of two of the healers wanted first to
consult their Ancestor Spirits before talking to us, and in these cases
we were allowed to have the interview. When the interview began,
the interviewer told the subject that she was a psychologist in the
United States, a healer somewhat comparable to themselves, and that
she was therefore interested in them, in their healing methods, their
lives, and their calling to become a healer, in order to understand
more about psychology and her work with her patients. At the end
of the interview the subject was invited to ask questions of the interviewer
and her experiences with healing, and they frequently did so.

Results

The pilot study, 1987, was a field questionnaire, consisting of twenty
questions, that was taken into KwaMashu, by a field worker. The
questions had to do with dreams, the meaning of dreams to the subjects,
their interpretation of dreams, and the personal history of the healer,
his or her calling, training, and methods of healing. The questionnaires
were transcribed and translated into English and later analysed. The
original idea was to compare and contrast the approaches of *isangomas*
with prophets, and to come up with some ideas about how these
two groups differ. It seemed that this might be one way to look at

cross-cultural change from a psychological point of view, because it could be argued that the role of the prophet is an evolving or changed form of the role of the *isangoma*.

In this first study, out of a total of 34 useable questionnaires, there were responses from 19 prophets (12 females and 7 males) and 15 *isangomas* (5 females and 10 males). This would be a statistically significant difference; a greater percentage of prophets were female and a greater percentage of *isangomas* were male in this particular sample. The average age of the prophets was 47.2, with a range from 23 to 75 years. The average age of the *isangomas* was 54.3, with a range from 23 to 72 years. In terms of training, the prophets had an average of 0.81 (less than a year) of training, versus the *isangomas* who had an average of 2.05 years of training. Some of the prophets said that they were called to be prophets and healers by the Holy Spirit and thus did not need to be trained. No *isangoma* made that claim. In terms of years of experience of being a healer, the two groups were similar, with eighteen years as the average for prophets and sixteen years for the *isangomas*. Both groups described having been called to become healers by having had a physical and/or psychological illness, and having been cured by other healers. How-ever, on the major variables involved in the study, there were no real differences between the two groups.

In 1988 the research team returned to the Durban area with the intention of going out into the field, primarily KwaMashu, to conduct lengthy clinical interviews with some of the original subjects from the 1987 study, to discover why there had been so little difference between the two groups, the prophets and the *isangomas*. A total of six healers were interviewed in their homes. Following up that study, a further seven healers were interviewed in 1989. In 1990, a total of 19 healers were interviewed, but because the transcriptions from this study are not yet complete, these results can only be suggestive.

Analysis

From analysing the data, it is clear that *isangomas* and prophets are nothing like the two discrete groups or categories that we had hypothesised them to be. In actually, it appears that *isangomas* and prophets could be viewed as two ends of a wide-ranging continuum. Of the first six healers interviewed in 1988, all of whom were women, one healer was just an *isangoma* and one was just a prophet. All of the other four healers were some kind of combination of prophet and *isangoma*, and they lived with that mixture with differing degrees of comfort. The words of one healer, a woman who is both a prophet and an *isangoma*, expressed her dilemma: "I have been praying to my ancestors asking them to become Christians."

In order to elucidate the dynamics of this process, a way to order and to categorise these differences was sought. A model, with a five-step continuum between *isangoma* in category I and prophet in category V, was found to be useful in ordering the data. Allocation of the subjects in one of the five categories is made by asking what is the mediating archetype between the ego of the healer and his or her connection with their higher power, God, *Unkulunkulu*, or, in psychological terms, the Self. Another way of putting this is to ask to whom do they pray, or, who gives them visions and power. In category I: *isangomas*, subjects are guided by and helped in their healing efforts by the Ancestor Spirits. In Category V: prophets, subjects are guided by and helped in their healing efforts by the Holy Spirit. In categories II, III and IV, the subjects are guided and helped in their healing efforts by both the Ancestor Spirits and the Holy Spirit, but in different degrees. In category II: *isangoma*/prophet, subjects respond that for them the Ancestor Spirit is more powerful than the Holy Spirit. In category IV, prophet/*isangoma*, subjects respond that the Holy Spirit is more powerful than the Ancestor Spirits. In category II: equal power, subjects respond that for them the power of the Ancestor Spirits and the Holy Spirit are equal, just the same in power.

In the samples gathered in 1988 and 1989, there were 13 subjects in all, 11 female and 2 male. The average age was 43. In terms of the categories, two subjects could be placed in category I, five subjects in category II, one subject in category III, two subjects in category IV, and three subjects in category V.

Some Case Examples

Category I: Isangoma

Subject IB is a married, 52 years old woman, who completed eleven years in school, was trained and worked as an assistant nurse in a hospital for 12 years. She experienced a number of different problems and difficulties between 1961 and 1985. "I was very much affected by the Spirit with the result that I lost control of myself and did not know what I was doing. My mind was not functioning well. I used to dream without being asleep and when I came back to my senses I became seriously ill." She attempted to avoid the Ancestor Spirit by going to a Zion church. "I joined the Zion church because I wanted to get rid of the Ancestor Spirit as I was not keen to accept it." She continued to have a tough time. "I was always running short of money and although I did not spend it I never seemed to have money. I used to put money away but when I looked for it, it had disappeared." She then had some powerful experiences, such as finding an *isangoma's* drum in her house, and other signs that an *isangoma* had been in her house. "Then I realized that I was in trouble." She finally accepted the call, and went to an *isangoma* for training. "I realized that I had to listen and do what my ancestors were telling me to do." Her training lasted two and a half years. She is now practising as an *isangoma* in her community.

Category II: Isangoma/prophet

Subject 7B is a married woman, aged 54, who was raised in a rural part of KwaZulu and did not attend school. She moved to the Durban area when she was 11 and began working as a housekeeper. She married when she was 40. She met her husband at a Zion church service that they both attended. Her husband has now founded his own Zion church. She became very irritable and it was predicted that she had the Ancestor Spirit. "I used to dream about different *mutis* (medicines) and how to use them to treat people." She dreamed four times about the person who was going to train her to be an *isangoma*. "I went to live with her in her home. I lived there for five months for *umdiki* and *umndawu* (that is the spirits of the ancestors)." She is now living at home and working as an *isangoma*. She attends the Zion church when her ancestors allow her to go. She says that in her dreams she sees herself "singing the isangoma's song very loudly, but when I dream about myself singing a Christian song I sing very softly." She says, "I use the Ancestors' Spirit, although I do sometimes call the Holy Spirit by giving them holy water to use, but I am not a prophet. The Ancestors' Spirit is stronger."

Category III: Equal Power

Subject 4A is a 51 year old married woman who lives in KwaMashu. She has been an *isangoma* a number of years and has people coming to her for help on the weekends. She specialises in treating young people with romantic problems. "Those who want to get married, I make a special *muti* for them so that the boyfriend will not have another girlfriend and he will marry her. . . . If your husband goes away, you must come to me and I will bring him back no matter where he is, even if he is in Johannesburg or Cape Town." However, she is now in a conflict. She now has the Holy Spirit as well. She dreams about church people laying their hands on her and praying, but the Ancestor Spirits do not want her to go to church. "The spirit of the ancestors is very powerful." She has fasted for days, and she prays to ask the spirit of the ancestors to lower its power so that the Holy Spirit can work on her. She says, "If both spirits are strong, it makes one sick. Therefore, one has to subside. This is the most difficult thing to do."

Category IV: Prophet/isangoma

Subject 2B is an unmarried 24 year old man who lives in a black township near Durban. In terms of education he has completed Standard 9. He was called to be a prophet through an illness in 1976, when his right hand became paralysed for about one year. He was forced to drop out of school for that time. He was healed by a prophet in a Zion kind of a church. His father was also the minister and a prophet and healer in a small AIC that he founded. Subject 2B was able to observe and to practise his own predicting and healing skills by working with his father. He became a prophet in 1978 and is considered to be a strong healer in his community. He says, "Previously, when I was praying I used to call the Ancestors' Spirit, but since I am a prophet I use both spirits, but mostly the Holy Spirit. It (the Ancestor Spirit) does help me but I use the Holy Spirit more as it is more powerful to me. I use my Ancestor Spirit in a Christian way. I am changing their spirit to a Christian spirit as I want my ancestors to come to me as Christians."

Category V: Prophet

Subject 6B is a widowed 60 year old female who lives in a black township near Durban. When she was young she had many dreams about her grandfather, whom she never knew, and when she described to her father the strange clothes that he was wearing, her father told her that the grandfather was an *isangoma*. This meant that she was to be called to be an *isangoma* as well. Subject 6B resisted this call for many years and many bad things happened to her. She said she resisted the call because "I did not like an *isangoma's* way of dressing. You cannot wear beautiful clothing and shoes. You only wear animal skins and look funny." The resolution came for her when she moved to the Durban area and joined one of the AICs. She dreamed about her grandfather. "He gave me a Zion church garment and told me to join the Zion church if I did not want to be an *isangoma*. (. . .) I do not usually read the Bible but I know all about it because my grandfather comes at night in my dreams and tells me what is in the Bible and which verse to read. When my grandfather comes to me he no longer wears an *isangoma* dress but appears in a long white gown which hides his legs." It appears that her ancestor, her grandfather, has become a Christian. She is a prophet in an AIC. When people come to her for healing in her home, she gives them holy water, tells them to light candles, and prays to the Holy Spirit.

Conclusions and Questions for Further Research

The research began with questioning why some healers are called to become *isangomas* and some healers called to become prophets, as a way to perhaps illuminate cross-cultural change from a psychological point of view.

The research indicates that one should not think about the healers, isangomas and prophets, as two distinct groups that can be compared and contrasted. Rather, the data suggests that the traditional healers and the prophet healers are two extremes of a continuum that has a considerable range of mixtures between the poles. *Isangomas* may be practising as traditional healers in one context and as prophets in another context, and vice versa. A model with five categories (I: *isangoma*; II: *isangoma*/prophet; III: equal power; IV: prophet/*isangoma*; V: prophet) was devised to order the data and to further elucidate the dynamics of the process that may be going on to determine whether one is called to become an *isangoma* or a prophet. So far, this model has proved useful in ordering the data collected as well as in providing direction for further research and research questions.

Only further research can answer some of the questions raised by this initial study. It appears that individual healers can be called to be *isangomas* or prophets. They can then move up or down the continuum until they reach a position that is supported by their unconscious (the

Self). There is a suggestion in the data that healers are called to become healers initially more often by the Ancestor Spirits, and that this spirit can then become cooperative with and/or changed into the Holy Spirit at a later time. The outcome seems to rest with the unconscious of the healer. There appears to be some resistance experienced in the ego of the healer to accepting the call to become an *isangoma* because it is expensive and unconventional from a "modern" perspective. This may be particularly true for those called to become healers who are living in an urban environment, as opposed to a rural environment. One could speculate, therefore, that throughout their histories as healers there is more movement of subjects from the lower categories to the higher categories than from higher categories to lower categories. If this is true, then one could conclude that at a cultural level the unconscious (the Self) is supporting a cross-cultural change by giving greater power to the Holy Sprit as opposed to giving greater power to the Ancestor Spirits as a mediating archetype for the healers in their work.

Further research will continue with the same methodology, lengthy interviews with individual healers about their personal life stories as healers. Greater attention will be given to focusing on healers who fall in the middle categories, particularly category II, to elucidate how a conflict between the Ancestor Spirits and the Holy Spirit can be resolved within the individual healer him/herself, and within what kinds of contexts, churches or environmental situations.

BIBLIOGRAPHY

Bureau for Information, *South Africa 1988/89. Official Yearbook of the Republic of South Africa* (Cape Town: CTP Book Printers, 1989, fourteenth edition).

Bührmann, M.V., *Living in two worlds* (Wilmette, Illinois: Chiron Publications, 1986).

Bührmann, M.V., "The feminine in witchcraft: Part I", *Journal of Analytical Psychology* 32 (1987) pp. 139–156.

Edinger, E., *Ego and archetype* (New York: G.P. Putnam's Sons, 1972).

Evans-Pritchard, E.E., *Theories of primitive religion* (Oxford: Clarendon Press, 1965).

Jung, C.G., "Psychology and alchemy", *The collected works of C.G. Jung* 12 (Princeton: Princeton University Press, 1953).

Krige, E.J., *The social system of the Zulus* (Pietermaritzburg: Shuter and Shooter, 1936).

Lessa, W.A. and Vogt, E.Z., *Reader in comparative religion, an anthropological approach* (New York: Harper Collins Publishers, 1979).

Linton, R., "Nativistic movements", *American Anthropologist* XLV (1943) pp. 230–240.

Tyrrell, B., *Suspicion is my name* (Cape Town: Gothic Printing Co. Ltd, 1971).

Vilakazi, A.; Mthethwa, B.; and Mpanza, M., *Shembe : The revitalisation of African society* (Johannesburg: Skotaville Publishers, 1986).

Wallace, A.F.C., "Revitalisation movements", *American Anthropologist* LVIII (1956) pp. 264–281.

MULTI-DISCIPLINARY AND INTER-CULTURAL RESEARCH WITH FAMILIES IN TRANSITION: A SEARCH FOR COMMON GROUND

A.S. VAN NIEKERK

Abstract

This paper represents the results of a multi-disciplinary research which aimed at understanding the situation and behaviour of a group of poor African people. The ultimate goal is the improvement of the quality of life of those people. The research, which was conducted from a holistic point of view, clearly showed the meeting and interaction of the modern Western world and the traditional African world with their different views of life, religions, values, technologies and social structures. The interfacing of these two worlds often causes not only tension and conflict but also suffering. Nevertheless, the traditional African thought-pattern was found to be inclusive: it tends to accommodate and assimilate new elements more readily than the Western patterns of thinking.

Introduction

Our multi-disciplinary research team has been working now since August 1989. The team consists of: Prof. D. Holm (Head, Dept Architecture, University of Pretoria; Dr J. Hugo (Dept of Family Medicine, MEDUNSA); Mr W.M.K. van Niekerk (Dept Chemical Engineering, UP); Rev Wilhelm van Deventer (DRCA Minister, Venda). The writer is the project leader. Several scholars have been working with us, including Dr Tseke Masemola of Nobody Village; Mrs Joyce Dali, a social worker, MEDUNSA; Rev Lehasa Mokoena, DRCA Minister, Balfour; Prof J.C. Marais of the University of the North; students who do fieldwork, including Mr M. Banda, Mr P. Ntshumayelo and Mr J. Taiwe. The families with whom we work are very much part of our team, and of the whole process.

Aim

Our aim is to understand the way in which all the different factors, some originating in traditional African culture, some in modern Western culture and some in the Christian churches, combine in the family life of the poor, in order to contribute to the improvement of the quality of their life through better designed methods of helping on all levels.

Approach

The family is a micro-structure that exists between the individual and the macro-structures of society. While the large political, economic, educational and ecological processes that take place have an impact on the individual, the responses and decisions of the individual often take place in the context of the family. Our approach is that the ability of the family to cope is crucial. The different scientific disciplines can contribute to the struggle of the family, provided that they do so in a co-ordinated or holistic way; but they have to adjust their "solutions" to the views, wishes and values of the poor themselves.

We work with a systems approach, where the family is seen as a subsystem of society, the family itself consisting of a number of subsystems. Our approach is holistic, in the sense that not only do the different subsystems combine in a system, but their combination constitutes a new reality, in which the whole determines the character of the constituting parts, and vice versa.

Including the poor in the search for better designs is in itself an empowerment of the poor, and has a humanising effect.

Our approach is open, but fundamentally based on Christian faith.

Themes

1. A place to feel at home: Designing with the poor (architecture).
2. The household and illness: healing of poor people (medical science).
3. Improving the quality of life of the poor: designing household technology (engineering).
4. Coping with life: designing support with the poor (theology).

Areas that we have not yet covered, but hope to do, include: nutrition, ecology, waste disposal, legal matters, education, etc.

Phases

Multi-disciplinary research is slow and sometimes cumbersome, but it can be very exciting.

First Phase

The first phase took almost ten years: it involved becoming aware of the situation of the poor and of the need for a multi-disciplinary and inter-cultural approach, and finding suitable people who were able and willing to participate.

Second Phase

The second phase is now almost complete. We first had to establish a common framework, next we had to start doing research, and then we had to begin to interpret the results of the fieldwork. We are now preparing publications to motivate the following statement: that there is a gap between the Western models (be it housing, technology, medical care or church liturgy and pastoral care), and the poor to whom these models are offered as solutions for their problems.

This may sound obvious. Why state the obvious? Because so many housing schemes, medical schemes and development schemes, so many courses offered at universities, even the "helping professions", give the impression that we are quite certain what the solutions are.

Many of those who do admit that there is a gap between "our" solutions and "their" (the poor's) problems conclude that "they' must change. They must be educated, so that "our" solutions will work for "them". Our team tries to make clear that education is not enough: "our" solutions must be re-designed in order to be relevant to the perceptions, needs and values of the poor as the poor see them.

Third Phase

We hope to be able soon to give our full attention to phase III, so that we can concentrate on designing such solutions, not only with scientists of other disciplines, but also with the poor themselves. This phase will, however, require more time and money than the first two. It needs hard work to convince people who decide on the allocation of money that Western solutions are defective. How do we convince them that yet another research project legitimates the allocation of scarce resources? Are we not merely taking more money away from the poor?

We still have to finalise phase II: to illustrate clearly and convincingly that "our" (middle-class, Western) solutions do not solve "their" problems, and that it is not only "they" who must adapt to "our" solutions (the education option), but that "our" solutions must adapt to "them" (the design option, we can also call it a client-centred approach).

From the viewpoint of the church we will sound another warning: somewhere along the line both the African tradition and the modern Western cultures will appear defective, and the need for conversion will present itself (the rebirth option). Without conversion, the correct, necessary conversion neither education nor new designs will solve the problems of poverty and human misery.

Common Ground

One may well ask: Have we found any common ground so far between the different sciences on the one hand, and the scientists and the poor on the other?

All the researchers have become aware that the poorest of the poor live, so to speak, in another world. We all agree that a gap exists between the researchers and the poor. This agreement constitutes some common ground.

Medical services

Our group decided to find out which illnesses the families suffer from, and to ask them to tell us the stories of their illness and healing. The medical doctor, Dr Hugo, noticed that the nearby hospital hardly played any role in the reports. In fact, one report stated: ". . . the people in the village have given the hospital the name *Re buile feela*, meaning "we come bare-handed, the person whom we were going to check had passed away". One reason for this is that the staff at the hospitals are rude.

The church, and specifically the AICs, on the other hand, feature strongly in the stories about healing.

One story of Mrs S. is quite revealing in this respect. The lady became sick. "The joints started to be loose and the head was aching right in front. The eyes grew dim and she couldn't see anymore." She didn't have money to go to the doctor, but the minister of her church (ZCC) came to her house and prepared tea for her. She drank tea twice a day, prayed, slept or relaxed, and kept her body warm. After six days she was still weak, but she was healed.

The approach of the ZCC minister contrasts in many ways with that of the hospital: it is affordable; it does not isolate the patient from her world and her family; it is not experienced as aggressive or hostile. The value of human contact, care, warm and loving relations for the healing process, and an interpretation of the causes and the care of the illness that makes sense to the patient, have impressed the medical doctor, Dr Hugo.

The theologian who studies pastoral care, the architect who is concerned with the human quality of the space in which we live, and the engineer, all find common ground here with the medical doctor: they can relate their science to such ideas.

Did we also succeed in finding common ground with the families, as far as the interpretation of the causes and healing of their illnesses are concerned?

As far as healing is concerned, the modern methods remain important, in spite of the fact that the hospital is hardly mentioned in the stories about healing. A young mother of twins said: "We live from hand to mouth. Whatever coin we find, or that is given as a gift to the children, we keep it for their health, that if they fall ill, we must be able to take them to hospital."

Two days later the infants did get ill; they were taken to hospital and one died there.

People take elaborate measures to try to ensure the success of modern medical care. When Mrs O. had to go to hospital for the birth of her child, she called her minister (ZCC). He came with a number of church members to her house, they sang and danced, put a girdle round her waist to protect her, and sprinkled her with holy water. She also drank some of the water. Immediately after they had left, Mrs O. went to the traditional healer, who gave her his full treatment. At home the family offered *(go phasa)* to the *badimo*, at the traditional place *(thitikwana)*. The next morning Mrs O.'s mother called the Lutheran minister, who laid his hands on her and prayed for her. When one of our researchers and student appeared on the same day, they were also asked to pray for Mrs O.'s coming visit to the hospital. The family now felt that all possible precautions had been taken, and they felt relaxed and confident for the visit to the hospital.

It seems that the family has bridged the gap between the modern medical services, the traditional methods and the Christian approach, by including all of these in an all-inclusive or holistic strategy that has been described as typically African (see van Niekerk, papers read at NERMIC in 1989 and 1990).

For their part, the researchers also made an effort to bridge the gap between the modern scientific approach and the "existentials" of the poor themselves.

Families complain about a wide variety of illnesses that have to do with witchcraft: multiple snakebites, the fire of lightning that slowly moves from the feet upwards in the body, lizards in the stomach, poison that turns into a living thing and begins to grow in the stomach, pains and swellings. The medical doctor examined evidence of the illnesses. Clearly, they belong to a category of illnesses that falls outside the scope of modern medical science as we know it.

So how does the medical doctor, with his scientific emphasis on physical evidence, find common ground with a person who suffers from these illnesses?

Dr Hugo and Mr Banda had a long discussion with Mrs M. She believed that her illnesses had been caused by her ex-husband, or his family, or one of his many lovers, or by her present husband, who was as unfaithful to her as the first one, or by jealous neighbours. Dr Hugo tried to establish common ground here: her strained relationships and the breaking up of her social system manifested in her body in the form of pains. If she could normalise her relationships her pains might disappear. This interpretation, seemingly, provided room for both of them: She could interpret it that she was healed because her people did not bewitch her anymore, while the medical doctor could interpret it in psychosomatic terms—but both could agree that the root of the illness was in the disintegrated social relationships.

Does this establish any common ground? Probably not, if we keep in mind that Mrs M's views are more complicated than we have seen so far. In her own words: "No, Mr Banda, you are still behind in knowing what I know."

In another interview she was asked if she would like to have a TV. She replied:

Badimo (the spirits of the forefathers) do not want TV. That is why we have a lot of people suffering from feet *(maoto)* and people die very young. For the mere fact that we gave the world to whites is a problem. All secret things are no longer followed. This fight is the revelation of the conflict between God and *badimo. Dingaka* (the traditional healers)

> with the help of *badimo* can try to stop this killing and unrest . . . Without
> the help of *badimo* and God things will not come well.

We considered another possibility of finding common ground. One
of our researchers, Rev W van Deventer, suffers from degeneration
of the nerves of the eyes. He is 95% blind, and the situation is still
degenerating. Mrs M. practises as a healer, and she promptly offered
to heal his eyes, claiming that she knows how. Rev van Deventer
put the matter before the group. How should he respond to her
offer? Just ignore it? Or should he go for treatment? How would
we know that her claim is unfounded, if we didn't go? In the end
we decided not to accept her offer. If he was treated, but not healed,
nothing was gained. If he was healed, how would he interpret it as
a Christian?

Our Christian faith is more exclusive than African Traditional
Religion, and common ground is not always possible.

In conclusion, then, we have made efforts to bridge the gap between
modern medical science and the traditional views of illness, but with
doubtful results. We have also not been able to bridge the gap between
our Christian faith and traditional methods of healing. Our exclusive
thought-patterns do not allow us. The families, with their inclusive
thought-patterns, experienced no problems to include all methods in
their strategies.

Engineering

The engineer on our research team, Willem van Niekerk of the
University of Pretoria, is working on a stove that works with sawdust,
a very cheap fuel. Two stoves have been placed with two families,
and we study the economic, social, religious ecological and other
practical aspects of the functioning of the stoves. With the feedback
from the families improvements are continuously made in the design
of the stove, with the aim of producing a product that will be accepted
as a good thing, both from the researchers' point of view and the
poor themselves.

Rev W van Deventer and Mr Ntshumayelo were discussing the
stove with the family of Mrs B. They spoke about the fire that we
use for cooking and heating, for light and for pleasant company. The
discussion moved to other types of fire, dangerous types, such as
lightning, the fire that is used to burn people and property, the fire
of necklace.

Where does fire come from? asked van Deventer. The traditional fire of cooking and heating comes from our forefathers, said one, a visitor. But this dangerous fire, the fire or lightning and necklace, comes from the whites. It is the same fire that is used in technology: the fire of electricity, the fire that makes the motorcar run (in Afrikaans the motorcar is also sometimes called *vuurwa*, or fire wagon).

That is why she doesn't want an electrical stove, said Mrs B. The first of the lightning is already in her feet, and it is slowly moving up, burning her life away. And electricity is the same fire.

Her daughter said that we should not be surprised about the many people who are killed these days by lightning, and in political murders by necklace, and the many witches that are burned nowadays. The Bible predicts that the world will be destroyed by the fire of God's judgment. It has already started, and we see it with our own eyes.

A full meeting of our researchers and associates (with only J.C. Marais, L. Mokoena and P. Mtshumayelo absent) came to the conclusion that we can indeed distinguish between "modern forces of fire" and "traditional forces of fire". We did not consider the possibility that the necklaces and burning of witches might be the first appearance of God's final judgement.

Prof Dieter Holm interpreted the views on fire with reference to the mythology of the ages. In mythology, fire is used to destroy the enemy, or rather, to transform it.

Mrs M. chopped down and burned the tree that provided shade for her squatter's dwelling, because, she said, there was a snake that lived in it. This snake, Mmamogashoa, is the mother of all snakes, and she stays in the sea. She flies through the air, and when she comes to land in the tree, she makes a dangerous wind. Therefore, the tree had to go.

In mythology, says Prof Holm, the snake and the tree often re-appear, e.g. in Genesis 3 and in alchemist mythology. The alchemists used fire in their efforts to turn base metals into gold. In *Genesis* 3, man is sent out of paradise, and the angel with the burning sword stands between him and paradise.

Western man has transformed his nature in the fire of the Industrial Revolution. It is not a threat to him anymore, said Prof Holm. Some in the group felt they could agree with the families who regard the modern forces of fire as dangerous. Some factories have high chimneys, with a burning flame that can be seen from far away. The smoke of the Industrial Revolution poisons the air, toxic waste consumes the earth. The ultimate danger of the modern world is a nuclear war, the most terrible fire in human experience. Such a war could perhaps point to the fires of hell.

According to Prof Holm, however, Mrs M. does not leave "paradise", that is, the mythological worldview. She has not been transformed by the fire of the Industrial Revolution, and neither has Africa.

The engineer has been somewhat baffled by all this. He wants to design a stove that would be of benefit. What should he do with all this mythology? It is the same pattern that we have seen with medical services: the modern medical services can be included in the all-inclusive, traditional thought-pattern, but the modern scientist finds it very difficult to find common ground on his own terms. In the same way, the families know how to interpret the post-Industrial Revolution's fire of the engineer, but the engineer hardly knows what to do with the mythological fire of traditional culture.

What he does recognise, however, is that a stove is not just a stove. It not only has economical and ecological significance, it also has strong emotional and religious significance, and the engineer must understand, intuitively if not rationally, something of this.

Architecture

Massive amounts of money are currently spent on housing schemes, but the media report many complications: the stealing of building materials, organised boycotts of loan repayments, destruction of houses in political violence, etc. Many private institutions have become reluctant to enter the market for black housing.

Such problems must be handled on the macro-level. In our research, however, we have become aware of problems on the micro-level, in the families' experience of the house in which they live. These problems cannot be solved by political or economic programmes. It requires the attention of scientists, to design, with the poor, a house in which people will feel at home, and that is also affordable and ecologically friendly.

Some families indicated that they did not feel at home in the modern type of house. One man said that they felt uncomfortable with the cement floors: people have to have contact with the soil, and therefore they want a floor smeared with cowdung. A cement floor separates one from the soil, and a carpet on the cement removes one even further.

Some people said that there must be at least one room with a grass roof, so that the sick members of the family can sleep there, and communicate with their ancestors.

The architect, Prof Holm, is interested in the way people experience their house: where are the boundaries between private places, holy places, public places, etc? How does the life of the family flow in the structures of the home?

He was struck by the strong element of fear in the way that people experience their homes. "A home—normally considered to be a haven of physical and spiritual safety—can turn into a veritable self-set death trap", he remarks.

If the ancestors are not honoured properly, they become angry and dangerous. When Mrs M. moved her house to another place, she took an extra day to inform the ancestors. "I am afraid that they will punish me. I do not want to make them angry with me . . . They either can wreck me or make it possible that we should stay without peace at Ga-Makanye, because they will be looking for me at this place I am now leaving."

The ancestors also visit Mrs M. in her sleep, and she then speaks in a strange language, while asleep. Her son Piet must sleep nearby, so that he can hear what she says. He understands the strange language. Once they did not carry out the instructions given in this way and the mother became ill. "She became too critical".

If a person becomes seriously ill because of the ancestors, the family invites all their relatives. Cattle is slaughtered, a very costly exercise. The ancestors are worshipped at the *thitikwane*, a specific plant in the house.

Mrs M. was asked if there is a specific place where the *thitikwane* is placed.

She said: "Oh, no. *Thitikwane* can be put anywhere in the *lapa*. It shouldn't be hidden. Remember, these are living people. They want to be seen also. If you hide it, the ancestors will tell you that they are not satisfied . . . You will have to do (i.e., hide it) only if you are instructed to do so."

Danger can also come from the neighbours. While Mr Banda was visiting Mrs M. at her new house, a neighbour came to complain that Mrs M.'s children destroyed the fence between them. Mrs M. said: "Mr Banda, now this is one of the type of problems I am going to face. Whatever wrong is done, people will say it is my children because I am very poor."

The fence was made of old branches, some with thorns. Mr Banda remarked that the fence did not provide adequate protection. His report on her previous house and her new house shows that the house itself has become a physical threat to her:

The house that Mrs M. and her sons have built, is open. It is one big room. The corrugated irons that were put on the roof of the old place are used even here. No nail is used, only stones at the top of the roof. The room is as follows: The plastics are intelligently used as walls from the sides. These plastics are supported by the old tins which are straightened. The aloe stalks are used as pillars in the sides and on the top of the roof. Corrugated irons are put on these stalks. To me I felt sorry about this because aloe stalks are too temporary. These are not strong enough at all. Jim said to me that the room took them only one day to erect. It was because they were afraid of the rain that was coming to wet their blankets. All property is packed in this room. The space is not enough for the family.

Stones that are put on top of the roof is a risk. This house is too temporary, and dangerous to live in. The door is made of an old maize-meal bag. When I had seen the inside of this room, it was for me a shame.

Now, I come to the house itself. She said: "That house was frightening us. Yes, because the wall had cracks. The roof was not nailed i.e. the corrugated irons were not nailed. These to me meant that I was risking the life of my children together with my own life. Instead of me being proud of the house, I was not proud of it. Although I had few visitors after a long period of time, I was really not proud of the house even the place itself. I was feeling uncomfortable and unsettled."

What can you say about the walls of your former house as compared to these ones here? She said, "The walls of my former house had an advantage for me only during windy days. But during the rainy days, they were a threat to me. I am saying this because if water penetrates the wall, the wall becomes more heavy with water. When this wall may fall, then it can kill a person. Secondly, the support of the stones we put on top of the houses, will press the corrugated irons and this also might kill a person by falling on him.

Now, as far as this house which I am staying in right now, I still have two problems. If it can rain heavily, there will be not enough warmness in the room. This will mean we may either die from coldness or may catch cold and be patients all of us in the family. I am saying this because of the papers and curtboxes we used for the wall. The roof itself still, is without strong poles. I used the same old poles because of lack of money to buy the new ones."

"Thus far, as far a your former house was concerned, were you worried about the inadequacy protection or maybe the house itself was frightening you?"

She said: "Yes, even the house itself was frightening me because I found the walls erected already. So people who wished to use the old walls for their own purpose were telling me to move away from the place. I couldn't do otherwise anything because I was not the person who built the walls but I found them there. What I could do was to move and get a place that would satisfy me. I sometimes thought that they wished to stay there again."

The breakdown of social relations that the medical doctor wrestled with, is again manifested in the way that the physical structures of the house are experienced. The house is frightening, not only because of the loose corrugated iron sheets on the roof, the heavy stones used to keep these sheets in place, the walls that may crumble and fall on you, the wind and the rain, but also because of sickness, of the neighbours, and the ancestors. The very same things that threaten one, are the things that protect one.

Conclusions

In the poorest rural families one witnesses the meeting and interaction of the modern Western and the traditional African worlds, as well as the Christian message. The meeting of different worlds—different worldviews, values, technologies and social structures—creates a lot of tension and suffering.

The traditional African thought-pattern is inclusive: it tends to accommodate and absorb new elements into the old pattern. It is remarkably tough, but also under great strain because of the impact of the Western world, and also, the Christian message. It is remarkable how aptly many families could include Western and Christian elements in their own framework of thinking, while the Western researchers, with their analytic Western patterns of thinking, and on occasion also because of the demands of our Christian faith to exclusivity, could not find common ground with traditional beliefs and practices. We are not convinced that we should always find common ground, for practical as well as theoretical reasons.

Education, design and conversion are all valid options, for rich as well as poor, Africans as well as Westerners. Our task remains to search for greater clarity on where and how each of these should be applied.

SECTION D

WOMEN IN MINISTRY

TOWARDS THE EMANCIPATION OF WOMEN IN A POST-APARTHEID SOUTH AFRICA: A CASE OF A PRAYER WOMAN IN A ZIONIST CHURCH

M. MKHIZE

Abstract

A positive image of the African prayer woman as a culture carrier who has survived dehumanisation and oppression is reflected in this essay. The paper is a result of a case study of a Soweto prayer woman. Details of the interview show that the researcher's conclusions are based on an interaction which flows easily from the prayer woman's membership of the Zionist Church, the healing power of the woman, her perspective on political developments in the country as well as the role women could play in the future of this country.

This paper which recognises the leadership of the prayer women in the African Independent Churches, concludes by challenging South African women to learn from the successes which the prayer woman and prophetesses have achieved against all odds.

Introduction

South Africa is going through a phase when gender relations are under scrutiny. While women are active locally, they are thinking internationally. They identify with women of the world who have communicated in no uncertain terms that women's liberation is part of the racial liberation package (Brodsky and Day, 1989; Davis, 1990; International Conference of Free Trade Unions (1949–1991); United Nations Decade for women (1975–1985 cf. Cook, 1991).

Issues raised during the two recent conferences entitled: "Women in Southern Africa" (cf. Agenda 1991) and "Black Women: About and for Ourselves" indicate that women of this country have reached a point where they call in no uncertain terms for a radical shift, not only away from racism but also away from sexism. However, black feminists are faced with a challenge to deal with the question of domination vs the subordination between men and women in ways which will not be perceived as a threat to the nation. For instance, when Angela Davis, a black American feminist and a political activist says industrialise domestic work, can we echo her words? What about cultural con-siderations? What about "Christian" teachings which are so important in a highly religious context like ours? These questions are pertinent in the context of black women, who in social terms are professional/businesswomen, factory workers, domestic workers, labourers in general, farm labourers, angry women who have spent a great deal of their lives alienated in exile, and housewives. I hope what I have said in no way implies a naive and simplistic way of outlining class differences amongst black women, as that will need qualification.

What is known about African women?

White women have played a major role in drawing the world's attention to black women's issue (Barret, Dawber, Klugman, Obery, Shindler and Yawitch, 1985; Cock, 1980). However such an alliance has been criticised by Letlaka-Rennert (1991). Her criticism of the aforementioned conference on gender in Southern Africa is as follows: "Ironically, the subjects of research in most of the presentations were black women but the conference did not include them. The consciously academic focus of this whole event excluded the majority of women in Southern Africa and consequently makes me doubt its value in the emancipation of women" (p. 23).

The challenge for black women is to identify and to document their own experiences. Admittedly, this might sound valid criticism but it has to be noted that some of the many black women who have been leaders in the liberation movement have been silenced by the Apartheid Government. Another aspect of violence against black women which could have dissuaded them from writing is that even at work the majority of them are under constant trauma as they are financially exploited (Kedijang, 1990); sexually harassed (Mkhize, 1991) or physically battered (Mkhize, 1990). Another major obstacle is that "Bantu" education was not meant to produce conveyers of knowledge.

However, no matter what is the case in women's lives they should validate Ngcobo's (1990) novel, entitled, *And they didn't die*. The title of this novel is interesting and encouraging since it portrays black women as conquerors who have survived multiple destruction: from racial oppression, unequal gender relations and adultism.

Still on the question of what is known about African women, Ngcobo (1990) has reviewed some novels of African writers (Mphahlele, 1967;

Mzamane, 1980). He avers that they are heavily burdened with male values and women's images are portrayed in ways which perpetuate sexist stereotypes. Ngcobo also reviews Ndebele's (1983) novel, which she identifies as remarkable in the manner in which it portrays the positive image of an African woman through the story of the 'Prophetess'. In this story it is said that women continue to be imbued with love and care, including the mysterious prophetess herself. Women are portrayed as repositories of mystery. The Prophetess is an old woman with certain mystical, superhuman qualities. There is an atmosphere of regeneration throughout the story; in one of the passages for instance the prophetess uses the following words, "have mercy on the desert— your hearts and in your thoughts . . . fill it with your power and may it bring rebirth". As Ngcobo has done in her analysis, I would also like to acclaim the portrayed positive image of an African prayer woman as a "culture" carrier, a powerful person, a repository of what is good and a person who has a "stake in society".

The question studied in this research is, how has the positive image of a prayer woman survived an era when all that is African in nature and character has been downgraded?

To seek an answer to this question an interview with a well-known prayer woman in Soweto will be presented in full.

The method used for the study

To obtain a qualitative understanding of the strengths of a prayer woman, an interviewing case analysis method was adopted. The advantage of this approach is that the meaning of a phenomenon is negotiated by both the interviewer and the interviewee (cf. Mishler, 1986). The approach thus democratises the research process and is a form of empowerment for the participant in that it draws her into a process of knowledge building. Thus, knowledge gained is not knowledge for its own sake but is action-oriented and involves decisions about what can be done to complete the democratic process. In short, the approach was not chosen because of any theoretical sophistication but because it was deemed fitting. The investigation took place in April 1991, in Senaone, Soweto.

The Interview

The prayer woman is 56 years old and is referred to as X. R stands for the researcher.

R: Eh, what can I say, perhaps we could begin by asking you to
      say a little bit about your membership of the Zionist church in
      South Africa.

X: My life is a mystery, people do not understand but I'll tell you
      something. I have been a member of the Zionist church for many
      years. I cannot remember the exact number of years but what
      I can say is that I joined this church during my youth.

R: Can you think of things which led you to join?

X: My grandmother was an active member of the Zionist church.
      I remember when we were still young she used to conduct prayer
      meetings and I was always the first one to arrive at her hut.
      As soon as I started to beat the drum all the children would
      come running. My grandmother would at times be invited by
      people living far away from home and I would accompany her.

R: You said people used to invite your grandmother. For what
      purpose?

X: Hm! Maybe I'll be able to think of a few instances. People had
      problems and they wanted her to help then. Some wanted to
      have children; some people were troubled by different illnesses.
      I won't forget a man who was possessed by demons; he used
      to speak to himself, sometimes he would go mad and refuse even
      to sleep. Each time he started to sing and dance wildly outside,
      people got scared of him. My grandmother would put on her
      gowns and robes, sing loudly on top of her voice and in a loud
      voice curse the demons, commanding them to flee from him and
      in most instances the possessed man would gradually calm down.
      My grandmother would hold him very tight and shout on top
      of her voice instructing the demons to come out of him and
      the family would sleep. It is difficult to recall each and every
      incidence but my grandmother helped people with different
      problems. In most instances we were woken up at night.

R: Do you think those experiences had a direct influence upon your
      life?

X: It is difficult to say but, somehow, since that time my character
      was strengthened. I learned not to easily give up. I developed
      a conviction that all things are possible to women of faith. I won't
      forget an experience which I had shortly before I got married.
      We were sleeping; my grandmother was away. I heard a woman
      shouting, it was as though I was dreaming. She was persistent;
      ultimately I woke up. I heard my parents telling her that the

prophet was away. It was like something in me said, "but you have your grandmother's gift too." In no time I was up. I wrapped a blanket around my body and I forced myself into the conversation. This woman was carrying a child at her back. She could have been 8. She was breathing with great difficulty. The mother of the sick child was with two other women. To my parents' greatest surprise I first said, well we'll do what I have seen my grandmother doing. I told the woman to get inside the house, I lit seven candles, I made fire and I took my holy water which I was given by my grandmother and I instructed the child to drink it.

For the first time it was like I could penetrate through the mother of the sick child's mind. I sang a song which was my grandmother's favourite whenever she was praying for the sick. I cannot tell you exactly what happened but it was like I got into a trance-like state and I perceived things which the "patient's" mother did not tell me about. I began to tell her what I thought were vast causes of the problem; she was angry, she was not happy, her heart was dusty. As I was talking she got frightened and ultimately she cried in a hysterical manner. In the meantime the child had fallen asleep. I made it clear to her that for the child to be healed she'll have to open up and talk about whatever was her problem. She looked at these other women as though she was checking with them whether it was OK with them for her to talk about herself and to discuss family matters with a stranger. They looked down and I picked up their reluctance and I reiterated that cleansing was a prerequisite for healing.

The patient's mother threw herself on the ground and said, "a month ago I was deeply hurt during my husband's visit from Johannesburg. My mother-in-law said bad things about me and my husband believed all what she said. Since then there has been no communication between me and my mother-in-law. She is the one who serves her with food. I don't know why would our ancestors attack her like this. She couldn't suffer like this.

Let me be brief, going back to your question, I would say yes, my grandmother had a great influence on me. Can you believe that after my involvement in the healing of that child I changed my mind completely about marriage. My parents had to take back my fiancé's *labola*. When we ultimately went back to this woman's community to complete the cleaning and healing in the context of the larger community, I experienced power of some kind and it became clear that I needed space to develop my gift and marriage was not an ideal place for that growth.

R: Do you imply that women who want to heal other people should not get married?

X: Not really, it depends, but for me it became clear that I have special powers, a special gift from the God of Israel and from my ancestors. If I got married I would have had to be subordinate not only to my husband but to the whole clan. My fear was that subordination characteristic of the patriarchal social order would compel me to repress my strengths.

R: What you are saying is interesting to me because in your church I have seen both men and women and I would be interested to know whether you would say men disempower you in your dealings with them?

X: Not really, the context is different. I help people with serious life problems; men are afraid of my healing powers. Some have no respect for women but when they talk to me they show great respect. There are many reasons for this; you know some of them joined the church when they were at the verge of death and they know that I have special powers.

R: Can you tell me more about your powers?

X: It is difficult to tell another person about such powers. You know I should think I was given this power by my ancestors, God assisted them of course. If I can tell you about my dreams and my life experience you'll be surprised. You know at times something wakes me up at night to pray and I see everything. I then ask for protection and I prevent terrible things. Sometimes God reveals things to me and sometimes my ancestors communicate with me directly. For my power to survive it is important to be sensitive to the Holy Spirit and to be obedient to my ancestors.

R: If you have attended any one women's society here in Soweto, you would agree that women's struggles revolve around racial oppression of black people and also unequal relations between men and women. If you were to talk to them, what would be your advice?

X: I would congratulate them. I don't agree with an English saying that a place of a woman is in the kitchen. Because of these societies women have become public figures and as far as I am concerned that is their rightful place. Women have done great things. I don't know where to start but I can tell you in no uncertain terms that all the houses which you see here in Soweto are run by women. They are the ones who make it a point that a meal is cooked, and also that children attend school. It is a pity that in these women's societies they would never invite a person like me. They consult me privately during odd hours but it is a shame to be associated with me. Besides helping each other with groceries, they have got to improve their circumstances. They should support each other, instead of competing with each other. The future of this country is in women's hands; men have failed. Have you seen what is happening between male-headed political organizations? They hate each other as though they have nothing in common.

R: While talking about political organisations, let me ask you a specific question. Earlier on in our talk you emphasised the fact that you have powers, but can't you make use of your powers in struggles for the liberation of the oppressed black masses?

X: I really don't know, but to me and all the members of the Zionist church in the whole of Africa, the African community and the struggles of black people are not fashionable. Our formation was not political in any way. We emerged as an alternative to mainstream churches, which were not geared towards the needs of people. Again, it depends on what you understand by political struggles. You will never see us carrying placards; we are not famous but we have always been there; we do not go to the press, we do not appear in the TV, but we are there. Our focus is on the African community. I don't think there'll ever be a shift in our focus. The most exciting aspect of our gatherings is its ability to unify black people beyond the limitations of age, sex and geographical origin. You know, for instance, in my church you'll never hear of conflicts between Zulus and Xhosas. So besides my powers, for members of my church, unity is important. We love each other and we share each other's joys and sorrows.

R: I just want to get your opinion of this. As you might be aware, recently there has been a march organised by lesbians and gays which I should think raised public awareness about people's right to practise sexual orientation of their choice.

X: It all depends, but for me there is nothing really new. As I told you earlier on, I decided not to get married because I wasn't sure whether my power could survive in the face of male

domination. Almost all my life I've been very close to some of
my sisters. We love each other, we share each other's joys and
sadness, we carry each other's burdens, and a person who is close
to me wouldn't leave Soweto without telling me. I cannot explain
this but it is like people should be accountable to each other.
Even in the olden days, members of the same sex could get very
close to each other. We talk intimately like man and wife but
we do not have sexual intercourse. There are many women who
established relationships with men for security reasons like to get
a four-roomed house or a permit to be in Johannesburg. Hence
the divorce rate is so high because people did not mean anything.
You'll be surprised as the laws change and women have the right
to determine their lives there'll be less attraction towards men.
Maybe as a prayer woman I am not supposed to say this, but
have you ever thought about reasons why the African culture
promotes subordination on the part of women, not so much respect and care for each other?

R: Like which ones?

X: It is difficult to think of any right now but even some of the
sayings like *indoda yindoda* (a man is a man) Uh! ja, have you
heard elderly women saying to a battered woman, *indlovu ayisindusa
umboko wayo* (an elephant cannot be burdened by its horns)? This
is interesting, whenever this proverb is used the proverb gives
a clear message to the woman that carry your cross but maybe
we need more time because you may not understand me. I am
one person who has great respect for people's cultures; that is
how I have survived. My ancestors would not communicate things
directly to me if I was not connected to them. Even the Bible
emphasises love first on the part of the man and respect on the
part of the woman. I know it is not easy for you to understand
some of these things but I can go on and on.

R: I understand.

R: Finally, what is the future of women in this country?

X: Good. Very good. Women are strong and they stand for their
convictions. I have no doubt that women are running the country.
Look at women's societies; they are so organised. If we had to
vote for a woman to rule the country she would not have to
struggle for support because women are already organised. One
thing I need to emphasise is that women should help their children
to learn *ubuntu* (personhood). The killings that have been going

on in this country have misguided the youth, but I don't want
to get to that but what I wanted to say is that our children need
to learn what is good and bad and to unlearn the evils of the
past. I don't know whether what I am saying is clear enough.
R: It is. Thank you.

Discussion of findings

The interview between the researcher and the prayer woman clearly
shows that Independent Churches cannot be ignored in development.
On the basis of the participant's responses, these churches are an
integral part of the communities they serve. Their origin was political
in the sense that their role has always been to meet people's total
needs. Healing, for instance, has always been their major focus. It
is a shared resource which the prayer woman makes available to all
throughout the community.

An interesting observation, for the purpose of this study, is that
the African prayer woman who is often the leader within the African
Independent Church has survived in a sexist era when women have
been subjected to subordination. She commands great respect within
the African community. She is trusted as a "goddess" of wisdom and
members of the community generally have faith in her as she is the
repository of mystery. She has direct communication with her ancestors
and God.

There are obviously many lessons that women's social formations
can learn from a prayer woman. Her successes need an in-depth
analysis.

It would be unrealistic to give prescriptions for women regarding
specific lessons, but a challenge can be raised that South African women
who are in a move towards womanism should look for great teachers
within their communities. The said teachers are not international
feminists, but are our own sisters, who have successfully struggled
against the psychological subversion that places women in an inferior
position. Amnesia about the presence of women who have sustained
and maintained womanhood might be brought about by the fear of
re-living the painful experiences of being black women under the sexist,
Apartheid Government, but it is a loss.

BIBLIOGRAPHY

Barrett, J.; Dawber, A.; Klugman, B.; Obery, I.; Shindler, J. and Yawitch, J. *Vukani makhosikazi—South African women speak* (London: Catholic Institute of International Relations, 1985).

Brodsky, G. and Day, S., *Canadian Charter equality rights for women: one step forward or two steps back?* Canadian Advisory Council on the Status of Women, 1989.

Cook, G., "Telling our own stories: experiences on the path to womanism", A paper read during the conference of the Family Institute, "Black women: about and for ourselves", June 21–23, Cape Town, (In press), 1991.

Davis, A., *Women, culture and politics* (London: The Women's Press Ltd., 1990).

International Confederation of Free Trade Unions, *Working Women*, ICFTU Policy and Programming, Belgium, 1949–1991.

Kedijang, M., "Domestic violence", Unpublished paper, WITS University, 1990.

Letlaka-Rennert, K., "What is the nature of the alliance between black and white women in South Africa?" See Cook.

Letlaka-Rennert, K., "Ambivalence in Impressions", Conference on Women and Gender in Southern Africa, *Agenda* 9 (1991) pp. 22–23.

Mishler, E.G., *Research Interviewing* (Cambridge: Harvard University Press, 1986).

Mkhize, H., "Families at work—a case against women", Unpublished paper presented during a seminar on legal aspects of women abuse—FAMSA, 1990.

Mkhize, H., "'Silences' in the gender agenda: the crisis of black women in South African white farms." See Cook.

Ngcobo, L., *And they didn't die* (London: Virgo Press Ltd, 1990).

Ngcobo, L., "Images of Women in South African Black Literature". In: Worsfold, B. (ed.), *Festschrift from Lleida for Professor Boireann Macdemott* (Lleida: University of Barcelona/Virgili and Pages, 1991).

WOMEN'S MINISTRY IN INDEPENDENT CHURCHES

L. AUGUST

Abstract

This paper discusses aspects of the ministry of women in the church. The ministry is rooted in the Bible and finds expression in procreation, prophetism, counselling prayer, salvation and evangelism. The paper argues that women's full humanhood derives from the liberating love of Jesus Christ.

In the African Independent Churches women and their ministry have always been in the forefront. Women have been founders and leaders of local churches.

The paper concludes that through empowerment and development women are well equipped to challenge old and obsolete church traditions. Through their dreams and visions, faith-healing and leadership many African Independent Churches become meaningful movements.

Introduction

Before we discuss a woman in the church and her ministry, we need to know whom we are talking about.

A woman is a mother, the fountain of life and very responsible when birth or death occurs in the family or in the community into which she is born. As women, we have come a long way on the road of harassment, discrimination and humiliation. As women who now, through God's mercy, see a little spark of hope following the prayer meetings we held in praying for the struggle and the release of our leaders, let us now stand firm and prepare ourselves for the most bitter and painful part of our lives as we pray for peace and harmony in our country. As fountains of life, mothers of the nation, we should stand firm against this blatant brutality and killing of our children and innocent people. As Christians we believe that the Almighty God will answer all our prayers and set all the nations free, not only in our country but throughout the whole universe. Our courage and determination as women has encouraged us to do something about ministry in our churches.

We are always encouraged by our mothers in the Bible who have

made up the great history in the world yesterday and today. Grandmother Eve is responsible for the ministry of Pro-Creation. She is
the mother and a woman whose intelligence above Grandfather Adam
has brought us thus far. If she had not brought the knowledge of
what is good and what is bad, the world could have been lonely
and desolate. Deborah was both a prophetess and the first woman
judge in Israel (Judges 4:4). In her ministry she judged and directed
Israel. She directed Barak to take up war and because God's hand
was on her, Barak defeated his enemies and, through the hands of
a brave woman named Jael, Sisera was killed.

Hannah's ministry was a ministry of Prayer in Song (1 Sam 2:1)
"My heart rejoiceth in the Lord, mine horn is exalted in the Lord,
my mouth is enlarged over mine enemies because I rejoice in Thy
Salvation". Hannah was barren, she prayed for a son and promised
God that she would give the child to the Lord's service. Her prayers
were answered and she was blessed with a son.

The ministry of Salvation came through the Virgin Mary, who was
called by God to present His son to the nations. Christ was born
and His birth brought Salvation and forgiveness of sin to the entire
world (Luke 1:28–31).

The ministry of Evangelism was brought by the women who first
went to the Tomb: Mary Magdelene, Mary, the mother of James
and Joana. They evangelised to the disciples but because they were
women, the disciple Thomas could not believe such mystery could
come through a woman. He wanted to put his fingers in the Lord's
wounds. Nonetheless, evangelism came through women. They proclaimed the Risen Christ.

It is through the experiences of our ancestors that today women
are falling in to evangelise, to change this world and make it a peaceful
home for all God's creatures.

Women in ministry

Women lived under restricted laws, like sheep marching to the shearers
they moved; they experienced all sorts of ill-treatments at home, at
work, at government level and within their communities.

Today's women are the elite of the world, they have attended the
same universities, seminaries and theological training colleges as men.
They question the male chauvinism in the church. They ask such

questions as: are our churches in solidarity with women? do our menfolk still regard our place as in the kitchen? do they still expect us shut up in the church, as St Paul suggested in the first century? In our journey to restructure our churches, we need to minister to our menfolk in the church hierarchies that women need to be ordained and be given full powers in the church equal to men.

As women we have a full humanhood restored, we have been given powers to choose—to follow Jesus as equal parties in new ways of life and service. We are liberated in Christ; the key to liberation lies in us as Christian women in our interaction with Jesus, who challenges us to participate in the creation of a new world that will give freedom to all human creatures, both males and females, to go into the world, into Judea and Samaria, into all corners of the world and preach to all nations. Young Kim, a Korean woman minister, believes her society has suffered enough by trading away the gifts and value of its women, its silver coin. Women are advancing in ministering to Africa and Asia today.

Women's ministry in independent churches

To discuss women's ministry in Independent Churches we first must say who these Independent Churches are. The birth of the African Independent Churches was an attempt by African Christians to live their Christian faith in their own national garb, without drifting away from the universal theology. They sought to establish a Christianity of the Bible as they saw it and believed in it.

The AICs have a positive role in expressing African Christian theology through their liturgy, worship and structures. Their services are alive with warm expressions of joy as they clap hands and speak in tongues.

The progress made by the AICs in Africa is tremendous. They have no link with mainline churches; they receive no assistance from overseas. They are self-governing, self-supporting and self-propagating. They gain more strength as thousands are presented to leave the mainline churches because their needs are met in the AICs, through faith healing or spiritual examinations and diagnosis of their physical, mental and cultural ailments. They have their own educators who know the needs and policy of their churches and who now train the church leaders, minister and all church workers.

Women as founders and local leaders

In Southern Africa a number of Independent Churches were founded by women. Today, the traditional role of men over women is being challenged. Women play a very important role and they are thereby given their share and position in the hierarchy in the church. Some women are not only local leaders, they are the founders of these churches. A number of Zionist churches are led by women and these churches grow tremendously. Women are very active and dedicated to their work, which involves faith healing, a potent symbol of care attracting many who have been healed of their different diseases.

Some women from these Independent Churches take over the leadership positions of their husbands when they die. For example, a woman called Annah from a Zulu Zionist Church became the leader after the prophet founder of the church died; she led the church and acquired a tremendous influence in the church. The widow of Rev P. Mabiletsa, the prominent Zionist Church leader, Mother Mabiletsa, successfully led the church and also became a prominent figure. She gave dignity and respect to the church and cared well for the church's progress.

The influence of women in the Independent Churches is striking evidence of the rise in their status. Women have been very active in the church, even in the Mission Churches.

The influence of African women is enhanced and they respond to their duties in a way which shows that they are appreciated for the work they are doing in the church. Most of the AIC congregations are principally composed of women and girls.

The Industrial Revolution has contributed much to the emancipation of women in their move from the rural areas to big cities, where they have introduced certain activities which spring from the Christian church. The self-help activities of women in the AIC are an important feature in the social life of the African women in the cities, showing how far women have advanced in self-reliance and self-expression.

Women founders in adjacent countries influenced by one church in South Africa

From the 1940s, in Botswana, Namibia, Swaziland and Lesotho, the history of Independent Churches has been greatly influenced by the unique healer and prophetess Mother Christinah Mokotudi Nku.

Mother Nku started prophesying in 1906, at the age of twelve and a half. In 1914 she was given the name of a church which she was to name after John the Baptist. At the same time, she was told the names she was to give to her children after birth. The first would be a boy who was to be named after John the Baptist, as was the church, thus St John's Apostolic Faith Mission.

In 1930 this church came into being. It started in her two-roomed house in Prospect Township near Jeppe. Large numbers of people came for prayers and healing and there was little space to accommodate them. She was then forced to use the premises of the Apostolic Faith Mission in Mooi River, Doornfontein. She travelled widely locally and nationally, and was also attending international conferences abroad. She prayed for those who came for healing and for other forms of physical help and spiritual guidance. She became internationally known.

In 1936, she stayed with her sister, Mother Annah Moloko in Evaton, and her fame followed her there. In 1937, Prospect Township was moved to Orlando. The empty space near her house was always full of patients, who gathered there every morning and afternoon to be prayed for. The space was found to be too small and they bought plots in Evaton, leaving the Orlando house to the children. Rooms were built to accommodate patients who were coming in great numbers. A church was erected for prayers and Sunday services. In 1938, the spirit sent her to Lesotho; hundreds followed her there and joined the church. In 1945, she went to South West Africa—Namibia, where a group of Hereros became converted. In Botswana, Swaziland, Lesotho and Namibia, Mother Christinah Mokotudi Nku has built many churches in the name of the St John's Apostolic Faith Mission. There are two extraordinary churches built by Mother Christinah Nku. One in Evaton with twelve doors was prophesied in 1924, dedicated in 1953, and is called *Jerusalem*. The other is built at the farm, her resting place on the outskirts of Rustenburg. It is called the *Tabernacle* and accommodates ±30,000 people. She also erected schools to help needy children. One mission school was built by her and her husband, Archbishop Lazarus Nku, in Evaton, in 1940. Two public schools came out of this mission school, namely Mosioa Community School, named after Archbishop Mosioa Nku, and Mokotudi Higher Primary School, named after Mother Mokotudi Nku. Motlollo Primary School at the farm in Bophutatswana and a Theological Training Centre founded by her daughter, are named after her. Though Mother Nku had no secular education, her spiritual education put her in the service of the community. She bought a farm at Brits for the poor, aged

and disabled in the church. There are church bands and drum major-
ettes, church choirs and youth fellowship groups. Various secessions took
place but the work of Mother Nku continues to prosper in various ways.

*Churches that broke away from Mother Nku's church and are said to be
founded by certain women*

1. Mother Boamaruri Molotsi founded the Apostolic Faith Healing
    Church, a breakaway from Father Jacob Motswasele, who broke
    away from the St John's Apostolic Faith Mission in Botswana.
2. Mother Evelyn Kobota started St Mathews Apostolic Faith Mission,
    a breakaway from St John's Apostolic Faith Mission.
3. Mother Lebotse broke away from Mother Kobota and started
    her own church. In Namibia, Swaziland and Lesotho we also
    have women who broke away from the St John's Apostolic Faith
    Mission and started their own churches.
4. Mother Tusnet Hambundja in Namibia.
5. Mother Mantsopa junior in Lesotho.
6. Mother Msibi in Swaziland.

The influence of St John's Apostolic Faith Mission has been very strong.
The church itself is very powerful. In these three countries St John's
Apostolic Faith Mission is still powerful with a very large following.

Conclusion

In concluding this paper, I feel privileged to be able to state that
there are more women in church ministry today throughout the whole
world who are challenging the old church tradition. In Korea, we
have the Women's Church of Korea with Young Kim as its first pastor.
In South Africa, women are defining their role and position in society.
Today's women speak about Empowerment and Development. In the
Independent Churches, women prophets are increasing their dreams
and visions; faith healing plays a very important part and they contribute
to making the Independent Churches a real force in this country.

BIBLIOGRAPHY

Lagerwerf, L., *They pray for you: Independent Churches and women in Botswana*
    (Leiden-Utrecht: Interuniversitair Instituut voor Missiologie en Oecumenica).
Mother Christinah Nku, unpublished biography manuscripts.
Sundkler, B.G.M., *Bantu Prophets in South Africa* (Oxford: Oxford University
    Press, 1961²).

THE ROLE OF WOMEN IN THE LEADERSHIP OF THE CHURCHES IN SWAZILAND

R.J. CAZZIOL

Abstract

This paper inquires into the reasons why women are often excluded from senior positions in the church. It also seeks to establish the extent to which international trends regarding the development of women's leadership in the church, have had an impact in Swaziland.

For the background to the development of the leadership of women in the church the paper draws from the Old Testament and the New Testament. The paper argues that in both the Hebrew society of the Old Testament and the offices of the primitive church in the New Testament there was male dominance. It is noted that these traditions persist in the contemporary churches, especially in those with a strong sacramental tradition. This practice was challenged by recent developments which gave impetus to feminist theology. For the purpose of this paper the writer's research methodology consisted of questionnaires and interviews. The paper concludes that in Swaziland the Church of the Nazarene and the National Baptist Church are the only two denominations where women are on a par with their male counterparts. In most indigenous churches women are excluded from the major positions of leadership.

Introduction

The last decade of this century has been widely publicised by the international community as the decade of women development. In recent years there has been considerable interest on the part of United Nations' organisations (e.g. UNESCO, WHO, FAO, and the World Bank) in investigating the role of women in the development of Third World countries.

In Africa, women have been prominent in agriculture, marketing, education, social work, and a lesser extent, science and medicine. Yet in most African countries decision-making remains firmly in the hands of men. Although women have occasionally occupied ministerial posts in Namibia, Sierra Leone, Botswana and Swaziland, politics in Africa is a male realm. Heads of State and Prime Ministers have consistently been made and even when a woman, like Queen Regent of Swaziland, has temporarily acted as head of state, her powers have been severely curtailed by tradition and by an entourage of male counsellors.

The Church is another institution where African women have not been able to exercise authority at the highest echelons. There have been charismatic women, like Lucy Mofokeng of the Holy Mission Church and Mama C. Nku of the St John's Apostolic Mission in South Africa, who have established their own churches—but they are notable exceptions, even within the Independent African churches.

Even fewer are African women from the former mission churches who have achieved international prominence, although one could mention Brigalia Bam of the YWCA in South Africa, Chief Justice Annie Jiagge of the Presbyterian Church of Ghana and Rena Karefa Smart of Sierra Leone, who was associate-secretary of the Inter-church Aid Division of the World Council of Churches.

Nevertheless, even in Europe and North America, women have been prevented until recently from holding positions of leadership in the church. The following section of this study gives an historical background to this problem.

Swaziland is still a male-dominated society where, until recently, married women were not allowed to hold property and could not acquire a passport without the husband's consent. Nevertheless, education has been responsible for a more enlightened attitude towards women, and today we have women medical doctors, magistrates, senior police officers, senior civil servants and university professors. Yet, leadership in the churches continues to be the prerogative of men, and women are only allowed to hold offices within women's church organisations (e.g. Mothers Union, Women Missionary Society) or to perform administrative duties under the supervision of a pastor or a priest.

The aim of this study is to find out why women are still excluded from senior positions in the church and to see if the new international trend which promotes the leadership of women in the church is becoming more acceptable in Swaziland.

Historical background

Although in all religions women have been assigned some specific duties, leadership has remained a prerogative of men. This is true not only of Christianity but also of the other major world religions (e.g. Islam, Judaism, Hinduism, Buddhism) where the priesthood, the highest role in the religious community, has been reserved for men.

In the case of Christianity, the absence of a sacerdotal role for women has often been attributed to the influence of Judaism as portrayed in the Old Testament. Yet, while partiarchalism is clearly the dominant orientation in the Old Testament, the masculine images of God are set forth as anthropomorphisms. Unlike the deities of the ancient Near East, the God of the Old Testament is a spirit and not to be depicted as either male or female. In fact, feminine imagery, though not common, is also used to describe Yahweh. He is described as a nursing mother (*Isa.* 49:15), a midwife (*Ps.* 22:9–10), a female homemaker (*Ps.* 123:2) and helpmate to humankind, as Eve was to Adam (*Ex.* 18:4; *Deut.* 33:26; *Ps.* 121:1–2).

Notwithstanding the male dominance in Hebrew society, women were not barred from holding the office of prophets (*2 Kgs.* 22:14), judges (*Judg.* 4:4) and even rulers (*2 Kgs.* 11:3), but unlike other contemporary religions in the ancient Near East, Judaism had no priestesses. According to Conn (*NDT* 1988 : 256), this was to avoid the dangers of fertility cults and sacred prostitution practised by the neighbouring Canaanites.

In the New Testament, all the offices in the primitive church such as apostles, prophets, evangelists, pastors and teacher (*Eph.* 4:8–11) are in the masculine gender, although Phoebe is mentioned as a minister of the congregation in Cenchreae (*Rom.* 16:1). She is referred to with the masculine *diakonos* (deacon) rather than the feminine *diakonissa* (deaconess). The apostle Paul, while allowing women to teach children and younger women with the congregation (*Tit.* 2:3–5), prohibited them from speaking in public meetings (*1 Cor.* 14:23–25, 31–35; *1 Tim.* 2:11–15). This prohibition was probably aimed at preventing the spread of some forms of Gnosticism which spoke of women as being intermediaries between God and man and gave to Eve a prior existence in which she consorted with celestial beings.

Nevertheless, Paul states also that in a spiritual sense there is no distinction between men and women (*Gal.* 3:26–28) and that their respective roles in the church are complementary rather than one gender dominating the other. Accusations of misogyny by Paul are not well substantiated because women appear to have been his staunchest supporters in the churches he established in Greece and Macedonia.

The same cannot be said for the early Fathers of the church, who either ignored women altogether or regarded them as inferior to men. Byrne in her book *Women before God* (1988 : 5) mentioned some of the vituperative views held by the Church Fathers:

> ... Women! You are the Devil's doorway; you have led astray one who the Devil would not dare attack directly. It is your fault that Son of God had to die; you should go in mourning and rags (Tertullian).
> ... Among all the savage beasts none is found so harmful as woman (John Chrysostom).
> ... Woman is a sick she-ass ... a hideous tapeworm ... the advance post of hell (John Damascene).
> ... Woman is an occasional and incomplete being, a misbegotten male. It is unchangeable that woman is destined to live under man's influence and has no authority from the Lord ... The image of God is found in the man, not the woman, for man is the beginning and end of woman (Thomas Aquinas).

While these views may not represent the official position of the church towards women during the patristic period, it appears that the leadership role of women in the church was doomed at an early stage.

The introduction of a hierarchy in the priesthood led to the virtual disappearance of a leadership role for the laity and the entrenched dominance by the clergy. The diaconate was no longer a prerogative of the laity and soon became the initial step into the clergy. Men and women who wanted to play a role in the life of the church had to join either a monastery or a convent. In the process, a separation of the sexes was introduced into monasticism, with men or women performing certain duties as required by the order to which they belonged.

As Bertolucci (1987 : 34) points out, the only role left to laity in the (Roman Catholic) church was bell ringing for men and the selling of candles for women. Even the role of sacristan, once performed by laymen, was taken over by lowly paid labourers supervised by the priest.

It was during the Reformation that the laity, both men and women, regained a leadership status in the church. Following Calvin's teachings on the priesthood of all believers, the government of Presbyterians and Reformed churches was taken over by laymen (presbyters), reducing the role of the pastor or predikant to that of preaching and of administering the sacraments. Yet, women were again excluded as all the presbyters were men. Some churches, like the Lutherans, had deaconesses but their duties were limited to teaching doctrine to children and to nursing the sick.

In 1667, the tract *Women's Speaking Justified by the Scriptures,* written by Margaret Fell, wife of George Fox, the founder of the Society of Friends (Quakers), proclaimed, on the basis of biblical hermeneutics, that women were equal to men in the leadership of the church. The Quakers were, in fact, the only denomination in which women enjoyed complete equality with men. Taking this position was relatively easy for the Quakers, who had neither priests nor sacraments. The purely administration position of secretary of the Quaker Meeting was open to both men and women.

It is interesting to note that opposition to the ordination of women to the priesthood is strongest in the church with a strong sacramental tradition (cf. Roman Catholic, Anglican, Orthodox), where the administration of the Eucharist is reserved for the male priest who is acting *in loco Christi.*

This is evidenced by the fact that women have been ordained with relatively little opposition in those denominations (e.g. Baptist, Methodist) where the Communion service is merely a commemoration of the Last Supper, rather than a sacrifice with the transubstantiation of the elements as found in the Eucharist.

Towards the end of the last century, the equality of rights demanded by the suffragist movements was felt in some churches. Charismatic leaders, such as Mary Eddy Baker, Ellen G. White and Aimee McPherson, founded respectively the Christian Science Church, the Seventh-Day Adventist and the Four-Square Pentecostal Church. They were the leaders of these sects in their lifetime, yet those who succeeded them in the leadership were all men.

It is only in recent years that women have begun to realise that although they have been accepted as equal to men in politics, the judiciary and the academic world, they are still playing a subservient role in the leadership of the churches. A milestone in the evolution of church leadership for women was the establishment by the World Council of Churches of the Commission on the Life and Work of Women in the Church (1949). Through a variety of consultations, conferences and programmes the WCC has played a vital role in more recent developments, leading to the formulation of feminist theology and an increased status for women in the work of the church. A record of the struggles by women for recognition by the WCC is well documented in S. Herzel, *A Voice for Women* (1981).

Contemporary feminist theology

The rise of the women's liberation movement from the mid-twentieth century helped to create a feminist critical consciousness which inevitably questioned the status of women within the church. Although women in some denominations constitute as much as 80% of active membership, and contribute a substantial share of the church finances, their leadership role is often minimal.

This has called for a new investigation into the traditional roles of men and women in decision-making within the churches. Hermeneutical questions have been raised by both male and female theologians. How do we interpret what is seen as the male orientation of the Bible? Books with such titles as Bloesch's *Is the Bible Sexist?* (1982), Fiorenza's *The Will to Choose or to Reject* (1983), Spencer's *Beyond the Curse* (1985) and Russel's *Feminist Interpretation of the Bible* (1985) have challenged the clergy and the laity alike. Feminist theology has recently become an increasingly significant feature of contemporary theology.

Questions such as "How do we interpret what is seen as the male orientation of the Bible?" and "Can we interpret the Bible from a feminist standpoint?" or "Is gender equality possible in church leadership?" have been tackled and have produced contrasting views. According to Cann (*NDT* 1988:255) three trends have emerged as models of hermeneutical interpretation:

(1)   the *rejectionist* view that sees the Bible as promoting an oppressive patriarchal structure and rejects the whole Judaeo-Christian tradition as hopelessly male-oriented. The most radical wing of this approach is attracted to a nature mysticism, based exclusively on women's consciousness, or to esoteric cults which are female-oriented.

(2)   the *loyalist* view that upholds the whole testimony of the Bible and justifies the alleged sexism of the Bible as being consonant with the customs and mores of the times in which the Bible was written. One group within this model accepts submission by women in the leadership of the church. Women leaders in the Russian Orthodox Church, for instance, do not feel the need to protest about the matter of ordination. For them, male priesthood is not a problem and they see the priest as representing Christ quite specifically (Herzel 1981:90). Another group argues that the full

biblical data call for egalitarianism and mutual submission, with ordination for both men and women. Women leaders in the Protestant denominations who ordain pastors (e.g. United Methodist Church, United church of Canada) adhere to such a view.

(3) the *reformist* (or liberation) model shares with the rejectionists the view of alleged patriarchal chauvinism in the Bible and Christian history, but wants to overcome it. The most radical wing goes to the extent of re-writing the Bible with a feminist bias (e.g. "Our Mother (Father) who is in Heaven, hallowed be thy name . . .") Chung Hyun-Kyung, a woman Presbyterian theologian from South Korea, for instance, caused a heated debate at the recent Canberra meeting of the World Council of Churches (WCC) by claiming that the Holy Spirit was female. The reformists want nothing less than equality between male and female members of the church and strive for a just society free from any kind of social, economic or sexist oppression.

There is no doubt that feminist theology will go a long way to redress the injustices of the past when women were denied a leadership role in the church. On the other hand, the excessive demands and dubious claims raised by the more radical women theologians may alienate the many people who sympathise with what is unquestionably a just cause.

Methodology used in the research

The methodology used for this research consisted of a questionnaire, which was sent to 32 churches, and interviews with ten men and women, who are either church leaders or prominent members of their churches. Since confidentiality was assured both in the questionnaires and in the interviews, names of individuals were omitted and they will be referred to as for example, Rev X., or Mrs M. The names of the churches were identified in the questionnaire.

The questionnaire (Appendix I) and the list of churches (Appendix II) are found at the end of this paper. Only nineteen out of thirty two churches returned the questionnaire and none of the nineteen respondents answered all the ten questions. The response to the questionnaire (60%) was disappointing but those who answered represented the major denominations in the country. The interviews were more satisfactory as the respondents were quite frank in expressing their views. The analysis of the questionnaires responses was based on the responses given to each of the ten questions. The analysis of the interviews was based on the response of each individual.

Analysis of the questionnaire

The response to each question was analysed as follows:

Question 1:   Eleven respondents answered "No" implying that women cannot be ordained as either priest/pastor or evangelist. The latter position was interpreted in different ways as in some churches an evangelist is not ordained to the priesthood. Four churches indicated that they have women evangelists who are not ordained. Two churches indicated that they have women who are theologically trained and are acting as pastors but are not ordained. Only two churches indicated that they obtain both men and women to be pastors, provided they have been trained for the position.

Question 2:   Fifteen respondents answered that women are allowed to occupy minor positions within the structure of their churches (e.g. church treasurer, lay preacher, *manyano* leader, prayer-group leader, church secretary, Sunday School teacher, Mothers' Union leader), either as laypersons or members of a religious order for women (e.g. sisterhood, deaconesses). In all these positions women are elected by the congregation or by a church organization. Some are appointed by a bishop or by an overseer. None of them are ordained, hence they are not allowed to preside over sacramental rituals (e.g. communion, weddings, funerals). Two respondents indicated that women are allowed to occupy any position in the hierarchy of their churches, including that of General Superintendent or Church Moderator, which are elective posts. One respondent indicated that the only two positions accessible to women are those of leader of the *manyano* and leader of the Wednesday prayer meeting. One respondent indicated that the leadership within an exclusively women's group has specific duties (e.g. caretakers of the church building).

Question 3:   Only sixteen respondents answered this question. The highest positions mentioned are the following: Pastor, Evangelist, Church Warden, Deaconess, Lay Minister, Administrative Secretary for the denomination, Chair of the Women's Federation, District Sunday School Director, Church Treasurer.

Question 4: Only ten respondents answered this question, six in the negative and four in the affirmative. As nearly half of the respondents did not answer, it is evident that the question is rather controversial. Among the negative responses, comments such as "no longer in practice", "applicable only in the past", "some biblical injunctions were only valid within that period", were quoted. Among the affirmative responses, the comments varied from "definitely so" to "the instructions of Bible are for ever", "the Bible is the same yesterday, today and tomorrow", "the church's structure need not change because of social pressure".

Question 5: Only eight respondents answered this question. The other questionnaires were left blank or N/A was placed in the allocated space. Comments by the respondents ranged from "I am not" and "I do not think there are any" to "we only believe what is in the Bible" and "there is no other reason except the verses quoted in the Bible". There was no indication that either Swazi traditions or the attitude of Swazi men towards women could be a factor limiting the leadership role of women in the church.

Question 6: Ten respondents answered this question. Seven of them felt that the cultural context in biblical times restricted women from occupying a leadership role in the church. One respondent felt that since men and women are equal in the sight of God this equality should extend to leadership roles in the church. Another felt that as women emancipate themselves the church cannot restrict them to a submissive role. The remaining respondent felt that, although the New Testament is not specific about what roles women should have in the church, there is mention of women such as Lydia and Phoebe (*Acts* 16, *Rom.* 16) who apparently were leaders in their respective churches.

Question 7: Fifteen respondents answered this question. Five felt that in their churches men do not resent women in positions of leadership. Nevertheless, the pastor or priest should still be a man. One suggested that as men are head of the family, they should also be the leaders of the church which is a family of believers. Three respondents felt that the Bible does not recognise religious leadership for women either in the Old Testament or in the New Testament. One respondent stressed that Jesus selected twelve men as disciples, despite the fact that several women were among His followers. Three other respondents felt that so far there has been no rivalry for leadership between men and women in their churches. One felt that as the King and Queen Mother jointly rule the country, the same should apply to the church. One quoted *Matt.* 28:18–20 and suggested that all church members must obey the Great Commission, irrespective of gender.

Question 8:   Twelve responses. Eight respondents agreed that men are predominant in the leadership of the church, yet they felt that was the pattern in all the other areas of social life. One suggested that in fact some churches have given comparatively more leadership responsibilities to women than either the civil service or the Swazi private sector. Another respondent felt that only in the teaching service do women occupy more positions of leadership than in the churches. One respondent felt that the church has it own values and rules and should be guided by what goes on in the outside world, rather than by theological or cultural reasons which may prevent women from becoming top leaders in their churches.

Question 9:   Fourteen responses. Three felt that present social changes are not necessarily for the better, hence the churches should not imitate what goes on in the outside world. One felt that any change that is not biblically sanctioned should not be adopted by the church. Another felt that the issue of women's leadership may cause severe division within the church, as has happened in England and the USA. One felt strongly that changes like that of women's priesthood will destroy the church and hasten the coming of the Anti-Christ. Nevertheless, a majority of nine respondents agreed, for different reasons, that, as with any other institution, the church is inevitably undergoing changes.

Question 10:   Only three respondents. One stressed that when God created Adam and Eve, he gave dominion to the man and Eve became his help-mate and not his equal. The second felt that the church has her own rules and traditions and does not need to change them because of social pressure. The third wished for the research to go beyond the issue of men vs women leadership and to find their sincere and true position in Christ.

Analysis of the interviews

Ten persons were interviewed, eight Swazi nationals and two foreigners. Five were male church leaders, three were women who are active church members and two were women church leaders.

1. Bishop X. claimed that in his church women occupy important positions as lay leaders but cannot be ordained as priests. Although personally he has no objection to women priests, he felt that most lay members, both men and women, and the older clergy do not favour the ordination of women. This opposition appears to be based more on church traditions or Swazi customs than biblical injunctions.

2. Bishop K. is the leader of an indigenous church which limits the involvement of women to minor positions of leadership. Personally he would like women, particularly those with some education, to be involved with responsibilities higher than manyano leader or congregational treasurer. After all, he observed, women represent about 80% of his church's membership. Nevertheless, he felt that both Swazi traditions and biblical injunctions preclude women from higher positions of leadership.

3. Rev Y. is an American missionary who has been in Swaziland for many years. His church in the USA ordains both men and women, provided they have successfully completed the ministerial course of study prescribed by the church's manual. Since the regulations in the manual apply also to the Swaziland branch of the church, there would be no problem with having women pastors. Nevertheless, so far, no Swazi women have been interested in the pastorate and the only two women pastors in Swaziland have been American missionaries.

4. Rev M. is a leader in a church originally established by Scandinavian missionaries. He firmly believes that although women have many important roles to play in the church, including lay-preaching, the headship of a congregation should be exclusively for men. This is in accordance with both the Bible and Swazi traditions, which accept only men as heads of the family.

5. Father W. reiterated the position of his church, which does not allow the ordination of women because it is contrary to ecclesiastical tradition. Women have important roles to play, nevertheless, as lay-persons or as members of a religious order. He pointed out that those churches which have accepted the ordination of women have experienced deep divisions and the loss of many members. He quoted the example of the Episcopal Church in the USA which has lost 1,500,000 members (about half of the total membership) since it began ordaining women ten years ago. Most of those who left have joined the Roman Catholic Church, thus confirming that the ordination of women leads to defection.

He also felt that the church should not oblige those who clamour for change because of social pressure or modern social trends.

6. Rev T. is a female missionary from the USA. Her church began to ordain women ministers only five years ago and she was among the first to be ordained. Her arrival in Swaziland as pastor of the largest church of the denomination caused quite a stir. Members of the congregation, both men and women, did not expect a female pastor and the men in particular resented it. Nevertheless, they have finally accepted what they regard as an anomaly.

7. Mrs P. has been occupying an important position in the Council of Churches and she is a prominent member of her church. While in theory she accepts the fact that women should be ordained, she sees a number of problems which prevent Swazi women from becoming priests and pastors. The priesthood, she claims, is demanding and requires undivided attention. It is not like working in an office from 8.30 am to 4.30 pm. Only an unmarried woman could be a successful priest. Without a husband and children she could give her undivided attention to pastoral duties. In Swazi society, where unmarried women are looked at askance, an unmarried woman priest would have a considerable problem in being accepted. This may not apply to foreign women as they are perceived as having quite different customs.

8. Miss R. is a leader in the women's organisation of her church. She graduated in the United States and is self-employed. She feels that, since women are accepted as lawyers, medical doctors and university lecturers, there is no reason why they should be excluded from being church ministers. Nevertheless, she admitted that there are social, cultural and financial reasons preventing a woman from becoming a priest or a pastor.

9. Mrs Z. is a teacher, married to a teacher, and she is a prominent church member. She is the secretary-treasurer of her congregation and has represented the women of her church in conferences outside Swaziland. She believes that women have many important roles to play in the leadership of the church. Nevertheless, she feels that the priest/pastor should be a man. In addition to what the Bible may say about a male priesthood, she feels that women have many limitations. She recalls, when attending a conference in Zambia, how worried she was about her children at home and the ineptitude of her husband in looking after them. Swazi

men, she rejoins, do not share domestic chores or responsibilities, as do men in America or Europe. They expect to be served by the wife, even if she has a full-time job. A Swazi man would not accept playing a secondary role to the wife, thus causing a situation which would force the wife to resign from the ministry. A Swazi unmarried woman serving as an ordained minister is, she felt, quite unacceptable.

10. Mrs. F. is a widow with grown-up sons and daughters. She has a pension and her children help her financially. She spends most of her time working for her church and a "Zenzele" club of which she is the chairperson. She is involved in the social work of the church, visitation of sick members, etc. She firmly believes that the *umfundisi* should be a man, and cannot envisage a congregation headed by a female minister. She felt that "it is not right for a woman to talk in the church. Women should be good mothers and good wives and that is quite enough for them to cope with". Mrs F felt that only older women as herself, with plenty of time on her hands, should be helping in the various activities of the church.

Conclusion

The analysis of the 10 questionnaires and the 10 interviews revealed that:

1. Women occupy important positions of responsibility in most churches but are still excluded from the priesthood/ministry. The ratio of women vs. men in the leadership of the churches compares favourably with similar positions in teaching, the civil service and the judiciary. The widely held notion that the churches lag behind in recognising women for leadership is quite unsubstantiated.

2. With two exceptions, women are excluded from the priesthood/ministry. Although some church leaders are personally sympathetic towards the ordination of women, they recognise a formidable opposition from both the clergy and the lay members of their churches. Those church leaders who rejected the leadership of women in the church on biblical grounds were a small minority.

3. Opposition to the ordination of women is not exclusively a male attitude. Many women oppose it as well, quite often for entirely different reasons. Reasons given for this opposition, in order of importance, are the following:

a) Swazi culture, which is male-dominated and rejects the concept of women as head of family, household, chiefdom etc. This is despite the fact that women are often the breadwinners in the family.

b) Biblical injunctions such as *1 Cor* 14:34–35 and *1 Tim* 2:11–13, which restrict the roles of women in the church.

c) Socio-economic reasons, which prevent women from joining the full-time church ministry (e.g. objections of husband, raising children, low salaries, traditional taboos affecting women).

d) Church traditions, which prevent the adoption of a more liberal view on the equality of men and women.

In conclusion, it appears that the church of the Nazarene and the National Baptist Church are the only two dominations which accept ordained female ministers on a par with their male counterparts. It is obvious that this attitude is due to the influence exercised by the "mother church" in the USA upon their missionary branches in Swaziland.

As a whole, the Protestant denominations (e.g. Anglican, Methodists) seem more sympathetic towards the ordination of women. The United Church of Zambia (UCZ), an amalgam of Protestant churches, has ordained women since 1973. The many objections raised by the respondents did not seem to have deterred Zambian women from joining the ministry. This may be due to the fact that many tribes in Zambia are "matrilineal" and women have traditionally enjoyed rights which were unheard of among the "patrilineal" Nguni tribes (e.g. Zulu, Swazi, Xhosa).

The indigenous churches (e.g. Zionists, Apostolic) exclude women from major positions of leadership and their leaders are more likely to give a literal interpretation to the biblical injunctions restricting the roles of women in the church.

The Roman Catholic Church, citing ancient church traditions, sees the roles of women as being enhanced within nubile monastic orders serving the entire community (e.g. teaching, nursing). Married women seem to be relegated to domestic roles. Such a position was made clear by Cardinal Gibbons of Baltimore, an early opponent of women's emancipation:

> ... When I deprecate female suffrage I am pleading for the dignity of women. I am contending for her honour, I am striving to perpetuate

those peerless prerogatives inherent in her sex, those charms and graces which exalt womanhood and make her the ornament and coveted companion of man. Woman is queen indeed, but her empire is the domestic kingdom.

This view, expressed in less lyrical terms, appears to be held by a majority of men and women in Swaziland. So long as it holds way and women are relegated to the "domestic kingdom", it is unlikely that they will take over major leadership roles, either in the church or elsewhere.

APPENDIX I
QUESTIONNAIRE ON THE ROLE OF WOMEN IN THE LEADERSHIP OF THE CHURCHES

Kindly return this questionnaire in the stamped envelope and address it to:
Dr Roger J. Cazziol
Dean, Education
University of Swaziland
P/B Kwaluseni, Swaziland

We would greatly appreciate whatever information you can provide. Avoid, if at all possible, the answers "YES" or "NO" which are of very little use in a questionnaire of this type.

1. Does your church allow women to occupy positions of leadership, either as priest/pastor/evangelist, which require official ordination? Please give details.
2. If your answer to question (1) above is in the negative, does your church allow women to occupy minor leadership roles (e.g. Prayer Leader, deaconess, chairperson of a committee, treasurer)? Kindly elaborate.
3. What is at the moment the highest position of leadership in your church which is occupied by a women?
4. Does your church regard *1 Cor.* 14:34–35 and *1 Tim.* 2:11–13 as biblical injunctions which limit the leadership roles of women in the church?
5. If you are in agreement with the injunctions in question (4), are there any other reasons, not specifically mentioned in the Bible, which limit the leadership roles for women in the church? Please explain.
6. If you are not in agreement with the injunctions in question (4), could you suggest reasons for which women should not be restricted to occupy certain roles of leadership in the church? Is there any quotation in the Bible that supports or justifies leadership roles for women in the church?
7. In the context of the church in Swaziland, it has been alleged that males in the church resent or object to giving women positions of leadership, because it is contrary to Swazi traditions which give to men a dominant role in society. Do men in your church subscribe to this belief?
8. It has been suggested in some quarters that women in Swaziland have

been able to achieve leadership roles in all areas of social life except in the churches. Would you agree with this suggestion?

9. Assuming that you agree with the suggestion in question (8) above, do you think that this attitude is going to change in the near future? Is there any evidence that a change of attitude is already in progress?

10. Is there anything else you would like to mention on this issue of women's leadership in the church which has not been taken care of by the previous questions in this questionnaire?

THANKS FOR YOUR KIND COOPERATION

Signed: _____ Name _____

Church/Affiliation: _____

NOTE: This information remains confidential and will not be revealed, but if you wish to remain completely anonymous, you need only mention the name of your church and you need not reveal your own name.

APPENDIX II
LIST OF CHURCHES

N.B.: The asterisk which churches returned the questionnaire.
1. African Evangelical Church *
2. African Gospel Church
3. African Methodist Episcopal Church (AMEC) *
4. Alliance Church *
5. Apostolic Faith Mission Church
6. Anglican Church *
7. Assemblies of God *
8. Christian Apostolic Holy Spirit Church in Zion
9. Church of the Nazarene *
10. Entokozweni Church of God
11. Evangelical Bible Church *
12. Evangelical Disciples Church
13. Free Evangelical Assemblies *
14. Independent Methodist Church *
15. Jericho Zion Church
16. Jehovah Witness Assembly
17. Lutheran Evangelical Church *
18. Methodist Church (SA) *
19. National Baptist Church *
20. Nazareth Zionist Church
21. New Apostolic Church
22. Old Apostolic Church
23. Pentecostal Assemblies of Africa
24. Roman Catholic Church *
25. Swedish Evangelical Church
26. Seventh Day Adventist Church *
27. St Enegena Zion Christian Church *
28. St John Apostolic Church *

29. Swazi Christian Church in Zion
30. United Pentecostal Church *
31. Wesleyan Emmanuel Church *
32. Zion Christian Church (ZCC) *

BIBLIOGRAPHY

Bacchiocchi, S., *Women in the Church* (Philadelphia: Trinity Press, 1987).
Bertolucci, A., *Lay Leadership in the Catholic Church* (New York: Orbis Press 1987).
Bloesch, D.G., *Is the Bible Sexist?* (Westchester: Crossway Books, 1982).
Byrne, L., *Women Before God* (London: S.P.C.K., 1990).
Herzel, S., *A Voice for Women* (Geneva: W.C.C. Press, 1981).
Hurley, J.B., *Men and Women in Biblical Perspective* (Grand Rapids: Zondervan, 1982).
Spencer, A.B., *Beyond the Curse: Women called to the Ministry* (Nashville: Nelson, 1985).
Zerbst, F., *The Office of Women in the Church* (St Louis: Concordia Press, 1955).
New Dictionary of Theology (Leicester: IVP, 1988).

SECTION E

PERSONAL AND SOCIAL TRANSFORMATION

THE SOUTH AFRICAN NEW AGE MOVEMENT AND THE AFRICAN INDIGENOUS CHURCH MOVEMENT—A COMPARISON

G.C. OOSTHUIZEN

Abstract

This article gives an overview of the origin and activities of the New Age Movement in South Africa. The comparative study mainly dwells on the *prima facie* similarities between the New Age Movement and the African Independent Churches. Similarities are found in their structures, house fellowships, reaction against empirical Christianity, forms and symbols of religious expression, their idea of the existence of a universal energy, and an emphasis on prophecy and healing. An assessment is made of the possible future of the New Age Movement in South Africa and the possible involvement of blacks in this movement, but also in the African Independent Churches.

Introduction

It took two aluminium poles, planted by the Movement for Peace through Prayer (which originated in Japan after World War II) to bring the New Age Movement to the attention of South Africans in general. One pole was planted in Cape Town on November 11, 1989 (Armistice Day) and the other on Table Mountain, behind Cape Town, on November 12, 1989 (Remembrance Day). Some were shocked that such "foreign" religious activities were carried out in this country—and in Cape Town, as well as on their most prominent mountain, of all places. Had the Cape of Good Hope become a symbol of foreign religious invasions? Had the Mayor of Cape Town with affinities to Sufism and the New Age Movement, become a traitor of all that is dear to so many conservative Christians? The Mayor of Cape Town, Gordon Oliver, made no excuses for his participation in the planting and consecration of these poles. On the contrary, he emphasised: "There are many paths to the same source. My role as Mayor is one of bridge-building with love" (*Cross Times*, January 1990). He himself goes to Jewish synagogues and takes part in Buddhist meditation sessions.

The Mayor further stated: "I am a Christian but not an orthodox one." He added: "I feel at home in any form of religion and support the idea of one world religion and one God" (*Die Burger*, November 15, 1989). He criticised Christians for being intolerant; stating that they need not accept the religious views of others, but could pray for peace with them. This was said at a time when the country was in deep turmoil especially within the black townships. He noted that it was the New Age Movement which had organised the activation of the "Energy Centre" but he did not wish to be described as a member of the Movement.

Table Mountain had special significance for General J.C. Smuts and his book entitled *Holism and Evolution* published in 1926 receives special attention from the New Agers in South Africa because of their holistic approach. Through the years, this book has not received the attention it deserves but the man who received inspiration from his regular walks and climbs in the mountains has been embraced by the New Age Movement in this country. His approach tried to overcome the Newtonian mechanistic concept of nature i.e. that all events in nature are merely physically-chemically directed. Smuts emphasised that an "inner energy", a *vis vitalis,* exists in matter; there is a theological factor which governs the material processes. In his *God in Process* (London: SCM, 1967, p. 97), Norman Pettinger states the following: "If one were looking for an ancestry to American process thought one would find it in the Philosophers of emergent evolution in the first three decades of this Century: in the work of such writers as C. Lloyd-Morgan, Samuel Alexander and Jan Smuts. The basic categories of process theology with its emphasis on event, becoming and relatedness, reject those of "substance" and "being". Reality is in process and, apart from the other characteristics of process thought the process approach has adopted some form of panpsychism. God has been brought "in" everything. Everything is seen as being "in" God. Smuts had difficulties with the Judaeo-Christian concept of the Divine. He preferred the concept of dynamic energy active in matter, rather than one of a mechanistic disposition. What was done on Table Mountain in November 1989 has affinity with his ideas. Holism and evolution have thus become important reference material in this context.

The two aluminium poles planted in Cape Town and on Table Mountain, carried the words "May Peace Prevail on Earth". It was an independent action of the Movement for World Peace through Prayer. At the same time, New Agers decided to "positively activate the negative energy" on Table Mountain through meditation, prayer and consultation of the astrological calender, which would bring a spirit of peace, love, friendship and harmony to Cape Town. An ecological act was also performed in the clearing away of litter. Songs were sung such as *Nkosi sikelela i Africa* (God Bless Africa)—an "anthem" (for blacks) which originated in South Africa and is translated and sung in many countries in Africa and further afield. It is a prayer directed to God, asking that Africa and its people be blessed. Whites often interpret this beautiful song as a kind of "War Cry". The songs on Table Mountain at the abovementioned ceremony were sung to the accompaniment of Buddhist gongs.

Very few were conscious of the fact that the New Age Movement had entered South Africa. Several incidents were reported of strong reactions by fundamentalist Christians, who chopped down the poles and accused New Agers of having imbibed the Spirit of Satan, a kind of satanic conspiracy. Most people are not even aware of the New Age Movement. Some Christians who have been in contact with it condemn it, while others are more careful. Everything is put under a magnifying glass, especially the symbols, such as the rainbow, pyramid, unicorn and star.

It is impossible to describe here every aspect of this fast growing "movement" in South Africa. There are differences between the various "communities" and between individuals, but certain specific attitudes prevail. It is described by some as an attitude to life; by others as a therapy. It emphasises love and peace, is strongly opposed to drugs; its music is described as creating a mood around the listener; its holistic approach to health and the treatment of the whole person is attractive to an increasing number of people.

The New Age Activities in South Africa

Many aspects of what is designated as "New Age" hail from ancient philosophies and religions, so that its title is actually a misnomer. One can hardly call it a "movement" in South Africa, as there is a large variety of attitudes towards the spiritual, physical, mental and emotional aspects of humankind and to the environment. Equally, so many activities are in progress—some groups acting in isolation from others. There is no unity, and yet there exists an understanding among most

of the groups that they are, in a sense, congenial spirits reacting against
the staleness of their churches, against the superficialities of the modern
society—and that they wish to live from the depth dimension of the
metaphysical world and be fully part of the cosmos. There are the
ingredients of a movement. In fact, the extent of its "mushrooming"
in South Africa during the last five years, especially in the cities, means
that it cannot be ignored.

Odyssey is the major magazine (bi-monthly) of the New Age Movement
(NAM) in this country. It was first published in 1977 and maintains
a high standard of presentation and content. In the first issue after
the aluminium pole incident, the editor states that it is "an adventure
into more conscious living and offering", and adds that it is an
"inspiration for creative, ethical and responsible life styles, a synthesis
of alternative realities, and a reverence for all life" (*Odyssey*, Feb/Mar
1990). Rose de la Hunt, the editor, emphasises further that the "new
age is not new age: it is a new consciousness." The new directions
in science, religion, etc., reject the term new age, "although their work
with all its creative power to bring a new world into being, is exactly
what is meant by new age. Those who do their work quietly refuse
the name 'new age'. They do not see themselves as the vanguards
of God and of history. History is not centred on them and their efforts—
a notion which they find repulsive" (p. 8).

Odyssey reacted against accusations of "occult" and "satanism" after
the planting of the peace poles and the Table Mountain celebrations.
With the sudden awakening of "defenders of the faith" to the existence
of NAM, the editor of *Odyssey* considered it necessary to restore balance
and clarity in a situation that could all too easily become polarised
in the usual, "'we-them' kind of stance" (p. 8). Admittedly, a definition
of the "New Age" is impossible because there are multiple perspectives
derived from a great variety of sources, but basic to these different
interpretations is the idea of evolution of consciousness and the understanding that "this is a time of transition and change; a time of opportunity for new birth and initiation, not only for individual souls, but
for the whole of humanity and for the planet Earth itself" (p. 8).

The New Age is seen as a maturing process, a movement in which
people become more consciously responsible for themselves and the
world they have co-created. The New Age in South Africa has an
influence on people who find little satisfaction in the secular and religious
status quo. Their agenda covers holistic health and healing, education,
relationships on all levels namely family, marriage, social and busi-

ness; various dimensions of ethics, alternate technology and conflict management, non-adversarial politics, non-adversarial law, new ways to care for the dying and the environment, green issues and peace issues. Not only is the intensity of activities of the New Age Movement increasing, but its scope is widening as more people become convinced that the new vision gives them hope and satisfaction. This leads to the assurance of self-empowerment, of being more creative and spiritually aware, and of reaching beyond the self, to be interconnected with others and with the environment. Many New Agers have a history of discontent with the churches, and of going through experiences of rejection, accused of being "unorthodox" and "heretical". The first link-up between New Agers in South Africa came in order to help such persons to make real contact with one another. This is referred to as "networking" and each region has its own Link-Up. It provides a communication service and gives free information on forthcoming events, workshops and talks, as well as details about many of the on-going groups and other activities available in and around the various cities.

Emphasis on Healing

The emphasis on alternative healing is one of the outstanding features of the New Age Movement in South Africa. Alternative healing also has a special place on the agenda of the African Independent/Indigenous Churches as will be indicated later. The Secretary of the (African) Traditional Healers' Council estimates that in South Africa, eighteen million blacks (out of a total black population of more than twenty six million), visit traditional healers, i.e. diviners and herbalists. The New Age healing methods come from various parts of the world, such as the so-called British Tai Chi Chuan and Shaolin Kung Fu Association. This is an ancient system of martial art, that has only recently been introduced in the West. It is considered to be a holistic means of attaining and maintaining optimum health. For the body it is a form of exercise and relaxation; for the mind a study in concentration, will-power and visualisation; for the soul, a system of meditation and spiritual development. These methods are applied in Cape Town. Shin Sen Do is practised *inter alia* in Johannesburg. This Taoist energy practice, which includes healing, diet, meditation, acupuncture, herbology and macrobiotics, is receiving much attention.

The Wholistic Health Centre in Constantia, Cape Town, concentrates on studies in medicinal herbs, massage courses, seminars on aromatherapy, energy balancing, crystals and building an immune system. Other such centres offer homeopathic remedies and phyto-therapeutic medicines.

In South Africa the NAM attracts the younger people, who see in this movement an answer to their longing for a more dynamic and meaningful expression of their convictions. The same aspirations are evident in the Pentecostal/Charismatic Churches which, however, are no longer expanding at the rate they did in the 60s up to the early 80s. The NAM started to make itself felt in South Africa only in the middle 80s. None of the Churches here have done an in-depth analysis on its influence on their Churches, although concern is expressed about its activities. More attention has been given to Satanism. As an inclusive movement, NAM also appeals because of its emphasis on a global stance, in contrast to the narrow approach that previously prevailed here. People seek wider contact in a country which has nine world religions, many new religious movements, Independent, Charismatic and Pentecostal Churches. A section of the youth find the NAM attractive because of its open, universalistic stance in a situation where the narrow *apartheid* syndrome destroyed real contact among people and what they hold dear. It is usually the more intellectualised and middle to higher income group who experiment with new possibilities. This leads some to occult practices with the emphasis on self-realisation and rediscovery of the Divine in oneself. The hidden knowledge, wisdom and power, outside the sensory and experiential reality have to be sought and found in extraordinary ways. The NAM is attractive because it teaches that each person determines his/her own values and norms. What the youth experienced in the South African context was not attractive, for many.

The NAM is nothing more than a longing from the heart of modern man for a more hopeful future and world. The NAM challenge to the Churches in South Africa will become more severe in the future. Many white youth are genuinely filled with guilt feelings and the NAM is especially attractive for a section among them, as it provides the opportunity for contact with congenial spirits. Many New Agers in South Africa are sincere people, believing firmly that they serve God in what they are doing. People who want to do good are also attracted. The NAM satisfies needs and those who are seeking mystical experiences seek help, even through occult practices.

The NAM has something for everybody, whatever kind of people

they are. Many of the New Agers are sad that intentions are mis-
understood and that they are not considered to be Christians. Many
of them would have been candidates for the Charismatic Churches
because of their deep longing to be meaningful, but the New Agers
got in first.

Movements of Spiritual Freedom in South Africa—NAM and Black Zionism (BZ)

In spite of specific differences, the New Age Movement and Black
Zionism have many similarities. In what sense, then, is the NAM
"new"? In the Southern African context, black Zionism is a vast
indigenous Pentecostal/Charismatic movement. It is one of three
sections—Ethiopian, Zionist and Apostolic—within the African
Independent Church (AIC) movement, which reacted against the
ecclesiastical establishment because of its association with missionary
control. The Zionists, which constitute the largest section, were
established as a result of influences from the Christian Catholic Church
in Zion (Illinois), USA. 80% of the 8,000,000 strong AIC movement
(and 28% or 6,500,000 of the total African population) belong to
the Zionists. (cf. G.C. Oosthuizen, "The Birth of Christian Zionism
in South Africa", University of Zululand, 1987).

Reaction against staleness in empirical Christianity

Like the Ethiopians and Apostolics, black Zionists reacted against
missionary control and mainly against the westernised expressions of
Christianity. The movement is, by and large, an expression of
ecclesiastical democracy, in fact ecclesiastical freedom, in a situation
of political oppression. To a large extent, church structures are
decentralised and many of the house congregations are fully fledged
denominations. These face-to-face church groups strengthen the
traditional sense of community. They reintegrate, as does the NAM,
individuals who have lost their relationships with family and extended
family, who have become alienated from traditional bonds. Many blacks
in South Africa migrated to the cities over a short space of time,
with the result that BZ became a major factor in reintegrating religiously
and culturally rudderless people.

The communal sense is as strong in the NAM as it is in Zionism.
The relatively small NAM groups transcend the barriers of race, of
narrow, closed, suffocating, and isolating communities. In spite of its

variety groups, the NAM cherishes wider contacts; Black Zionism also. Through its numerous different activities, the small NAM groups have grown at a great pace during the last few years. New Agers themselves find it surprising that there is such a genuine and deep interest in the various aspects of their movement. In the faceless cities and in the context of faceless churches many find the NAM activities "refreshing and inspiring".

Both the NAM and Black Zionism feel themselves free to choose their own religious expressions. The former do so by borrowing from East and West, the ancient Middle East and also Africa—while the latter combine religious expressions from African traditional religion and Christianity. Both broke through conventional boundaries in order to reach the people. Black Zionists express their liturgy through singing, dancing, handclapping—in a spontaneous manner that is not evident in most of the so-called mainline churches. Such spontaneity is also found in many of the New Age groups.

In both, symbols play an important role. Sacred power is relayed by way of symbols—in BZ, through crosses, staves, holy water, colour symbolism, candles, stars and certain acts; in the NAM, through the rainbow and other symbols associated with ancient mythologies, utilised in order to obtain secret or sacred power. In BZ, there is much emphasis upon the Spirit (Holy Spirit) as a powerful force. This is due mainly to their members' experience of powerlessness in the South African situation of powerful negative forces. The Spirit, as a powerful macrocosmic counterforce to the realities of their situation, acts within the microcosmic context i.e. within the group. These small communities or denominations isolate themselves from the wider context of human existence, with the idea of retaining their spiritual power in order to be, in a centripetal manner, the salt of the earth. The Spirit, with its sacred power identifies itself with their group—it is for them a vivid experience, especially through dancing, singing and hand clapping.

The NAM also comprises numerous relatively small groups, most of which strongly believe in the omnipotent mystical power which transforms them through various spiritual acts, such as meditation, spiritual or sacred dancing and singing, chanting (especially in Eastern influenced groups), and various types of yoga.

BZ and NAM react against structural institutionalism

Like the NAM, black Zionism, by and large, reacts against structural institutionalism, with the result that there are no fewer than 6000

denominations of the movement in South Africa. Only a relatively
few groups have authoritarian structures, some, however, with large
followings. Their finances are not spent on keeping the organisation
going as an institution, but on the needs of their flock and others
who need their help. Ministers or leaders are often not paid for their
services—BZ is largely a "tent-making ministry". Personal charisma
is the major "gift" expected for ministry, without undue emphasis
on theological training. Thousands upon thousands of small groups
gather for services in houses or natural open spaces (only about 5%
meet in church buildings). Many of these groups become closely knit
entities with hardly any form of structure. Various people who assist
with different tasks—such as the leader, the evangelist who is a
probationer, the lay preacher, the prayer healer, the prophet and the
women's leader. The latter three offices could all be held by women
for their role here is as prominent as it is with the New Agers. BZ
emphasis on the free flow of "the Spirit" and contact with the traditional
African worldview as well as the healing procedures practised, make
them attractive to the Africans.

The anti-establishment and anti-institutional character of the New
Age Movement is very evident. However, many New Agers remain
in "mainline" churches, especially the more "liberal" ones. A tremendous
variety of activities go on under the designation "New Age" as is
evident in the *Link-Ups* and *Odyssey,* the bi-monthly magazine. Many
of the groups know about each other through various types of
communication, including personal contacts, newsletters, *Link-Up* and
sharing of information. Every New Ager decides for him/herself what
direction is the most advantageous to his/her spiritual taste and
longings. Certain elements of eastern universalist spirituality are
attractive for a section of the New Agers. The New Age Movement
attracts mainly urban whites and a small number of Indians—Hindus
rather than Indian Christians.

The role of universal energy in BZ and NAM

Most NAM and all Black Zionists accept the existence of a universal
energy. For the African, there is a life force or energy in everything—
some objects and people have more of this mysterious energy than
others. It is referred to in black Zionism as "power"; an energy, a
force that effects healing, that gives a person the power to heal, to
prophesy, to exorcise. As does NAM, BZ believes in the universal
power which permeates all existence. Some places, like mountains,

rivers and the sea, have special power; dancing and praying on a special mountain is more effective than other places; the sea, with its white, blue and green "coloured" water and salt is effective in transforming this power and in making contact with the "living dead" ancestors in the beyond. The sea serves as a contact medium with the forces in the metaphysical world.

Although New Agers see this power as a natural energy that permeates everything in the cosmos, certain persons with supernatural qualities convey it more effectively than others. They receive contact with the higher form of energy through specific methods which enable a person to tune in on it and relay it to others.

Channelling and prophecy in NAM and BZ

In the traditional African society the diviner plays a prominent role. This important office has been compensated for in BZ by the faith healer *(Umthandazi)* and the prophet *(Umprofeti)*. The prophets, especially, work through visions and transfer the healing powers which they receive from the "Holy Spirit" and the ancestors, onto the sick; they exorcise, counsel and transfer healing energies and powers to patients. They are also seers, with the gift of "prophecy". They speak in tongues and another has to interpret what they say when they are in a state of trance. The prophet in BZ is a medium or channel through whom specific ancestors operate often when in a state of trance, so that the Holy Spirit and ancestor can contact people here. Such contact from the ancestors is important for the diviner in traditional African religion and so also for the prophet, the substitute for the diviner in most of BZ. New Agers also concern themselves with "channelling". For both New Agers and BZ, these powers make contact in a dramatic manner, not because they are remote but because of the significance of such contact.

Negative evil forces—The BZ and NAM

While the traditional Pentecostal/Charismatic Churches place much emphasis on Satan and demonic powers, in BZ Satan is in the background and demonic evil spirits are the greatest enemies of a group as they are used by sorcerers to harm people. The reaction against these forces by black Zionists holds them together. One of the most important activities in Black Zionism is the removal of various kinds of demons from the flock and this is usually done at dams, rivers and the sea. The Christian religion of the first few centuries after the ascension of Jesus Christ had much to do with exorcism, especially after this religion was declared the religion of the Roman Empire in the fourth century AD. As for those Christians, so for the second-century Christians of BZ, evil and well-meaning spirits are a reality, affecting health, well-being, inter-relationships and the future.

On the whole, New Agers do not evade the issue of negative spirit influences, yet they do not give much attention to the concept of an evil disposition in the unseen world being a threat to mankind. The spirit world is rather benevolent and helpful to human existence. For both black Zionists and New Agers, the metaphysical world is a world of sacred power, from which enlightenment and revelations are received for personal life and human existence.

Healing in BZ and NAM

Healing in the holistic sense is a central issue in BZ. This is one of the main reasons for the rapid growth of this movement (cf. G.C. Oosthuizen, S.D. Edwards, J. Hexham and W.H. Wessels, *Afro-Christian religion and healing in Southern Africa* (Lewiston: Edwin Mellen Press, 1988)). They understand the psyche of their people, they speak the "language" of adherents at the grassroots, and they address the problems these people encounter with cultural diseases such as the effects of evil spirit possession, witchcraft and sorcery, as well as the usual diseases. The world of spirits is still very real for most of the adherents of BZ. Much of their concentration on evil spirits is due to the fact that socio-economic and political issues are professed evil forces. Bewitchment and sorcery lead to deprivation, annihilation—they are the destroyers of life, often through mysterious events and diseases. BZ concentrates on purification rites as a fortification against misfortune and the forces of evil (cf. G.C. Oosthuizen, "Baptism in the context of the African Indigenous/Independent Churches", University of Zululand, 1985). Because typical African diseases are ignored by the so-called "mainline" church leadership, people are not able to fortify themselves against their onslaughts. They then either go to herbalists or diviners, or to the prayer healers and prophets of the African Independent Churches. These Churches are spiritual "freedom fighters"—they free their flock from the oppression of evil forces projected into evil spirits. They have their own approach to group dynamics, based on sensitive and in-depth understanding of the African psyche.

Many NAM activities are associated with a very extensive variety
of healing procedures. All kinds of healing techniques are utilised in
NAM, including spiritual therapies, meditation techniques, mind
healing procedures, New Thought teachings, visualisation, various types
of yoga and various physical techniques. NAM's deep involvement
in holistic healing procedures attracts many people at the crucial age
of twenty to forty-five years.

The healing and empowerment of the body, the soul and the mind
(the latter perhaps indirectly in Black Zionism) accounts for the growth
of both the BZ and NAM—the one deeply associated with traditional
Africa at grassroots level and the other with a combination of East
especially and West.

Both Black Zionism and New Age emphasise the role of holy power
personally experienced in individual lives. The duality between this
world and the world out there has been broken down—there is a
deep, sensitive relationship between the physical and the spiritual world.
In both movements personal experiences with the numinous power
are emphasised. In Black Zionism this experience is manifested through
speaking in tongues, prophesying, praying, intercession, laying on of
hands, singing, handclapping, shiverings in the body, jerks, shouting
and exorcism; while in the NAM personal experience with sacred
powers comes through channelling, prophesying, meditation and
exorcism. Experiences of the sacred are thus not the exclusive
prerogative of the "mainline" churches but of every individual.

The stability and care that an individual experiences in these
movements make them feel at home. They have been seeking for
this in the hustle and bustle of urban life, but the churches could
not give it. In the meaningful house congregations of BZ and the
sacred communities of NAM they have found it.

The healing of people through non-medical means, giving wholeness
to their lives is a great attraction in both movements. Here they
experience a freedom through the metaphysical forces that support
them, a freedom that they did not experience in the so-called "mainline"
churches. Mystical experience and revelation are not limited to a few
but are the birthright that every human being can claim, without
any reference to an institution or any hierarchy.

While the NAM venture to synthesise the scientific, metaphysical
and religious worldviews, Black Zionism concentrates on the metaphysical
and religious worldviews without regard for the scientific worldview.

Black Zionism seriously takes into account the traditional roots of the Blacks. No fewer than five million traditionalist blacks have joined Black Zionism during the last quarter of a century. For them a new future has opened up. BZ is much more open to black people's needs than is classical westernised Pentecostalism. In the black community, black Zionism has proved itself as the church of the future in South Africa. The NAM, in spite of its "newness" on the South African scene, has momentum on its side among those who seek more dynamic responses to their quest for meaning than the mainline churches can give. However, some combine their churches and the NAM. For the majority the NAM is still new and challenging. There are clear indications that this movement will become a force to be reckoned with in the South African context—much depending upon how active the Pentecostal/Charismatic Churches become especially among the youth. Many "mainline" churches have lost the dynamic stance which attracts the youth, with whom lies the future.

Conclusion

The NAM has only recently come to the attention of South Africans. It seems that this movement will extend its influence among whites, especially between the ages of twenty and forty-five. The average New Ager is a seeker and could have been a candidate for the Charismatic movement. The movement has an influence on the middle income group in South Africa, among those who have become marginal in the so-called "mainline" churches (including the Afrikaans language churches) and those who have already left these churches. Those who wish to overcome what they consider to be the narrow and biased outlook of the white section in South Africa will feel themselves attracted to such movements as the NAM. In a country which is a microcosm of the "global village" many will try to overcome the narrow, biased approaches of the past, some feeling that this can best be achieved through the NAM. As NAM gains momentum, fundamentalist Christianity will feel itself threatened and will react strongly. The Hindu section—the Muslims will remain unmoved—will discover more and more the central role that aspects of their religion play in the NAM. Whether the Pentecostal/Charismatic movement will be able to expand its influence in this context remains to be seen. The black community, deeply religious and not easily moved by other than Christian-orientated movements, will not produce many New Agers. Black Zionism, in fact the African Independent Church movement, will be the main force in the lives of those who look for a dynamic expression of religiosity, although contemporary black youth will challenge these churches to take an active interest in the socio-economic and political situation of blacks and of the country as a whole. Black Zionism will continue to be a force among blacks as an indigenous Pentecostal/Charismatic movement. It could be that NAM will attract increasing numbers of blacks from the intelligentsia. A small number of them visit the NAM bookshops but they are not as yet actively involved.

An interesting aspect of NAM's development in South Africa is Johanna Brand's position as the very first person to highlight the contours of the NAM during the first quarter of this century, in spite of her Calvinist upbringing. That Jan Christiaan Smuts, another with a Calvinist upbringing, also became a forerunner of the NAM, through his *Holism and Evolution*, is indeed remarkable. Thus, in spite of NAM's empirical "newness" in South Africa, it has been in this country for decades, existentially. Furthermore, as is the case with the AICs and similar groups, it attracts many who are dissatisfied with the so-called "mainline" churches.

BIBLIOGRAPHY

Ashe, G., *The Ancient Wisdom* (London: MacMillan, 1979).
Campbell and Brennan, J.H., *The aquarian guide to the New Age* (Wellingborough: The Aquarian Press, 1990).
Capra, F., *Uncommon Wisdom* (New York: Fontana, 1989).
Cheetham, R.W.S. and Griffiths, K.A., "The traditional healer-diviner as psychotherapist", *South African Medical Journal* 62 (Dec. 11, 1982).
"On the 'Movement for Peace through Prayer'", *Cross Times*, January 1990.
"On the World Peace Movement in South Africa", *Die Burger*, November 15, 1989.
Green, C., *Out of body experiences* (Oxford: Institute of Psychophysical research, 1968).
Happold, F.C., *Mysticism, a study and an anthropology* (Penguin, 1970).
Harner, M., *Hallucinogens and Shamanism* (London: Oxford University Press, 1973).
Mkhize, M.,"Indigenous healing systems and western psychotherapies", M.A. Thesis, University of Natal, Pietermaritzburg, 1981.
Mkhwanazi, M.,"An investigation of the therapeutic methods of Zulu diviners", M.A. Dissertation, University of South Africa, 1986.
Odyssey 1986–1992.
Oosthuizen, G.C., "Baptism in the context of the African Indigenous/ Independent Churches" (KwaDlangezwa: University of Zululand, 1985).
Oosthuizen, G.C., "The birth of christian Zionism in South Africa", (KwaDlangezwa: University of Zululand, 1987).

Oosthuizen G.C., Edwards, S.D., Hexham, J., Wessels, W.H., *Afro-christian religion and healing in Southern Africa* (Lewiston: Edwin Mellen Press, 1988).

Pettinger, N., *God in process* (London: SCM, 1967).

Schlosser, K., *Eingeborenenkirchen in Süd- und Südwest-Afrika* (Kiel: Mühlau, 1958).

Schweitzer, R.D., "Indigenous therapy in Southern Africa", *Bulletin of the British Psychological Society* 33 (1926) pp. 278–81.

Smuts, J.C., *Holism and Evolution* (London: Oxford University Press, 1926).

Taylor, J., *Primal Vision* (London: SCM, 1963).

STORIES OF FAITH AMONG THE ZIONISTS

D. HOSTETTER

Abstract

The content of the stories differs. Some of the following matters are treated in the stories of faith: the call to Christian ministry and its power over indigenous beliefs; understanding the Bible message of Christian love; confession of sin and an indication that sin is not to be taken lightly; the role of confession in dealing with the consequences of sin; fellowship versus chaos; hospitality with reservation; response to a prayer of faith; God's provision in surprising ways; indigenous heritage and the communication of the Gospel; transformation of indigenous practices for Christian use.

These stories illustrate important aspects of the lives of the Zionists. Through stories of faith like these, one gets a better insight into the world-view of the Zionists and into the process of transformation of African traditions.

Introduction

There is a tendency by us, as Westerners, to attempt to research, analyse and explain something which is not familiar to us. The Zionists have been one of those groups which we have not understood well. Their history, traditions, beliefs and practices have been researched and studied, but they also have stories of faith which need to be recorded and learned from.

This paper will be a compilation of stories which comes out of my personal experience and relationships with Zionists, while working for the Faith Bible School (FBS) for the past eight years. FBS is a ministry of Zionists, from various denominations, who have a vision for the Bible to be taught, studied and lived among their people.

From bondage to freedom

Isaac Dlamini did not know of Christ as a child as his parents were not Christians. His father spent eleven months of each year working on the railway in Johannesburg. In fact, as a young boy he did not even know his father. Isaac's mother remarried while Isaac was still young and her new husband did not want Isaac around as he was afraid Isaac would cause trouble. So Isaac spent most of his early years living with an uncle.

Finally, at the age of twelve, Isaac saw his father for the first time that he could remember. He decided he wanted to live with his father, so he ran away and set out to find him. Shortly after joining his father, he became very ill. He was taken to a hospital and the doctor found that his lungs were badly diseased. He eventually had surgery and one lung was removed. But he still remained sick and was in and out of the hospital for nine months. The hospital doctors told his father that Isaac did not have more than five years to live. His father took him to traditional doctors, as well as western doctors, but no treatment seemed to help him much. He remained sickly for the next four years.

Because of Isaac's persistent illness and the fact that his grandmother was a *sangoma*, it appeared to many that Isaac was being called by the *emadloti* (ancestral spirits) to become a *sangoma* and to carry on this role in his family. Therefore, Isaac's father sent him away to be trained. He had not been in training long when he received these words in a dream, "Go, preach and you will be healed!" Since Isaac had no direct contact with Christianity, he had no idea what these words meant. The longer he stayed in his training, the more penetrating these words became to his soul. He finally felt compelled to leave his training in order to follow the words of the dream, even though he knew that this could mean his death. (It is thought that leaving the *sangoma* training is dangerous and could result in a curse or death by the ancestors).

Shortly after arriving home, he again had a dream and this time he understood that he was to see a blind man, who would help him. There happened to be a blind evangelist visiting a neighbouring homestead so he went to see him. This evangelist told Isaac that he had many demons and should stay with him for some time, while he fasted and prayed for his complete deliverance. After about a month, Isaac was completely delivered and healed. The evangelist told him to give his life to Jesus, or else the demons would return.

Isaac did not fully understand what it meant to give his life to Jesus. When another evangelist preached in his area, Isaac immediately responded to an altar-call as his heart had been prepared.

Now Isaac finally understood his dream and the words. "Go, preach and you will be healed." Isaac felt that God wanted him to work

with the Zionists, so he joined the Zionist Church near his home.
He felt a tremendous need for training in the Bible, but when he
tried to attend a mission Bible school they told him that they would
only receive him if he left his Zionist Church. It was not possible
for him to leave the people that he felt called to minister to, so he
took three years of training by correspondence.

Today, Isaac is well known among Christians in Swaziland as a
real man of God. He is president of his church, the Pentecost East
Star Jerusalem Church in Sabbath. He continues to teach the Bible
with the Zionists and enjoys good health.

Unlimited love

While I was teaching a Bible class in Mankayane about "the Sermon
on the Mount" from Luke 6:27-49, we discussed whether Jesus really
meant us to live out this kind of love today. I was amazed at how
quickly they responded with, "God wants us to turn the other cheek
and love our enemies, even today". I had expected a long discussion
and many questions as to how we could be expected to live out God's
unlimited love. I used in my teaching Clarence Jordan's descriptions
of love; limited love—loving those who love us, and unlimited love—
loving those who hate us as well.

Little did I know that these people were seeing in Scripture what
they had experienced in their community very recently. The brother
of uMfundisi Msibi of the Zion Apostolic Swaziland Church of South
Africa was working in his maize field when his neighbour approached
him and accused him of planting on his land. The neighbour was
so very angry that he struck Mr Msibi across the forehead with a
hatchet. Then the neighbour ran off, but not empty-handed as he
also helped himself to Mr Msibi's fertilizer. UMfundisi Msibi was
notified of his brother's injury and took him to the closest hospital,
where his head was stitched.

As uMfundisi Msibi and his brother conferred together on what
to do, they decided to report their neighbour to the police. The
neighbour was arrested and put in jail the same day. A few days
later the Msibi brothers reconsidered their decision. Their neighbour
would probably be incarcerated for up to a year and this would mean
being separated from his wife and children. They wondered, who
would take care of the neighbour's family, fields and cattle, who would
pay for his children's school fees. Would their neighbour's imprisonment

really bring peace to the community or divide it? The Msibi brothers felt the need to forgive their neighbour and investigate whether the case could be dropped, since it had not gone to court yet. They went to the prison and visited their neighbour, asking him to forgive them. Their neighbour was delighted with their visit and apologised as well. Then the brothers went to the police and explained that they wanted to drop the case against their neighbour. The policeman was shocked and asked, "What do you want to do? Don't you know that this man will continue to give you trouble?" The policeman, on realising the Msibi brothers' request was a firm decision, hesitantly began to write the report necessary to close the case. Their neighbour was released and returned to his home with the Msibi brothers.

This forgiving love has affected the church and community. No longer is there any conflict between the families involved. People from the church have gone to this neighbour to visit and pray with him. While time brought healing to Msibi's head, forgiveness brought healing to wounds of broken relationships.

After our Bible class that day, the Msibi brothers were so excited because they understood scripturally what they put into practice with their neighbour. They explained to me that Jesus' teaching is very difficult to obey, but their forgiving love was a living demonstration and example of what God's unlimited love means. They recognised the cost and suffering that comes with unlimited love—scars on the head, hospital bills and loss of fertilizer. But the result was well worth the price, as now there is peace and goodwill in the community.

Acceptance in spite of rejection

The Faith Bible School (FBS) committee, comprising Zionist ministers and leaders, holds weekend seminars, five or six times a year, around Swaziland. These weekend seminars are times of intensive teaching for anyone who wishes to attend. They are often held at schools during the school holidays.

On one occasion, the FBS decided to hold a weekend seminar in a school in another part of the country from where we usually meet. The FBS committee made prior arrangements for food and lodging, with the headmaster of a high school which was cooperatively run by the government and a church denomination.

On Friday afternoon, people began to arrive from all over the country, even as far away as 150 kms. When we arrived the headmaster informed us that the head of the denominational mission was not aware that "Zionists" were using their facility until that day, and he was insulted about this lack of communication.

So four of us men who had arrived early went to speak to the head of the church on the school compound. He invited us into his home and proceeded to explain that a church group wanting to use the school premises must make a written application to a particular committee of the church. The FBS chairman told him that we were not aware of this procedure and had understood that arrangements made with the headmaster were adequate.

The chairman of FBS then graciously asked the mission administrator what we were to do with all the people arriving that night. He replied that he was extremely sorry but since we hadn't worked through the proper channels, we would need to leave the next morning unless the president overruled. He said he would consult with the president by phone and give us his response later that evening. He informed us that we were not allowed to sing, pray, teach or worship while we waited for the president's response.

Our response was disbelief. "It wasn't our fault that they hadn't informed us of the proper procedure." Many of us wondered, "How could this Christian group just throw us out and not even allow us to hold our Friday night meeting?"

Instead of being angry, the general secretary of FBS suggested, "If this church leader won't allow us to have our teaching session tonight, why don't we ask him to come and speak to us instead?" So the chairman of the FBS turned around and went back into the home of this minister and invited him to speak to all of us who were gathered for the seminar.

About nine o' clock that evening the minister returned to inform us that we must leave the next day. He also obliged us by giving a 15 minute devotional on "Don't forget God."

During the evening the Zionists could be heard asking one another, "How can our Christian brothers treat us like this?" One did not sense that they were angry or resentful, but puzzled. What a beautiful Christlike response it was to invite the minister to speak. In essence, the Zionist leaders were saying that they respected him as a brother in Christ, even though the acceptance was not mutual. Their willingness to learn from those who were rejecting them, was a beautiful example of Christian love.

Confessing all known sin

One of the Zionist Churches which I have often visited, Philip II of the Christian Catholic Apostolic Holy Spirit Church in Zion, has an interesting preparation for baptism. Each individual must confess specifically all known sin that he has committed. This is done publicly in the all-night service, prior to baptism in the morning. The leaders of the church are not satisfied if those wanting to be baptised have not mentioned all known sin in their lives. Often they will ask about premarital sex, stealing, etc., if the individual is slow to confess his sin. Some of the sins which I have heard confessed are: smoking, drinking alcohol, eating pork, having an abortion, lying, stealing, premarital sex (sometimes the number of different individuals is mentioned), going to the disco, etc. Sometimes, the church leaders will ask the boy who has confessed his sin of impregnating a girl whether he has confessed to the parents of the girl.

It appears that they do not take sin lightly. I heard one leader ask someone who had just confessed his sin, "Are you going to leave these sins now?" The leader stressed that "we are forgiven, but we do not play in Zion!"

After this time of confession and further preparation for baptism, anyone who remembers any other sin before reaching the river is instructed to confess it openly before everyone. I saw this done by a few before they entered the water.

An invitation to a confession

Mr Msibi, the younger brother of the minister, has been a member of the church and a leader of the youth for years. One day he invited all his neighbours, friends and family to come to the church because he had something important to share with them.

After the usual singing and prayer at the beginning of the service, Mr Msibi stood and opened the Bible to Luke 8 : 26–39. He began to read about the demon-possessed man who was crying out to Jesus, "What do you want with me?" Mr Msibi told us that he was like this man. He had heard about Jesus since he was young, but yet he remained condemned in his sins. He had failed his family, the church and his brothers, who had tried to advise him to turn from his sin of adultery. In the Bible, many had tried to help the demon-possessed man by binding him with chains, but like Mr Msibi, he had broken them and gone his own way.

The Holy Spirit spoke to Mr Msibi from the conversation between

Jesus and the demon-possessed man. When Jesus had asked him what his name was, the man had replied, "Legion" because there were many demons. Mr Msibi realised that Jesus was talking to him, not about his many demons, but about his many children conceived by women outside his marriage relationship. He confessed that he had often hid his sin by pretending to be going to an all-night service, when actually he intended to visit one of these women. Mr Msibi confessed his sins and asked forgiveness from all who attended the service.

He exposed how good it felt now to be "clothed and in his right mind", when he had been naked and controlled by his own pleasures for the past ten years. Just as the demon-possessed man met Jesus and was humbled and changed, so was Mr Msibi. Jesus had told the demon-freed man to return home and tell how much God had done for him. This is why Mr Msibi was sharing his testimony and confession to the community on that day.

Mr Msibi said that now, through the power of God, he wanted to deal with the consequences of his sin and lift up the name of Christ in his home, church and community.

Fellowship out of chaos

The invitations for our forthcoming Zionist weekend Bible teaching seminar had been mailed. All the persons asked to teach had accepted. We felt relieved that the planning had been done early and delegated responsibilities had been carried out. From all appearances, this should be a well-organised teaching seminar.

A week before the scheduled seminar we discovered that a mistake had been made. Some of the invitations sent out failed to indicate the date of the seminar. There was no time to repeat the mailing. We felt frustrated that some persons would have no way of knowing when the seminar would be held.

The day before the seminar was to begin, the first evening's speaker called to say he would be unable to teach, after all. There was no time to find another speaker. We were beginning to feel more stress over this seminar. Surely, nothing else could go wrong with our well-planned weekend.

Isaac Dlamini and I had tried to service early at the seminar so as to register persons attending. On Friday afternoon, I collected Isaac and his wife earlier than usual as I had also promised to pick up an old Zionist minister who needed transport. To my dismay, the road to this man's home was full of large rocks and gullies and we had to drive very slowly with much concentration. When we finally arrived at the house, the sun was beginning to set.

We found the minister leisurely sitting outside his house in his work clothes. My heart sank as I realised he was not ready to go. After the customary exchanging of greetings which are too time-consuming to our Western judgement in such a situation, the old minister explained he thought we were coming for him the next day. His eyesight was poor so he did not want to pack at that time of day. He asked us to return the following day to collect him, but when I explained that wasn't possible, he made the decision to remain at home.

After getting in the car and starting the long trip back over the deteriorated road, I realised we would arrive at the seminar after the scheduled time for registration and dinner.

Upon arrival we found everyone eating, but soon discovered that none of the other committee members had arrived early either, and therefore no one had been registered. I felt embarrassed and upset that these people had travelled from all parts of Swaziland and then on arrival at the centre had not been able to get a key to a room, but had no choice but to sit and wait.

It was 7 o'clock and time for the first session to begin, but no one had been registered, the meeting room was not set up, and there was no speaker for the evening. What a disaster! If we, as Westerners, had been the ones attending the seminar, it would have been very easy at this point to criticise and complain and wonder why we had spent our hard-earned money to attend such an unorganized seminar!

I apologetically asked different persons for their help. Some set up chairs, others helped set up the bookstand, and others showed persons to their rooms. During registration we filled all 70 beds at the centre. How could there have been such a good turnout, in spite of some of the invitations lacking such vital information as the date?

At 8.30 our meeting finally began with enthusiastic singing and praise. No one seemed offended or upset by the delays. Amazingly, everyone appeared happy to be there.

Oh, if only we didn't have to announce on top of all of this that there wasn't a speaker for the evening. How would the chairman handle this problem? After explaining that the speaker was unable to attend, he asked for two older women and a minister to come forward to join him as a panel to discuss the topic of the evening.

There was good input and discussion, and the session was an unbelievable success.

That night we slept well as we were relieved that the seminar had finally got off to a good start. Just before entering the meeting room the next morning, I learned that our second speaker had passed his assignment on to another couple who was unknown to us. In talking quickly with the couple, so that I would be able to introduce them, I discovered that they had not received a clear message on their assigned topic.

Fortunately, this couple was very adept in changing the focus of their input. Again, there was good discussion and I was amazed to see how what had appeared to be complete disarray turn out to be a helpful session for all of us.

During the second session a van load of 15 people arrived from South Africa. How could we accommodate all these people when the centre was already full? And shouldn't we work at solving this problem now? No, it wasn't until after the last session at 9.45 that we as a committee tried to rearrange the accommodation. Some persons changed rooms, others offered their beds and slept on the floor, until all the South African guests had beds to sleep on.

I was struck by the unselfish, giving attitude of these people, who did not view any of these problems as too burdensome to ruin their joy or excitement in being there. I, as a Westerner, in a situation such as this, often focus in on who is to blame for all the inefficiency, disorder and confusion. I then find myself angry and resentful and this brings a lot of stress to relationships at a time when quick solutions need to be found and everyone needs to work together in unity. One's attitudes also have an effect on the whole atmosphere of the meeting.

Our Zionist brothers and sisters do not seem to get upset when expectations are not fulfilled. They view problems as part of life and see the unexpected as an opportunity to get involved in helping. They willingly gave of themselves in order that everyone could benefit and go away blessed.

Although we, as Westerners, would probably say there was no excuse for all the mistakes, inefficiency and lack of communication, the Zionists went away from the seminar declaring that "All things work together for good to them who are called according to His purposes." Perhaps we in the West have overstressed efficiency and organisation, and therefore we lose sight of seeing God bring joy and a spirit of community out of confusion through the selfless giving of His people.

Hospitality without reservations

One day, when I stopped to visit Rev. Hlophe of the Nazaretha Christian Church in Zion, he told me about the visitor he had received a few days before.

His visitor was a stranger to him and his family and had arrived after dark and appeared to be needing a place to stay. He was an old man, but did not seem to know much siSwati or siZulu. It was not possible to discover where this man came from or where he was going. They gave him an evening meal and a room to sleep in that night, expecting that he would leave the following day. But their visitor never came out of his room the next day and food was taken to him.

On the second day, the visitor got up and had breakfast and left the homestead with some money which Rev. Hlophe had given him, but returned in the evening.

Finally, on the third day, the visitor left with the few things he had with him. When he left, the Hlophes did not feel that they really had got to know him, but nevertheless they felt that God had sent him to them for those three days, despite the fact that they did not know where he came from or where he was going.

I arrived at their homestead about noon on the day the visitor left. I had never visited their homestead, nor did I know Rev. Hlophe. A neighbour had encouraged me to visit him when I had informed her that I visit Zionist pastors. As soon as I met Rev. Hlophe he asked one of his boys to go to the store and buy me a litre of Sprite and some buns to eat. Then we began to chat together.

Rev. Hlophe had a different view of visitors than I had. When someone strange arrives he welcomes them with warmth and hospitality. I think he takes literally the exhortation from Hebrews, which says, "Do not forget to entertain strangers, for by so doing some people have entertained angels without knowing it." He likened my visit to one of an angel who came to visit him the same day that his other visitor left.

When I prepared to leave Rev Hlophe and his family, he insisted on giving me ten rand towards a drink and/or my ministry.

The prayer of faith

One day after visiting an old Zionist bishop from the Church of Christ Itshe LeGumbi, I felt led to give them twenty rand as a gift. Afterwards, I was amazed to learn that this gift was a direct answer to their prayers.

They had run out of money and food in their house. They asked their congregation if anyone could help them, but there was no one who could immediately do so. One of their congregation had just been laid off work and his family was struggling also. They all prayed together that God would meet their needs and bring them food.

The next day I arrived, but they had no idea that I might visit them. Their faith had been tested, but God proved again His faithfulness to them.

God's provision in surprising ways

Mr Isaac Dlamini, a watchmaker, had begun his business in Manzini and was renting a place to live with his wife and two daughters. One day, while he was fixing watches, an old man, whom he did not know, entered his shop and tried to encourage Dlamini to buy his house in a township of Manzini. Dlamini explained that he would not be able to do this because he had only started his watch repair business a short time before and he did not have the money. The old man did not take a no for an answer and continued for a number of weeks to beg Dlamini to buy his house.

Then Dlamini did not see the old man for almost a year. When he returned he still wanted Isaac to buy his house. In fact, he told Dlamini that he felt that the Lord had told him to sell the house to him. After much persuasion, Dlamini went with this old man to the bank to negotiate a loan so Dlamini could buy the house. As soon as they began to talk to the loan officer, the old man explained that Dlamini was not trying to buy his house, but rather he was trying to sell it to Dlamini. The old man said that he now wanted to reduce the price of the house from 15,000 rand to 9,000 rand. The loan was obtained by Dlamini and he bought the house. A month later the old man died.

Now Dlamini is still paying off his house, but he is able to provide for his six children and wife because God was faithful in providing for their needs, even when they did not know what their needs would be. Today, Dlamini is a pastor and his congregation meets in his garage.

The ancestral spirits prepare the way of Christ

When I visited another Zionist leader, Preacher Khumalo in the Christian Catholic Apostolic Holy Spirit Church in Zion, we began to talk about the ancestral spirits and how we address this issue when presenting the gospel to Swazi people. We agreed that Jesus is the Great Ancestor who supersedes and rules over all the other ancestors. We also discussed that our ancestors are not demons, but are part of us in many ways. It must have been difficult for many Swazis when missionaries came to tell them about Jesus and they were told that their ancestor "worship" was really demon worship.

As we continued to talk about this issue, suddenly Khumalo became excited and told me a story about the Swazi King Somhlolo. The king had a dream/vision in which he saw coming to his land some strange people who were the colour of the crest of the waves of the sea. In his dream, these people brought to the Swazi people two things: a book and a dazzling piece of metal. He was instructed to take the book, but leave the dazzling piece of metal.

Khumalo explained that no missionaries had arrived yet in Swaziland and all the people "worshipped" the ancestors. Any dreams or visions were the ancestral spirits trying to speak to them. When the king first saw this dream/vision, he left his house and went out under a tree to forget it, but it came again. He again fled to the cattle kraal where it came again. This time he received this vision as from his ancestral spirits.

Khumalo suggested that perhaps a better way to approach unbelievers in Swaziland would be to explain how the ancestral spirits told King Somhlolo that all Swazis should take the book, which practically all Swazis interpret as the Bible. Khumalo suggested that it was, in fact, the ancestors who first began to tell the Swazis that someone greater than themselves would be found in this book, the Bible. He thought that if Jesus is presented as the Great Ancestor, who is described in the book which the ancestor spirits told King Somhlolo to take and follow, surely they would be open to the gospel of Christ.

Transforming their traditions

Some of the Zionist leaders have begun to change some of the traditional rites and make them Christian. Some of them are taking the *Kugeza emanti* (a purification rite after death) and suggesting that, instead of this practice, which happens approximately one month after death, there should be a service to comfort the family and relatives. One month after the death of a relative is about the time when many friends of the relatives have begun to forget about the pain of losing a loved one; therefore it is a very pertinent time to be comforting those who are grieving.

Conclusion

For many people who have never seen or experienced these stories of faith, there is still laughter and mockery of the "Zionists", even by Christians. So, is it not important that we learn to listen to their stories, in their setting, and in their way of telling them? If we enter Zionist worship just for research, analysis and study, perhaps we have missed one of the most important parts of their lives, their stories of faith, that have a way of challenging each one of us.

These people have shown me the importance of relationships. It is important to visit one another, thank one another and pray for one another. Without living and working with these people, I would have tended to make a quick and premature judgement of them, perhaps missing these dynamic stories of their walk with Jesus.

INDEX